HOUGHTON MIFFLIN SOCIAL STUDIES

A More Perfect Union

Reading Support Workbook

KENNEDY MIDDLE SCHOOL
EUGENE, OREGON

HOUGHTON MIFFLIN

Boston • Atlanta • Dallas • Geneva, Illinois • Palo Alto • Princeton

Copyright © 1999 by Houghton Mifflin Company. All rights reserved.

No part of this work may be reproduced or transmitted in any form or by any means, electronic or mechanical, including photocopying and recording, or by any information storage or retrieval system without the prior written permission of the copyright owner, unless such copying is expressly permitted by federal copyright law. Address requests for permission to make copies of Houghton Mifflin materials to School Permissions, Houghton Mifflin Company, 222 Berkeley Street, Boston, MA 02116.

Printed in U. S. A.

ISBN: 0-395-94702-2

3456789-B-02 01 00 99

Table of Contents

Chapter 1: Reviewing Exploration and Settlement

Chapter Overview 1
Lesson 1 Preview 2
      Reading Strategy 3
      Summary 4
Lesson 2 Preview 6
      Reading Strategy 7
      Summary 8
Lesson 3 Preview 10
      Reading Strategy 11
      Summary 12
Lesson 4 Preview 14
      Reading Strategy 15
      Summary 16

Chapter 2: Reviewing the American Revolution

Chapter Overview 18
Lesson 1 Preview 19
      Reading Strategy 20
      Summary 21
Lesson 2 Preview 23
      Reading Strategy 24
      Summary 25
Lesson 3 Preview 27
      Reading Strategy 28
      Summary 29
Lesson 4 Preview 31
      Reading Strategy 32
      Summary 33

Chapter 3: Toward the Constitution

Chapter Overview 35
Lesson 1 Preview 36
      Reading Strategy 37
      Summary 38
Lesson 2 Preview 40
      Reading Strategy 41
      Summary 42
Lesson 3 Preview 44
      Reading Strategy 45
      Summary 46

Chapter 4: The Constitutional Convention

Chapter Overview 48
Lesson 1 Preview 49
      Reading Strategy 50
      Summary 51
Lesson 2 Preview 53
      Reading Strategy 54
      Summary 55
Lesson 3 Preview 57
      Reading Strategy 58
      Summary 59

Chapter 5: The Creation of a Party System

Chapter Overview 61
Lesson 1 Preview 62
      Reading Strategy 63
      Summary 64
Lesson 2 Preview 66
      Reading Strategy 67
      Summary 68

Table of Contents (continued)

Lesson 3 Preview. 70
    Reading Strategy. 71
    Summary 72

Chapter 6: The Maturing Republic
Chapter Overview 74
Lesson 1 Preview. 75
    Reading Strategy. 76
    Summary 77

Lesson 2 Preview. 79
    Reading Strategy. 80
    Summary 81

Lesson 3 Preview. 83
    Reading Strategy. 84
    Summary 85

Chapter 7: People of the New Nation
Chapter Overview 87
Lesson 1 Preview. 88
    Reading Strategy. 89
    Summary 90

Lesson 2 Preview. 92
    Reading Strategy. 93
    Summary 94

Lesson 3 Preview. 96
    Reading Strategy. 97
    Summary 98

Lesson 4 Preview. 100
    Reading Strategy. 101
    Summary 102

Chapter 8: The West
Chapter Overview 104
Lesson 1 Preview. 105
    Reading Strategy. 106
    Summary 107

Lesson 2 Preview. 109
    Reading Strategy. 110
    Summary 111

Lesson 3 Preview. 113
    Reading Strategy. 114
    Summary 115

Lesson 4 Preview. 117
    Reading Strategy. 118
    Summary 119

Chapter 9: The North
Chapter Overview 121
Lesson 1 Preview. 122
    Reading Strategy. 123
    Summary 124

Lesson 2 Preview. 126
    Reading Strategy. 127
    Summary 128

Lesson 3 Preview. 130
    Reading Strategy. 131
    Summary 132

Chapter 10: The South
Chapter Overview 134
Lesson 1 Preview. 135
    Reading Strategy. 136
    Summary 137

Lesson 2 Preview. 139
    Reading Strategy. 140
    Summary 141

Lesson 3 Preview. 143
    Reading Strategy. 144
    Summary 145

Table of Contents (continued)

Chapter 11: Causes of the Civil War
Chapter Overview. 147
Lesson 1 Preview. 148
    Reading Strategy. 149
    Summary 150

Lesson 2 Preview. 152
    Reading Strategy. 153
    Summary 154

Lesson 3 Preview. 156
    Reading Strategy. 157
    Summary 158

Lesson 4 Preview. 160
    Reading Strategy. 161
    Summary 162

Chapter 12: A Nation Divided
Chapter Overview. 164
Lesson 1 Preview. 165
    Reading Strategy. 166
    Summary 167

Lesson 2 Preview. 169
    Reading Strategy. 170
    Summary 171

Lesson 3 Preview. 173
    Reading Strategy. 174
    Summary 175

Lesson 4 Preview. 177
    Reading Strategy. 178
    Summary 179

Chapter 13: Reconstruction
Chapter Overview. 181
Lesson 1 Preview. 182
    Reading Strategy. 183
    Summary 184

Lesson 2 Preview. 186
    Reading Strategy. 187
    Summary 188

Lesson 3 Preview. 190
    Reading Strategy. 191
    Summary 192

Chapter 14: Reshaping the Great Plains
Chapter Overview. 194
Lesson 1 Preview. 195
    Reading Strategy. 196
    Summary 197

Lesson 2 Preview. 199
    Reading Strategy. 200
    Summary 201

Lesson 3 Preview. 203
    Reading Strategy. 204
    Summary 205

Lesson 4 Preview. 207
    Reading Strategy. 208
    Summary 209

Chapter 15: Industry and Workers
Chapter Overview. 211
Lesson 1 Preview. 212
    Reading Strategy. 213
    Summary 214

Lesson 2 Preview. 216
    Reading Strategy. 217
    Summary 218

Table of Contents (continued)

Lesson 3 Preview. 220
    Reading Strategy. 221
    Summary 222

Lesson 4 Preview. 224
    Reading Strategy. 225
    Summary 226

Chapter 16: The Gilded Age
Chapter Overview. 228
Lesson 1 Preview. 229
    Reading Strategy. 230
    Summary 231

Lesson 2 Preview. 233
    Reading Strategy. 234
    Summary 235

Lesson 3 Preview. 237
    Reading Strategy. 238
    Summary 239

Chapter 17: The Reform Era
Chapter Overview. 241
Lesson 1 Preview. 242
    Reading Strategy. 243
    Summary 244

Lesson 2 Preview. 246
    Reading Strategy. 247
    Summary 248

Lesson 3 Preview. 250
    Reading Strategy. 251
    Summary 252

Chapter 18: America Emerges as a World Power
Chapter Overview. 254
Lesson 1 Preview. 255
    Reading Strategy. 256
    Summary 257

Lesson 2 Preview. 259
    Reading Strategy. 260
    Summary 261

Lesson 3 Preview. 263
    Reading Strategy. 264
    Summary 265

Lesson 4 Preview. 267
    Reading Strategy. 268
    Summary 269

Chapter 19: Pluralism
Chapter Overview. 271
Lesson 1 Preview. 272
    Reading Strategy. 273
    Summary 274

Lesson 2 Preview. 276
    Reading Strategy. 277
    Summary 278

Lesson 3 Preview. 280
    Reading Strategy. 281
    Summary 282

Chapter 20: Modern American Democracy
Chapter Overview. 284
Lesson 1 Preview. 285
    Reading Strategy. 286
    Summary 287

Lesson 2 Preview. 289
    Reading Strategy. 290
    Summary 291

Lesson 3 Preview. 293
    Reading Strategy. 294
    Summary 295

Use with *A More Perfect Union* Pages 2–45

Chapter Overview
Reviewing Exploration and Settlement

Fill in the blanks with information from the chapter.

When: 1492–1775

Where: The American Colonies

Who: European Settlers and Native Peoples

Coming to America

The Land
- Landscape
- Climate
- _____

The Europeans
- Spain Leads the Way
- _____
- Settlements

Europeans Meet Native Americans
- Trade
- _____
- _____

English Colonial Life
- _____
- Middle Colonies
- _____

Reading Support Resources — Chapter Overview • Chapter 1 — **1**

Name: _____ Date: _____

CHAPTER 1
Lesson 1 Preview
The American Land

(*A More Perfect Union* pp. 4–13)

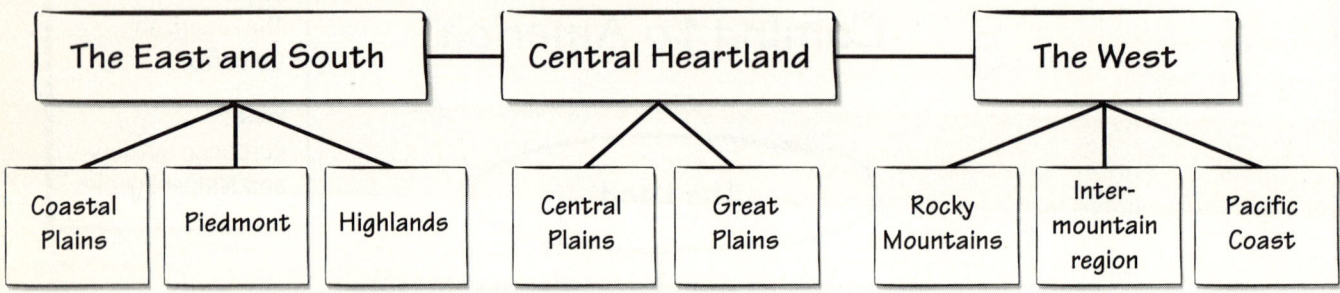

1. Look at the graphic organizer above. Read each sentence and then fill in the blank.

    a. The three areas of the eastern and southern United States are the Coastal Plains, the Piedmont, and the _____.

    b. Between the eastern and southern United States and the West is the _____.

    c. The Rocky Mountains, the Intermountain region, and the Pacific Coast are all part of the _____.

2. Look at the map on page 5 in your text. On the lines below write the color the map shows for each geographical area.

    Appalachian Highlands _____

    Great Basin _____

    Rocky Mountains _____

    Pacific Coast _____

2 Chapter 1, Lesson 1 • Lesson Preview   Reading Support Resources

Name: _____ Date: _____

CHAPTER 1
Lesson 1 Reading Strategy
The American Land
(*A More Perfect Union* pp. 4–13)

Self-Question This reading strategy helps you stay focused on what you read. Ask yourself questions before you read a section. Then read to see if you can find the answer to your questions.

1. Read the heading "The Relationship Between Geography and History" on page 4. Check the question you think this section will answer?

   ___ How does the land affect what happens in history?

   ___ How does history affect our lives today?

   ___ What parts of America are most interesting?

2. Look at the pictures on pages 6 and 7 and read the captions. Which question asks about all the pictures?

   ___ How might mountains, rocky coasts, and swamps have helped or hurt the colonists?

   ___ Why did mountains make it hard for the colonists to travel to the West?

   ___ What causes swamps?

3. Read the heading "The Eastern and Southern United States" on page 6. Write a question in the space below that you expect might be answered as you read the section.

   _____
   _____

4. Look at the pictures and read the captions on pages 8 through 13. Write a question in the space below that you expect might be answered as you read these pages.

   _____
   _____

Reading Support Resources   Reading Strategy • Chapter 1, Lesson 1

CHAPTER 1

Lesson 1 Summary
The American Land

(*A More Perfect Union* pp. 4–13)

Thinking Focus: How does the geography of the United States vary from one part of the nation to another?

The Relationship Between Geography and History

Physical geography is the study of **landforms** such as hills and mountains. **Human geography** is the study of how the land and people affect each other. You can find clues to America's history by looking at its land. For example, geography often determined the way of life of American Indian groups. Geography also helped determine where European settlers chose to live. Early settlers had to learn to meet the challenges of living in a vast, new land. Meeting these challenges helped them develop a strong sense of independence and self-reliance.

❓ In what ways is geography important to the study of history?

The Eastern and Southern United States

There are three main parts of the eastern United States: (1) The Coastal Plains stretch along the eastern edge of the country. This area has many **estuaries,** or places where rivers meet the ocean. It also gets a lot of **precipitation.** (2) The Piedmont is a rolling, hilly area between the Coastal Plains and the Appalachian Mountains. (3) The Appalachian Highlands stretch from northern Alabama to Maine.

❓ What are the main geographic features of the eastern and southern United States?

---

physical geography
(fĭz´ĭ-kəl jē-ŏg´rə-fē)
the study of the natural world

landform
(lănd´fôrm)
a natural land part, such as a hill, canyon, or plain

human geography
(hyōō´mən jē-ŏg´rə-fē)
the study of the ways the land and the people affect each other

estuary
(ĕs´chōō-ĕr´ē)
the mouth of a river where it meets the ocean

precipitation
(prĭ-sĭp´ĭ-tā´shən)
rain or snow

Summary continues on next page

The American Land *(Lesson 1 Summary continued)*

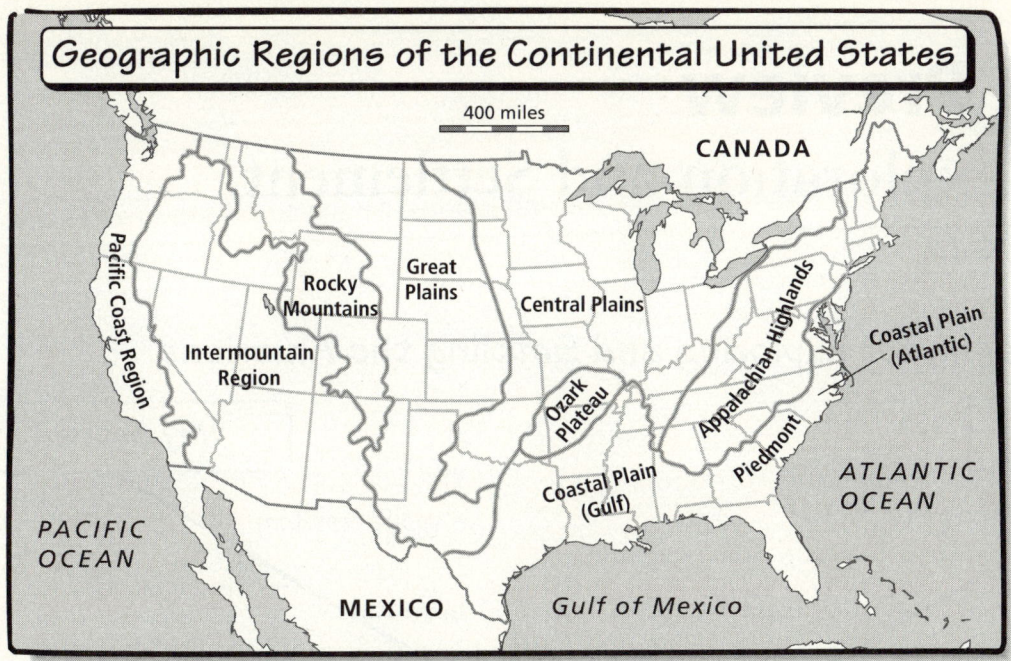

The Central Heartland

When settlers crossed over the Appalachian Mountains, they found land mostly covered by grassy **prairie**. This land is known as the Central Heartland. It covers the middle part of the United States and is an excellent area for farming. There are two main parts: the Central Plains and the Great Plains.

[?] What are the main geographic features of the central interior of the United States?

prairie
(prâr´ē)
hilly, grassy land

plateau
(plă-tō´)
high, flat land

The American West

There are three main parts of the American West: (1) The Rocky Mountains are very high. Early settlers had a hard time going over them. (2) The Intermountain region lies between the Rocky Mountains and the Sierra Nevada. The Intermountain region has many **plateaus,** including the Colorado Plateau. (3) The Pacific Coast is the western edge of the United States.

[?] What are the main geographic features of the western United States?

Name: _____ Date: _____

CHAPTER 1

Lesson 2 Preview
European Exploration and Settlement

(*A More Perfect Union* pp. 16–23)

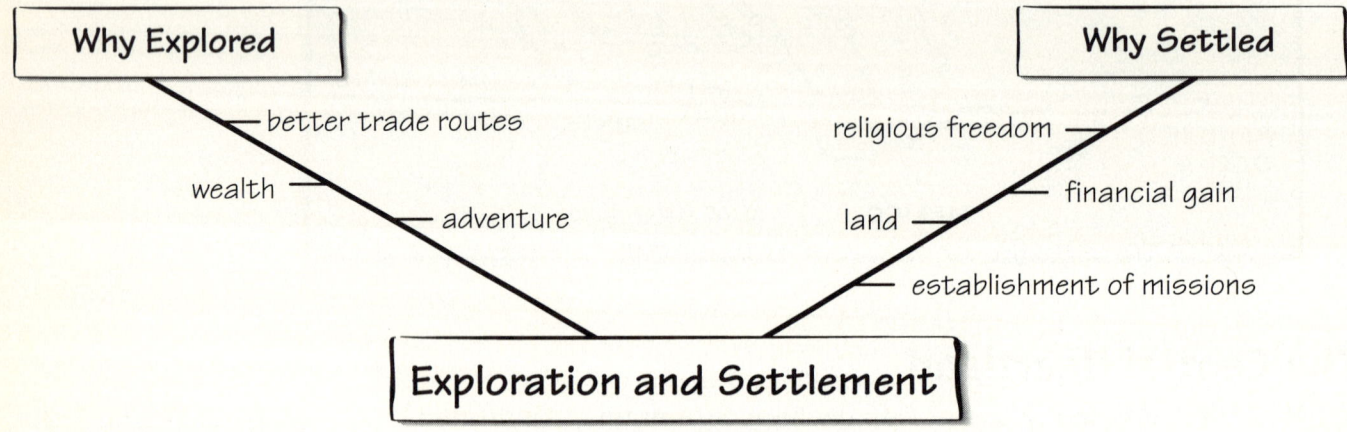

Reasons for Exploring and Settling the Americas

Why Explored: better trade routes, wealth, adventure

Why Settled: religious freedom, financial gain, land, establishment of missions

Exploration and Settlement

1. **Look at the graphic organizer above. Read each sentence and then fill in the blank.**

   a. Write one reason why people explored the Americas.

   _____
   _____
   _____

   b. Write one reason why people settled in the Americas.

   _____
   _____
   _____

2. **Look at the map and key on page 21. Which country had the most land in 1650?**

   _____

Name: _____ Date: _____

CHAPTER 1
Lesson 2 Reading Strategy
European Exploration and Settlement

(*A More Perfect Union* pp. 16–23)

Using the Visuals This reading strategy helps you use photographs, maps, charts, and illustrations to understand what you read. As you read, be sure to study the visuals and carefully read the captions.

1. Study the map on page 19 and answer the questions below.

   a. What time period does the map show? _____

   b. Which country did the most exploring during the years the map shows? _____

   c. What two oceans does the map show? _____

2. Now study the map on page 21 and answer the questions below.

   a. What time period does the map show? _____

   b. Which group has the largest amount of land? _____

   c. Which group has the smallest amount of land? _____

3. Compare the maps on pages 19 and 20. Name at least two places that are shown on both maps.

   _____

4. Look at the maps and pictures on pages 19–23. Then fill in the timeline below.

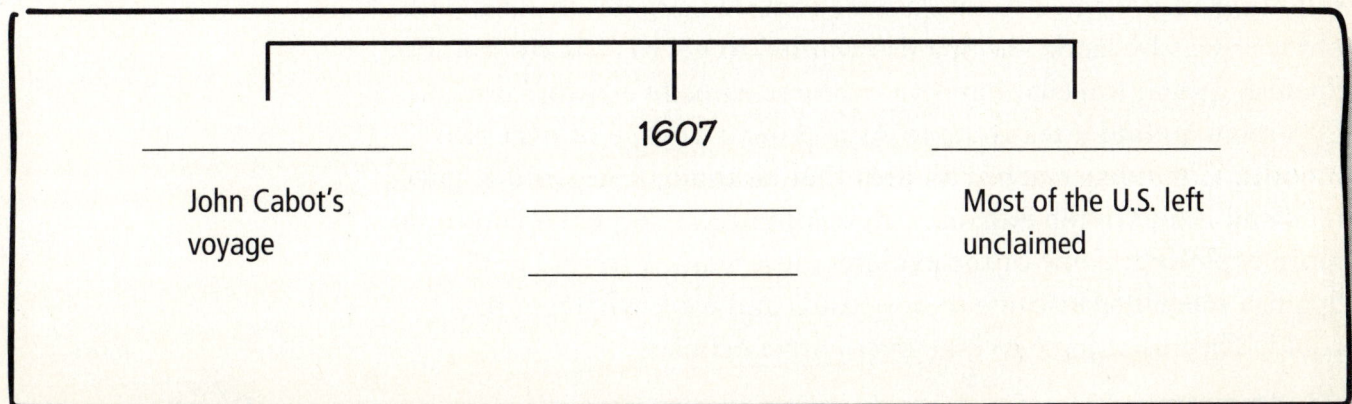

_____ 1607 _____
John Cabot's voyage _____ Most of the U.S. left unclaimed

Reading Support Resources Reading Strategy • Chapter 1, Lesson 2 **7**

CHAPTER 1
Lesson 2 Summary
European Exploration and Settlement

(*A More Perfect Union* pp. 16–23)

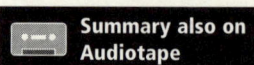 Summary also on Audiotape

Thinking Focus: Why did the Europeans leave their homes in the 1500s and 1600s to explore and settle new continents?

Europeans Look to New Worlds

Many Europeans in the 1400s and 1500s explored new lands. There were many reasons for this exploration.

- It was a time of great learning. People wanted to know more about the world they lived in.
- Many people wanted to find a place where they could freely practice their own religion.
- The rulers of some countries wanted to find faster ways of getting to Asia, a rich center of trade.
- Travel had become safer. Ships were faster and stronger. New tools helped sailors understand more about **navigation**.

[?] What historical events and developments led Europeans to explore the world beyond their borders?

Spain Leads the Way

The rulers of Spain wanted Asian goods, such as gold, silk, jewels, and salt. They also wanted to find a new, faster way to get to Asia. The old way was by land. The Spanish wanted to get to Asia by sea. The Spanish queen, Isabella, hired an explorer named Christopher Columbus to find a sea route to Asia. After a voyage of over two months, Columbus reached an area that he thought was India. It was really an island in the Bahamas. But Columbus's trip led Spain to do more exploring. Some of the explorers just wanted to find gold. Spanish **conquistadors** came to new lands and took whatever they could. They used force to take over native peoples.

[?] What was the chief motive of Spanish explorers in going to the New World?

navigation
(năv´ĭ-gā´ shən)
the way a ship's course is figured out

conquistador
(kŏng-kē´ stə-dôr´)
the Spanish word for "conqueror"

Summary continues on next page

European Exploration and Settlement *(Lesson 2 Summary continued)*

England, France, and the Netherlands Stake Claims

As Spain explored more of the New World, other countries in Europe worried that Spain would get too powerful. So England, France, and the Netherlands sent out explorers. These explorers sailed along the eastern coast of North America. They explored much of what is now Canada and the United States.

[?] Why did European nations other than Spain begin sending explorers to the New World?

Europeans Settle the New World

The population of Europe grew rapidly in the late 1500s and early 1600s. As a result, many people did not have jobs or land. They looked to the Americas for new opportunities. In addition, small religious **sects** broke off from older religions. This led to trouble between the older religions and the new sects. So, many people came to the New World to worship in peace.

The Spanish settled in South America, Central America, and Mexico. The French settled in Canada and the Great Lakes region. The Dutch settled in the state of New York.

In 1607, English settlers came to Jamestown, Virginia. Life was hard there. The land was not good for farming. The winters were long. Often there was not enough food. In 1620, another English group, the Pilgrims, settled at Plymouth, Massachusetts. The Pilgrims came to the New World to practice their religion freely.

[?] What factors led English settlers to leave their home for the New World?

sect
(sĕkt)
a small religious group that breaks off from a larger group

Name: _____ Date: _____

CHAPTER 1
Lesson 3 Preview
Europeans and Native Peoples

(*A More Perfect Union* pp. 26–31)

1. **Look at the graphic organizer above. Answer the questions.**

   a. What were two things the European colonists brought to America?
   _____
   _____

   b. What were two effects, or results, of the things that European colonists brought to America?
   _____
   _____

2. **Read the lesson title. Then read the main heading at the top of page 27. Which of the following sentences is true? Circle the letter of your answer.**

   a. The first Americans were Indians.
   b. The first Americans were Europeans.

Name: _____ Date: _____

CHAPTER 1
Lesson 3 Reading Strategy
Europeans and Native Peoples

(*A More Perfect Union* pp. 26–31)

Summarize This reading strategy helps you remember key points about what you have read. When you get to a good break in your reading, stop and write down the main ideas of what you have read.

1. Read the section "The First Americans" on page 27. Check the best summary of what life was like for American Indians.

    ___ Indians had their own languages and rich cultures long before the Europeans came.

    ___ Indians grew many different crops.

    ___ Five Indian tribes joined together and formed the Iroquois League.

2. Read from the heading "Early Contacts with American Indians" on page 27 to the heading "Relations with English Colonists" on page 29. Check the best summary of what happened when Europeans met American Indians.

    ___ The Europeans came to America in large boats to seek their fortunes.

    ___ Europeans and Indians were afraid of each other.

    ___ Indians caught European diseases, and the two groups traded with each other.

3. Read from the heading "Relations with English Colonists" on page 29 to the end of the lesson. Write a brief summary of relations between Colonists and Indians below.

_____
_____
_____
_____
_____
_____
_____
_____

Reading Support Resources

CHAPTER 1

Lesson 3 Summary
Europeans and Native Peoples

(*A More Perfect Union* pp. 26–31)

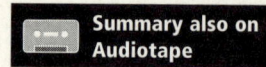 Summary also on Audiotape

Thinking Focus: What impact did European exploration and settlement have on the native inhabitants of the Americas?

The First Americans

European settlers were not the first people to come to the New World. Hundreds of Indian tribes already lived there. These tribes followed different ways of life and spoke different languages. Some tribes were **nomads.** They did not settle in one place. They moved around and hunted and fished. Other tribes were farmers. Sometimes the tribes formed **alliances** with each other. This helped them to defend themselves against attackers.

[?] In what ways were Indian tribes similar to European nations?

Early Contacts with American Indians

When European settlers came to America, some Indian groups were afraid. Others wanted to trade with the settlers. But any kind of contact with Europeans was a disaster for the Indians. The settlers brought a disease called smallpox, which killed more than half the Indians in North America. The Europeans had many things the Indians wanted. See the chart on the next page for things that Indians and Europeans traded and learned from each other.

[?] How did trade between whites and native peoples affect the daily lives of both Europeans and Indians?

nomad
(nō′măd′)
a person who has no home but moves from place to place

alliance
(ə-lī′əns)
an agreement because of common interests

Summary continues on next page

Europeans and Native Peoples (Lesson 3 Summary continued)

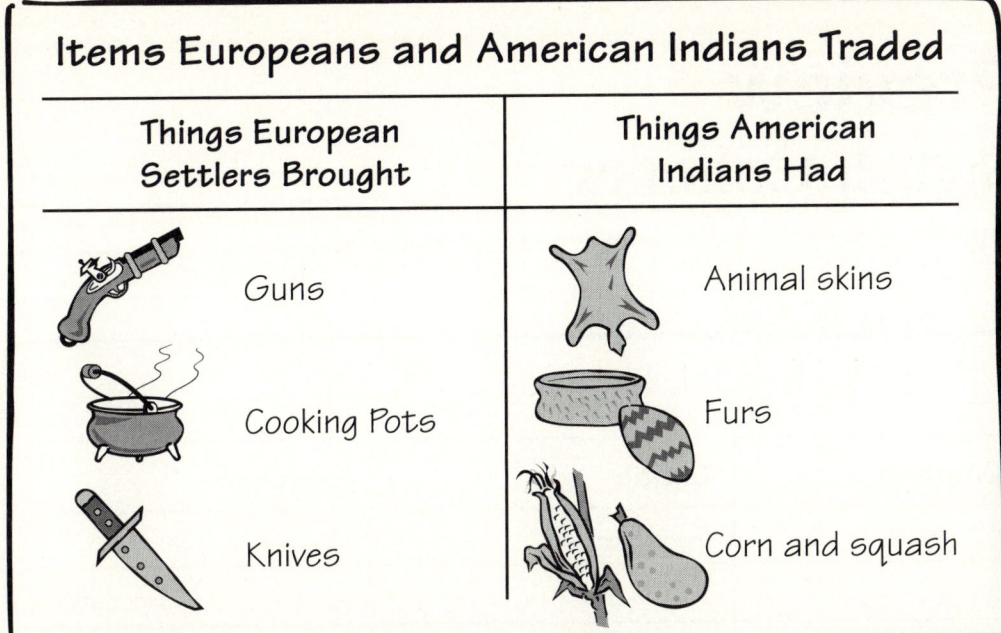

Relations with English Colonists

In some colonies, Europeans and Indians lived together in peace. Plymouth is a good example. The first winter in Plymouth killed half of the European settlers known as the Pilgrims. When spring came they had run out of food. But the Pemaquid Indians showed the Pilgrims where to hunt and fish and how to grow corn. In William Penn's colony, Pennsylvania, Quakers and Indians lived in peace for almost 70 years.

In Virginia, however, settlers cleared large pieces of land to raise tobacco. This made the local Indians angry. When white settlers killed an Indian leader, the Indians attacked and killed many settlers. This was the start of long years of fighting. Sometimes settlers turned Indian tribes against each other. In New England, settlers and members of one tribe fought against members of another tribe in Metacom's War.

? What caused most of the conflicts between European colonists and American Indians?

Name: _____ Date: _____

CHAPTER 1
Lesson 4 Preview
Life in the English Colonies

(*A More Perfect Union* pp. 33–39)

The English Colonies

	New England	Middle	Southern
Heritage	English, Scots	most diverse	moderately diverse
Community	small towns	spread out	plantations, backcountry
Livelihood	subsistence farming, fishing	cash crops, manufacturing	large-scale farming
Labor	mostly self, a few slaves	self, indentured servants, slaves	self, indentured servants, slaves

1. Look at the graphic organizer above. Read each sentence and then fill in the blank.

    a. The colonists in _____ lived mostly in small towns.

    b. Many people in the Southern colonies made their living from _____.

2. Look at the map on page 38. Tell which colonies are shown by the colors below.

    Green _____

    Purple _____

    Orange _____

Name: _____ Date: _____

CHAPTER 1
Lesson 4 Reading Strategy
Life in the English Colonies

(*A More Perfect Union* pp. 33–39)

Predict/Infer This reading strategy helps you understand what you have read and what you will read next. Before you read a section, think about the titles, pictures, and captions. Then think about what will happen in the selection.

1. Read the lesson title "Life in the English Colonies" and then look at the timeline at the top of page 33. What do you predict this chapter will be about?

    ___ the trip from England to the colonies in the early 1600s

    ___ the way the English colonists treated the Indians

    ___ the way of life of English colonists from 1700 to 1775

2. Look at the picture of the loading plan for the slave ship shown at the bottom of page 34. What does this picture tell you about the treatment of slaves?

    ___ Slaves were treated horribly, with no concern for their health.

    ___ The slaves came from all different parts of Africa.

    ___ The English colonists used slaves to work on their farms.

3. Read the red heading "Regional Differences" on page 35. Then read the blue headings and look at the pictures on pages 35–38. Based on these headings and pictures, what do you predict this section will be about?

    _____

4. Read the first paragraph on page 39 under "Patterns of Colonial Life." Then fill in the chart below with what you know and predict about life in the colonies.

What I Know	What I Predict

Reading Support Resources   Reading Strategy • Chapter 1, Lesson 4   **15**

CHAPTER 1

Lesson 4 Summary
Life in the English Colonies

(*A More Perfect Union* pp. 33–39)

Thinking Focus: What were some of the main characteristics of daily life in the English colonies in the early 1700s?

The Demand for Labor

Many farmers in the colonies used **indentured servants** to work on their farms. These servants worked as a way to pay for their voyage to the colonies. But in the late 1600s, more and more farmers bought black slaves. England had become active in the slave trade, so it was easy for colonists to get slaves. Also, conditions in England had gotten better, so fewer people became indentured servants in order to come to America.

Slave traders bought slaves in West Africa. The slaves were taken from their families and packed onto ships. Many died on the voyage. Those who lived were sold to farmers. Most would be slaves for the rest of their lives.

> **indentured servant**
> (ĭn-dĕn´chərd sûr´vənt)
> a person who works for someone in exchange for a boat trip from Europe to the colonies

❓ What factors led to the rapid growth of slavery in the English colonies?

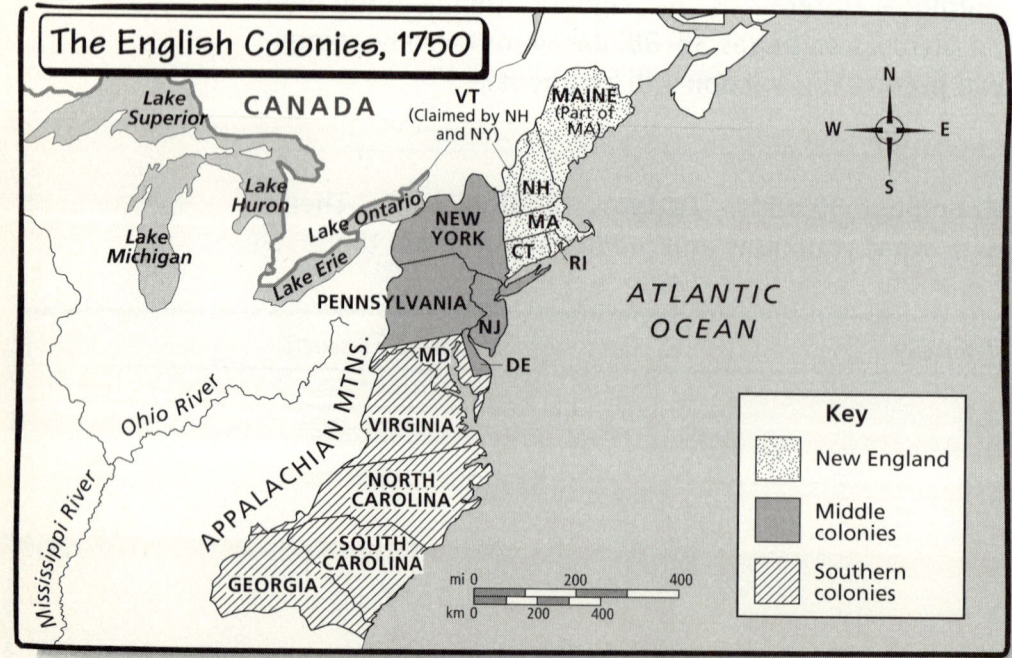

Summary continues on next page

Life in the English Colonies *(Lesson 4 Summary continued)*

Regional Differences

There were three main colonial regions: the New England colonies, the Middle colonies, and the Southern colonies.

Most people in New England were from England. Many New Englanders were **subsistence farmers**. The land was rocky and hard to farm. Farmers could only grow enough to feed their families. New Englanders who lived along the coast were fishermen and shipbuilders.

People in the Middle colonies were mainly from Germany, Scotland, and the Netherlands. Farmers in the Middle colonies could grow more than enough to feed their families. They were able to sell some of their crops. Other Middle colonists made glass, paper, or cloth.

Southern colonists grew tobacco and rice on huge farms called plantations. Many farmers got rich from these crops. But there were many poor people, too. The rich plantation owners were mostly English. The smaller farmers were usually German or Irish.

[?] What were the chief differences between life in the New England, Middle, and Southern colonies?

subsistence farmer (səb-sĭs′təns fär′mər) a person who grows only enough food to feed the family

Patterns of Colonial Life

There were many differences among the colonies. But the three colonial regions also had some things in common. Each region had a few port cities along the ocean. These cities were busy places where colonists could buy things from other countries and get news about the rest of the world.

When colonists traveled, they often stayed the night at one of the taverns along the road. These taverns gave travelers a meal and a bed. Taverns were also meeting places where different kinds of people came together.

[?] What features of daily life were common to all the English colonies?

Use with *A More Perfect Union* Pages 46–77

Chapter Overview
Reviewing the American Revolution

Fill in the blanks with information from the chapter.

When: 1700–1783
Where: The British Colonies
Who: British Government, American Colonists

Stages of the American Revolution

A New American Identity
- Population growth
- _____
- Colonial governments want some independence

↓

Growing Conflict
- _____
- British taxes and laws
- Colonists' reactions

↓

Fighting the Revolution
- _____
- Declaration of Independence
- Northern battles
- _____

↓

End of the War
- Treaty of Paris
- _____
- New state governments

Name: _____ Date: _____

CHAPTER 2
Lesson 1 Preview
An Emerging American Identity

(*A More Perfect Union* pp. 48–53)

Causes and Effects of Diversity in the Colonies

Diverse Origins
- British Isles
- Germany
- France
- Sweden
- Switzerland
- Africa

→ **American Colonies** →

A New Culture
- art
- language
- food
- religion
- farming/fishing

1. **Look at the graphic organizer above. Read each sentence and then fill in the blank.**

   a. People of diverse origins migrated to the _____.

   b. _____ was the result of the variety of people living in the American colonies.

   c. One result of the variety of people living in the United States that still exists today is _____ _____.

2. **Look at the pie chart of ethnic population in 1775 on page 49 in your text. Then look at the chart on page 50 of the 1997 U.S. Census. Describe at least one difference between the two charts.**

   _____
   _____
   _____
   _____
   _____

Reading Support Resources   Lesson Preview • Chapter 2, Lesson 1   **19**

Name: _____ Date: _____

CHAPTER 2
Lesson 1 Reading Strategy
An Emerging American Identity

(*A More Perfect Union* pp. 48–53)

Self-Question This reading strategy helps you stay focused on what you read. Ask yourself questions before you read a section. Then read to see if you can find the answer to your questions.

1. Read the red heading on page 48. Which question do you think you will be able to answer after you read the section? Circle the letter next to your answer.

   a. What new groups of people came to the colonies?

   b. What is the Northwest Passage?

   c. What was the most important crop in the Southern colonies?

2. Look at the pictures on pages 48–53 and read the captions. Which question can be answered from one of the pictures on these pages? Circle the letter next to your answer.

   a. What furniture did colonial homes contain?

   b. What foods did the colonists eat?

   c. What were the main ethnic groups in the colonies?

3. Read the red heading on page 51. Then write a question that you expect might be answered as you read the section.

   _____

   _____

4. Read the red heading on page 52. Fill in the left hand column of the chart with questions you expect to have answered as you read the section that follows. After you read the section, fill in the right-hand column of the chart.

My Questions	What I Learned by Reading

CHAPTER 2
Lesson 1 Summary
An Emerging American Identity
(*A More Perfect Union* pp. 48–53)

Thinking Focus: How did many kinds of new immigrants help to create a distinct American culture?

The Colonial Population Grows and Changes

In the early to mid-1700s, a new wave of **immigrants** settled in the colonies. The majority of these newcomers were from Ireland, Scotland, Germany, and Sweden. Most moved due to difficult economic times or political unrest. Some came to escape religious persecution. America became an example of **pluralism**, or a nation in which many ethnic, religious, and cultural groups live together. But not all of the new arrivals came voluntarily. Black slaves were brought from Africa. Many of them worked on southern plantations.

[?] How did the make-up of the American population change between 1700 and 1775?

immigrant
(ĭm´ĭ-grənt)
a person born in one country who moves into and lives in another country

pluralism
(ploŏr´ə-lĭz´əm)
the existence of many different ethnic, religious, or cultural groups living together in one nation

A Varied Population Creates a Unique New Culture

By 1750, different peoples had created a new culture that became known as "American." Each culture brought new words to the language. Different immigrants also brought a variety of religious traditions.

A religious revival known as the Great Awakening moved through the colonies from 1730 to 1750. Ministers gathered followers by attacking powerful religious and political leaders. They also spoke out against the Church of England. The Awakening led to a sense of greater independence from Britain.

[?] What features of everyday life in the colonies were distinctly American?

Summary continues on next page

An Emerging American Identity (Lesson 1 Summary continued)

Colonial Governments Seek Greater Independence

For much of the late 1600s and 1700s, the British government practiced a policy known as **salutary neglect**. England was too busy with conflicts in Europe to worry about the colonies.

By the 1730s, colonial assemblies—which were elected by the colonists—had won the right to approve plans for spending money. The king had the right to **veto** a bill from a colonial assembly. But the assembly often passed a similar bill to replace the vetoed bill. In this way, the assembly—not the king—held most of the power in the colonial government.

Soon, however, England began to try to regain its authority.

salutary neglect
(săl´yə-tĕr´ē nĭ-glĕkt´)
the policy of weakly enforcing laws that England used to rule the colonies in the late 1600s and early 1700s

veto
(vē´tō)
to prevent a bill from becoming a law

[?] How did the British policy of salutary neglect contribute to the development of colonial governments?

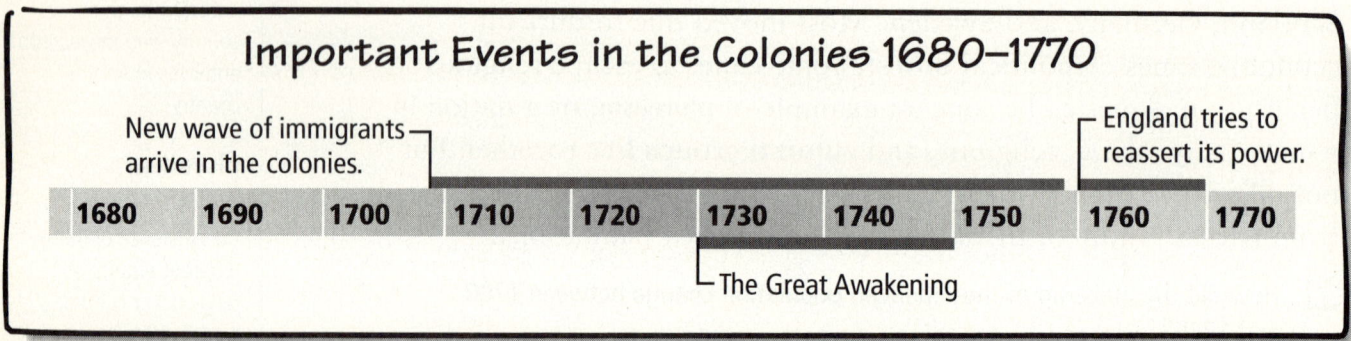

Name: _____ Date: _____

CHAPTER 2
Lesson 2 Preview
Growing Conflict with England

(*A More Perfect Union* pp. 54–59)

Causes and Effects of British Laws

1. Look at the graphic organizer above. Read each sentence and then fill in the blank.

   a. The Stamp Act and other laws were passed because England needed to pay off its _____.

   b. The British laws upset the colonists and led to boycotts, the _____, and the First Continental Congress.

2. Look at the map on page 55 in your text. Read the map key and the caption. Use this information to tell which two countries claimed the most land in North America in 1763.

   _____
   _____

CHAPTER 2

Lesson 2 Reading Strategy
Growing Conflict with England

(*A More Perfect Union* pp. 54–59)

Sequence This reading strategy helps you follow what is happening in your reading. As you read, pay attention to dates and times, as well as to words such as *before*, *finally*, *after*, and *then*.

1. Read page 54. Place the following events in order by writing *1*, *2*, and *3* in the blanks.

   ___ Andrew Oliver resigns as stamp distributor.

   ___ The colonists hang an image of Andrew Oliver.

   ___ The colonists destroy Oliver's office and home.

2. Read page 55. Then look back at the paragraph that begins "Braddock's defeat did not discourage the British."

   What year did the Seven Years' War start? _____

   What word or words helped you find the answer?

   _____

3. Read the section "British Policies Stir Colonial Protests." Then place the following events in order by writing *1* or *2* in the blanks.

   ___ Chief Pontiac attacked British forts.

   ___ The king issued a Proclamation closing the territories west of the Appalachians.

4. Read the section "Tensions Reach the Breaking Point." Then complete the timeline below.

   March 5, 1770   _____   _____
   _____   Boston Tea Party   First Continental
                                                    Congress Meets

CHAPTER 2

Lesson 2 Summary
Growing Conflict with England

(*A More Perfect Union* pp. 54–59)

Thinking Focus: What were the causes of the colonists' growing resentment of British rule?

Rivalry for North America Leads to Seven Years' War

Both England and France wanted control of North America, and each claimed land along the Ohio River Valley. In 1755, British general Edward Braddock and his troops tried to take over the region. But the French drove the British back. Braddock's defeat led the British to strengthen their military forces in North America. The Seven Years' War broke out between the French and British in 1756. By 1760, the British had taken all of Canada. In 1763, the British and the French signed the Treaty of Paris, which ended the war. This treaty gave England control of Canada, as well as of all lands east of the Mississippi River that had belonged to the French.

? What did England gain as a result of the Seven Years' War?

British Policies Stir Colonial Protests

The war left Britain deeply in debt. The British government thought that the colonists should help pay this debt. It also wanted to strengthen its control over the colonies.

First, Britain passed the Proclamation of 1763, which closed lands west of the Appalachians to colonists. Next, it passed the Quartering Act, which forced the colonists to provide food and housing for British troops. In 1765, the British passed the Stamp Act. This law forced colonists to pay a special tax every time they bought any printed material.

Summary continues on next page

Acts of Parliament Affecting the Colonies

Proclamation of 1763	Quartering Act	Stamp Act	Townshend Acts	Intolerable Acts
Closed all territory west of the Appalachians to colonists.	Required that colonists give food and housing to British troops.	Required colonists to buy a stamp each time they bought printed items such as newspapers.	Taxed paint, glass, paper, and tea.	Punished colonists for the Boston Tea Party.

The colonists felt they should not be taxed unless they were given a voice in the British Parliament. So colonists calling themselves the Sons of Liberty protested against the Stamp Act. Their protest was successful, and the British Parliament took back the Stamp Act in 1766.

? How did the Seven Years' War change the relationship between England and the colonies?

Tensions Reach the Breaking Point

In 1776, Parliament passed the Townshend Acts, which taxed the colonists on things like imported paper, glass, and tea. Customs officials were granted **writs of assistance**. The angry colonists responded by calling for a **boycott** against imported goods. On March 5, 1770, colonial workers attacked a guard at the Boston Customs House. British soldiers came to break up the fight. Five rioters were killed. This fight is known as the Boston Massacre.

Tensions continued to rise. In December 1773, colonists boarded ships in Boston Harbor and dumped hundreds of boxes of tea overboard. The "Boston Tea Party" made the British very angry. They passed another set of strict laws, which colonists called the Intolerable Acts. In the fall of 1774, delegates from all 13 colonies met in Philadelphia for the First Continental Congress. The Congress called for an **embargo** against England. The Congress also told the colonies to train soldiers for a possible war.

? What actions taken by Parliament contributed to the growing tension between England and the colonies?

---

writs of assistance
(rĭts ŭv ə-sĭs′təns)
papers from the British government that allowed officials to search colonists' homes and businesses without their consent

boycott
(boi′kŏt′)
a group protest in which people refuse to buy or use a product in order to force a government, person, or company to take some action

embargo
(ĕm-bär′gō)
a ban on trade with another nation

Name: _____ Date: _____

CHAPTER 2
Lesson 3 Preview
Fighting the American Revolution
(*A More Perfect Union* pp. 62–70)

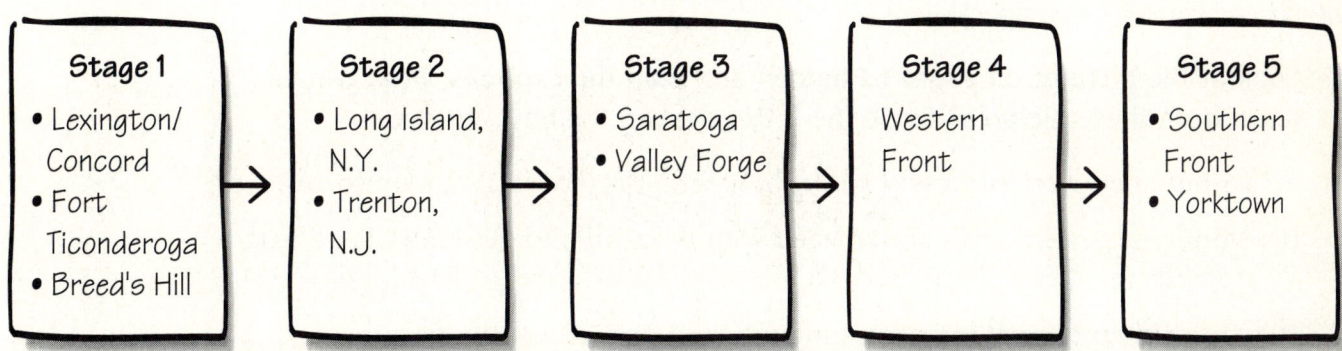

1. **Look at the graphic organizer above. Then read the following list of events. Place the events in order according to which happened first, second, and so forth.**

    ___ General Washington's men capture troops at Trenton, New Jersey

    ___ Battle of Lexington/Concord

    ___ Battle of Yorktown

    ___ Washington's troops camp at Valley Forge

2. **Look at the picture of the Battle of Lexington on page 62. Name at least one difference you notice between the British soldiers and the colonists.**

    _____
    _____
    _____
    _____

Name: Date:

CHAPTER 2
Lesson 3 Reading Strategy
Fighting the American Revolution
(*A More Perfect Union* pp. 62–70)

Using the Visuals This reading strategy helps you use photographs, maps, charts, and illustrations to help you understand what you read. As you read, be sure to study the visuals and carefully read the captions.

1. Look at the pictures on pages 62 and 64 and read the captions. What can you learn from these pictures? Circle the letter next to the best answer.

    a. Minutemen were professional soldiers who dressed in fancy uniforms.

    b. Minutemen were ordinary citizens who were able to get ready for battle quickly.

    c. Minutemen carried large amounts of food and other supplies.

2. Look at the picture on page 65 and read the caption. Write a sentence describing what is happening in the picture.
   _____

3. Look at the picture of the surrender of Burgoyne at Saratoga on the timeline on page 66. How might the landscape have affected the outcome of the battle of Saratoga?
   _____
   _____

4. Study the timeline on pages 66–67 and the map on page 69. Then answer the questions below.

    a. What kinds of information can you learn from a timeline?
       _____
       _____

    b. What kinds of information can you learn from a map?
       _____
       _____

CHAPTER 2

Lesson 3 Summary
Fighting the American Revolution

(*A More Perfect Union* pp. 62–70)

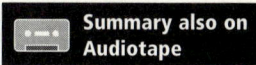

Thinking Focus: How did the colonies manage to defeat the most powerful nation in the world?

Early Battles of the Revolution

The first battles between colonists and the British took place on April 19, 1775, at Lexington and Concord, Massachusetts. The British had planned to arrest a group of colonial leaders. But the Americans found out about the plan, and the colonial **militia** was waiting when the British arrived. They blocked the British soldiers' path. The British fired their guns, killing eight **minutemen**. Then in May 1775, colonial soldiers surprised British troops at Fort Ticonderoga in New York. The Battle of Bunker Hill followed. Colonial forces let British troops come close to them and then fired at close range. The Americans retreated only when they ran out of ammunition.

[?] Find evidence to support the following statement: The early battles showed that the Revolution was likely to be a long and difficult war.

militia
(mə-lĭsh´ə)
a citizen army

minutemen
(mĭn´ĭt-măn´)
members of the colonial Massachusetts militia

republic
(rĭ-pŭb´lĭk)
a form of government in which people have a voice through the representatives they choose

The Road to the Declaration of Independence

Many colonists still wanted to avoid a major war with England. So the colonists sent the Olive Branch Petition asking King George to keep the peace. Instead, the king told his troops to crush the colonial rebellion. In January 1776, Thomas Paine published *Common Sense,* which said that the colonists had a right to form their own **republic**. Many colonists agreed. In the spring of 1776, Thomas Jefferson wrote a document declaring the colonies' independence. On July 4, 1776, delegates from each colony signed this document, called the Declaration of Independence.

[?] What events finally convinced many colonists that they should declare their independence from England?

Summary continues on next page

Reading Support Resources

Fighting the American Revolution *(Lesson 3 Summary continued)*

War in the North

Congress asked George Washington to lead an American army. The army's first big battle was a disaster. But Americans later claimed an important victory at Saratoga, New York. This victory convinced France that the Americans were strong enough to win the war. So France agreed to help the colonists. But not everything went well for the colonists. During the winter of 1777–1778, Washington's troops camped in the bitter cold at Valley Forge, Pennsylvania. More than 2,500 men died from starvation and sickness.

[?] Why did the French decide to enter the Revolution on the side of the colonists?

War in the West and South

In early 1778, most of the fighting took place in the West and South. In the West, the Americans knew the trails through the forests and took the British by surprise. But in the South, British General Cornwallis won many victories. When Cornwallis moved west, however, American General Nathaniel Greene weakened him with sneak attacks. Cornwallis finally retreated to Yorktown, Virginia. At Yorktown, George Washington trapped Cornwallis's army. On October 19, 1781, Cornwallis surrendered to General Washington.

[?] What factors led to Cornwallis's surrender at Yorktown?

The Treaty of Paris

The surrender at Yorktown forced the British to ask for peace. France and its ally Spain wanted to limit the land the British gave up to the Americans. Spain did not want a strong United States to threaten its own American colonies. To avoid conflict, the Americans met secretly with the British. They agreed to set the border of the United States at the Mississippi River. They signed the Treaty of Paris, which ended the war, in 1783.

[?] Why did the delegates for the United States meet secretly with the British to negotiate the Treaty of Paris?

Name: _____   Date: _____

CHAPTER 2
Lesson 4 Preview
Fighting the War at Home

(*A More Perfect Union* pp. 71–75)

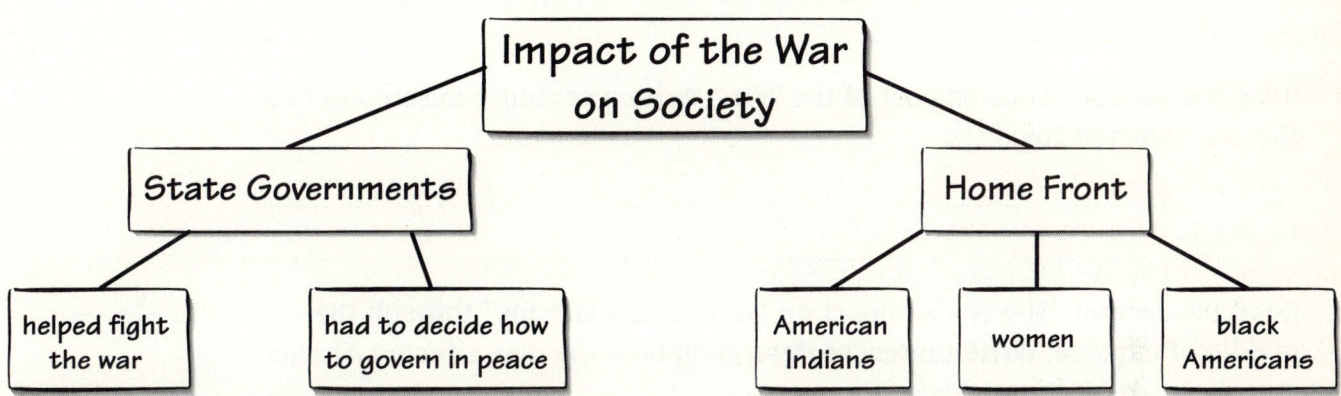

1. **Look at the graphic organizer above. Read each sentence and then fill in the blank.**

    a. The American Revolution had a great impact on _____ and the home front.

    b. Some groups of people who made up the home front were _____, _____, and _____.

2. **Look at the graph of wartime exports and imports on page 73. Answer the following questions:**

    a. In what year were exports highest? _____

    b. In what year were imports highest? _____

    c. What can you tell about the effect of the war on foreign trade?
    _____
    _____
    _____
    _____

Reading Support Resources   Lesson Preview • Chapter 2, Lesson 4   **31**

CHAPTER 2
Lesson 4 Reading Strategy
Fighting the War at Home

(*A More Perfect Union* pp. 71–75)

Compare and Contrast This reading strategy helps you understand how events are similar and different. As you read about historical events, think about how they compare and contrast with events you already know.

1. Read the section "Local Impact of the War." Write a sentence describing how the war affected Loyalists.

   _____

   _____

2. Read the section "The War's Impact on Some Social Groups" through the middle of page 74. Write sentences describing how the war affected African Americans and Native Americans.

   _____

   _____

3. Read the section "Women Join the Battle." Write a sentence describing the role women had in the war.

   _____

   _____

4. Fill in the chart below with information from the lesson.

	Negative Effects of the War	Positive Effects of the War
African Americans		
Native Americans		
Women		

CHAPTER 2

Lesson 4 Summary
Fighting the War at Home

(*A More Perfect Union* pp. 71–75)

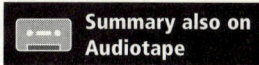
Summary also on Audiotape

Thinking Focus: How did the American Revolution affect the people of the colonies?

Local Impact of the War

Many colonists had supported the British during the Revolution. These people were called Loyalists. There were hard feelings between the Patriots and the Loyalists, and many Loyalists were forced to leave their homes. The war was also hard on the economy. Soldiers on both sides burned crops and settlements. The British took over most port cities and cut the colonies off from trade. Without foreign trade, the economy fell apart and many businesses failed. The colonies began printing their own **currency**. But as more and more money was printed, it became worth less and less. This led to higher prices, or **inflation**.

[?] How did the war affect American agriculture, manufacturing, and trade?

The War's Impact on Some Social Groups

Early in the war, the British promised freedom to slaves who would fight on the British side. So many slaves joined the British army. Later, many African Americans fought on the colonial side. But few blacks benefited from the ideals set forth in the Declaration of Independence.

The war was very hard on American Indians. Early in the fighting, the most powerful Indian group, the Iroquois Confederacy, broke apart. Most of the tribes fought on the British side. After the war, the colonists responded by burning Iroquois villages and killing the people. The Iroquois and the Cherokee were also forced to **cede** much of their land to the newly formed United States government.

Women were important to the war effort on both the British and

currency
(kŭr´ən-sē)
money

inflation
(ĭn-flā´shən)
rising prices

cede
(sēd)
to give up land in a formal agreement

Summary continues on next page

colonial sides. Some took part in the fighting. Others stayed home and ran family farms or businesses.

[?] What impact did the war have on the Iroquois Confederacy?

Impact of War on Some Social Groups

Black Americans	American Indians	Women
Some slaves won their freedom by fighting for the British. Some free black Americans fought bravely for the colonists. But few black Americans saw the ideals of equality and justice put into practice.	Most sympathized with their trading partners, the British. In revenge, Americans burned Indian villages and forced Indians to give up much of their land.	Women marched with the armies on both sides. They served as cooks, laundresses, nurses, guides and porters. They also published pamphlets and wrote about the war.

Colonies Form New Governments

During the war, the colonies formed state governments. Each state had a militia and paid taxes to help the war effort. When the war ended, the states faced new problems. They had to get the economy working again, and they had to figure out important laws. Each state was used to working alone. Now they had to work as a group. It would take a long time before the states could work together as a united national government.

[?] Why was it more difficult for the colonies to work together after the war than during the war?

Use with *A More Perfect Union* Pages 80–103

Chapter Overview
Toward the Constitution

Fill in the blank spaces below with information from the chapter.

When: 1775–1787

Where: The Thirteen States

The Articles of Confederation

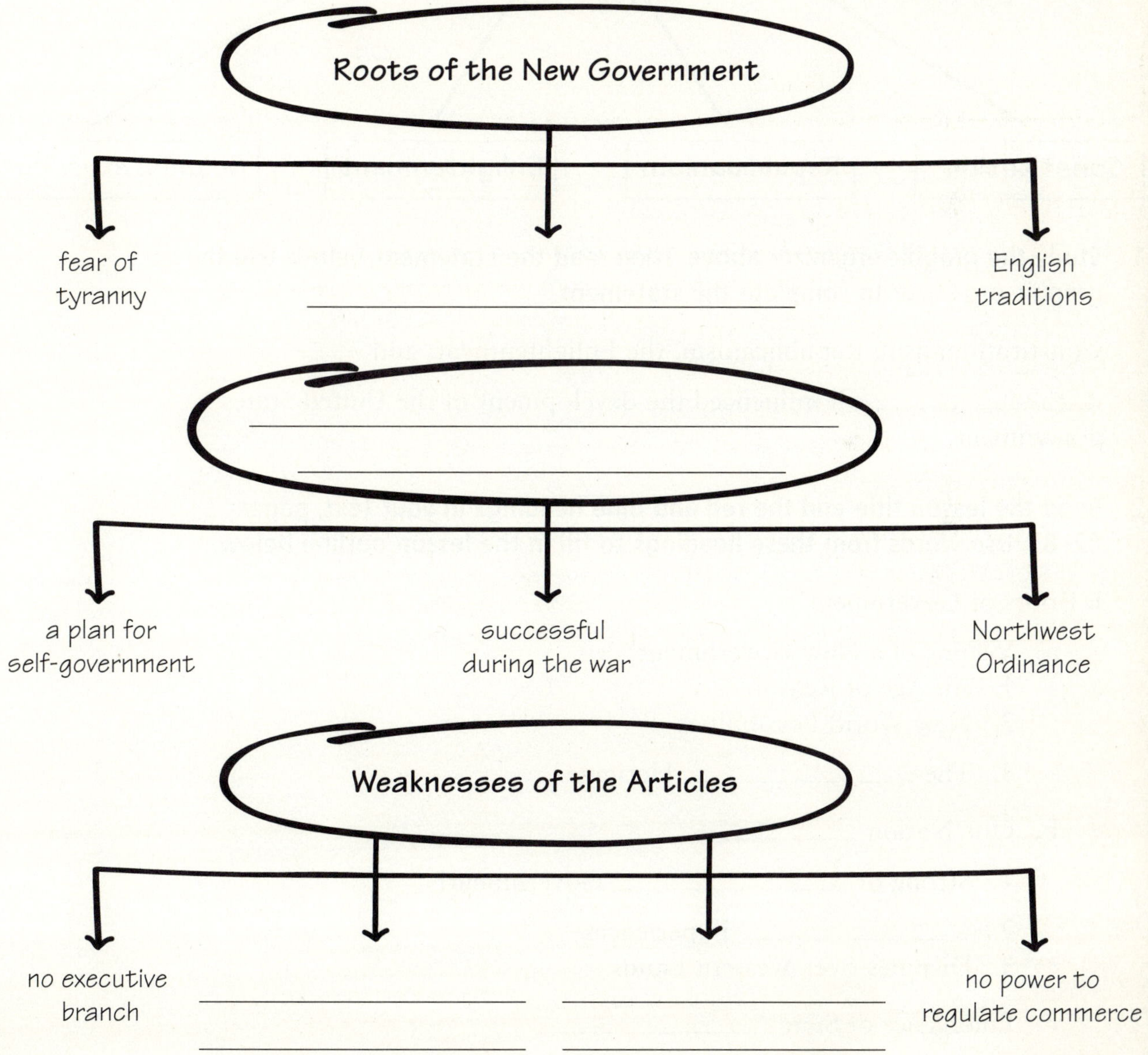

Roots of the New Government

- fear of tyranny
- _____
- English traditions

(_____)

- a plan for self-government
- successful during the war
- Northwest Ordinance

Weaknesses of the Articles

- no executive branch
- _____
- _____
- no power to regulate commerce

Reading Support Resources · Chapter Overview • Chapter 3 · 35

Name: _____ Date: _____

CHAPTER 3
Lesson 1 Preview
Roots of Government

(A More Perfect Union pp. 82–87)

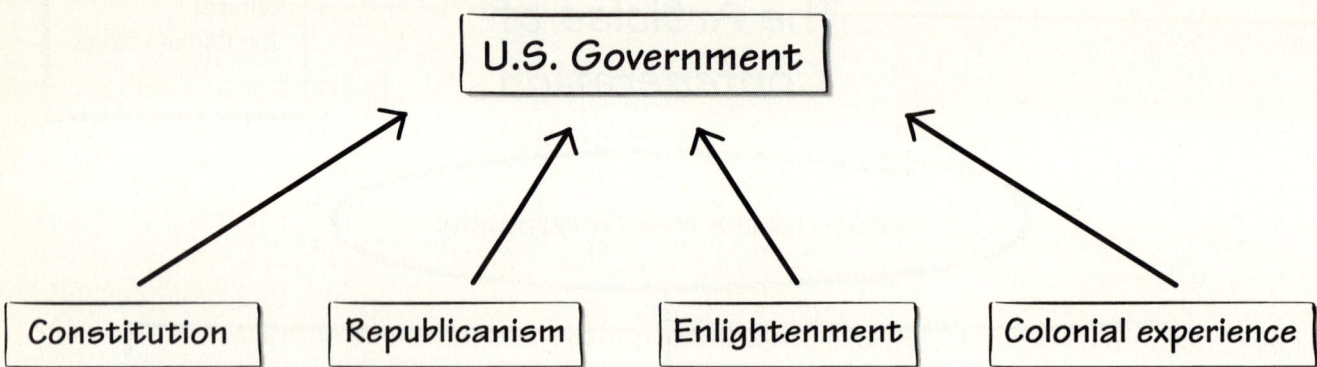

1. Study the graphic organizer above. Then read the statement below. Use the graphic organizer to complete the statement.

   Constitutionalism, Republicanism, the Enlightenment, and _____ all influenced the development of the United States government.

2. Read the lesson title and the red and blue headings in your text, pages 82–87. Use words from these headings to fill in the lesson outline below.

   I. Roots of Government

       a. Visions of a New Government
           1. An Age of Reason
           2. New World Possibilities
           3. The _____ Heritage

       b. One Nation _____
           1. Strong or _____ Government?
           2. _____ Experiences
           3. Disputes over Western Lands

       c. Emergence of State _____
           1. _____ in the States
           2. Variety Among the _____

Name: _____   Date: _____

CHAPTER 3

Lesson 1 Reading Strategy
Roots of Government

(*A More Perfect Union* pp. 82–87)

Summarize This reading strategy helps you remember key points about what you have read. When you get to a good break in your reading, stop and write down the main ideas of what you have read.

1. Read from the top of page 82 until the heading "New World Possibilities." What is the best summary of the ideas of the Enlightenment?
   a. Thomas Jefferson was influenced by the ideas of the Enlightenment.
   b. People could solve religious, social, political, and economic issues by using reason.
   c. People should revolt against authority.

2. Continue reading to the red square at the top of page 84. What is the best summary of the kind of constitution Americans wanted for their new government? Circle the letter next to your answer.
   a. They wanted a written document that would spell out their rights.
   b. They wanted a Magna Carta.
   c. They didn't want a king.

3. Read the section "One Nation United." Then fill in the chart below with a brief summary explaining why the Articles of Confederation were not immediately approved.

   Delays in Approving the Articles
   _____
   _____
   _____
   _____

4. Read the section "Emergence of State Governments." Then write a sentence or two summarizing the features of Pennsylvania's first constitution.

   _____

Reading Support Resources   Reading Strategy • Chapter 3, Lesson 1

CHAPTER 3

Lesson 1 Summary
Roots of Government

(*A More Perfect Union* pp. 82–87)

Thinking Focus: What major ideas went into the shaping of the new American government?

Visions of a New Government

The Americans who were working to set up a new national government in the 1700s were influenced by the ideas of a European movement known as the Enlightenment. One idea of interest to them was that people did not have to follow one authority (like a king). Instead, they could make society and government better by using reason. Republicanism, or government based on the decisions of the people, came from this idea. Americans were also influenced by the Magna Carta of 1215. This English document set up the right to a trial by jury. They also looked carefully at the English Bill of Rights. This gave Parliament more power to run the country and weakened the power of the king. The American writers wanted to have a single written **constitution** that would spell out their rights and be acceptable to all of the people in the 13 colonies.

How did Americans hope to improve upon the English tradition of constitutional law?

constitution
(kŏn'stĭ-tōō'shən)
a document that outlines the basic rules of government

British Influences on the American Government	
1215, Magna Carta	1689, English Bill of Rights
• Royal power limited • King to seek advice on laws and taxes • Due process of law • Trial by jury of peers	• King needed consent of Parliament to levy taxes • Free election of members of lower house of Parliament • Restricted King from maintaining an army in peacetime

Summary continues on next page

Roots of Government *(Lesson 1 Summary continued)*

One Nation United

In June 1776, the men of the Second Continental Congress began writing a plan for a new government. It was called the Articles of Confederation. They called for a **federal** government that would have power over the states. The colonists had just broken away from England, which had a strong central government and king. They were worried about having the same kind of government in America. Arguments had often broken out between the colonies' **legislatures**, who spoke for the colonists, and their governors, who were chosen by the king. Some delegates in the Second Continental Congress wanted the government to be a **confederation** that gave each state more power. They finally agreed that each state would have equal power in the new Congress and that there would be no national **executive**.

In 1777, the final Articles of Confederation were sent to the 13 states for approval. But there were differences of opinion among several states over western lands. This delayed the passage of the Articles. Three years later, in 1781, New York, Maryland, and Virginia agreed to transfer their western lands to the central government. The Articles were then approved.

[?] What issues contributed to the reluctance of Americans to establish a strong national government?

Emergence of State Governments

After declaring independence from Great Britain, each new state set up its own government. All the states had legislatures made up of elected representatives. In most states, representatives had to live in, and own property in, the communities they represented. But state governments were not all the same. In some states, like Pennsylvania and North Carolina, it was not necessary to own property to be able to vote. The Massachusetts constitution stated that all men were "born free and equal." This helped to end slavery in that state. Writing these state constitutions helped Americans learn about how republicanism really worked.

[?] Predict which aspects of the early state constitutions would eventually be adopted for the national government.

---

federal
(fĕd′ər-əl)
relating to a system of government that divides power between a central authority and a number of smaller states

legislature
(lĕj′ĭ-slā′chər)
an officially selected group responsible for making laws

confederation
(kən-fĕd′ə-rā′shən)
a group of states joined loosely for a common purpose

executive
(ĭg-zĕk′yə-tĭv)
a person or group that has authority over others; in this instance, no one person would be given authority to control the government

Name: _____ Date: _____

CHAPTER 3
Lesson 2 Preview
The Articles of Confederation

(*A More Perfect Union* pp. 90–94)

Responsibilities of Central and State Governments

	Central Government	State Governments
Diplomacy	control foreign affairs	enforce treaties
Finance and Commerce	set value of coins, weights, and measures	tax citizens, imports, and exports
Military	appoint army officers	
Law	negotiate between states	direct court system

1. **Look at the graphic organizer above. Then read the following sentences and fill in the blanks.**

    a. The _____ government set the value of coins, but the _____ governments had the power to tax citizens.

    b. In matters of law, the central government could _____.

    c. A direct court system was the responsibility of _____ government.

2. **Read the lesson title and the red and blue headings on pages 90–94 in your text. Use words from those headings to fill in the lesson outline below.**

    The Articles of Confederation

        I. Confederation Works for Wartime

        II. The _____ Define Government

            A. _____ Powers

            B. Limited Sovereignty

        III. Morris Funds the National _____

Name: _____ Date: _____

CHAPTER 3

Lesson 2 Reading Strategy
The Articles of Confederation

(*A More Perfect Nation* pp. 90–94)

Predict/Infer This reading strategy helps you understand what you have read about and what you will read next. Before you read a section, think about the titles, pictures, and captions. Then think about what will happen in the selection.

1. **Read page 90. What do you predict will be an important idea discussed in the lesson? Circle the letter next to the best answer.**

    a. free trade among the states

    b. the need for a strong central government

    c. the cost of goods in different states

2. **Read from the top of page 91 to the bottom of page 92. What do you predict the states will do when Congress tries to collect taxes from them? Circle the letter next to the best answer.**

    a. They will not pay the taxes.

    b. They will overthrow the government.

    c. They will happily pay the taxes.

3. **Name one clue from your reading that helped you make your prediction.**

    _____

4. **The last section of the lesson is titled "Morris Funds the National Treasury." Based on this title and on what you have already read, complete the chart below. Then check your predictions as you read the section.**

What I Know	What I Predict

Reading Support Resources   Reading Strategy • Chapter 3, Lesson 2   **41**

CHAPTER 3
Lesson 2 Summary
The Articles of Confederation

(*A More Perfect Union* pp. 90–94)

Thinking Focus: How did the Articles of Confederation divide power between the new national government and the state governments?

Confederation Works for Wartime

Even before all the states agreed to the Articles of Confederation, Congress used them as their plan for the government. Congress sent diplomats to Europe to get support for the fight for independence from Great Britain. The Articles of Confederation helped prove to Europeans that Americans were serious about setting up a new nation. This helped Congress get help from European nations during the war and when they were working on the peace treaty.

[?] How did the Articles help win support from Europeans for the American cause?

The Articles Define Government

Under the Articles of Confederation, Congress was not strong. The states still had a lot of power. But the Articles did give Congress a few important powers:

- Congress had **sovereignty** to work with foreign countries and make treaties with them.
- Congress created four important national departments: foreign affairs, war, finance, and the post office.

sovereignty
(sŏv′ər-ĭn-tē)
the authority that an independent country or state has within its borders

Congressional Powers Under the Articles of Confederation

Control the national army

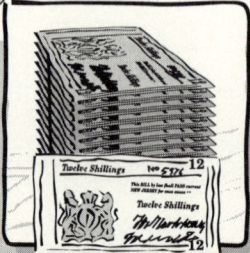
Issue money

Set up a system of weights and measures

Summary continues on next page

The Articles of Confederation (Lesson 2 Summary continued)

The central government's limited power caused problems.
- Conflicts between states were hard to solve because there was no national court system.
- Members of Congress were elected for only a one-year **term of office**. They could not serve more than three terms in a six-year period. Members often found that their terms were finished before they could do all they had planned.
- Although Congress could make decisions and treaties with other countries, it could not enforce them.

term of office
(tûrm ŭv ô´fĭs)
a limited period of time during which an elected official serves the public

[?] What was the national government's most serious weakness under the Articles of Confederation?

Morris Funds the National Treasury

The central government did not have the power to tax citizens directly. Each state was supposed to collect taxes and give the money to the national government. Often the states did not. As a result, the government did not have the money to pay Revolutionary War soldiers.

The lack of money became so serious that Robert Morris, the Superintendent of Finance for the Congress, used his own money to pay for army wages and supplies. Still, many soldiers were not paid. Congress had been printing paper money, but the money was worthless. So states started making their own money. People had to use a different kind of money in each state. Business suffered because it was hard to use so many different kinds of money.

[?] If the states still issued their own money today, how would trade and travel within the country be different?

Name: _____   Date: _____

CHAPTER 3
Lesson 3 Preview
The Crisis of Confederation

(*A More Perfect Union* pp. 95–99)

Causes and Effects of U.S. Financial Problems

Causes
- central government has no power to tax
- central government has no power to regulate commerce

→ Worthless Money

No Import Taxes →

Effects
- government can't pay soldiers
- farmers rebel
- U.S. has little income
- states compete
- U.S. can't retaliate against Britain

1. Look at the graphic organizer above. Use the following words to fill in the blanks below.

   | causes   effects |

   a. The central government's inability to tax was one of the _____ of worthless money.

   b. One of the _____ of worthless money was that soldiers couldn't be paid.

2. Look at the map on page 98 in your text and read its caption. Then read the following questions and fill in the blanks.

   a. In what year was the map made?
   _____

   b. What four lakes are shown completely on the map?
   _____
   _____
   _____
   _____

44 Chapter 3, Lesson 3 • Lesson Preview   Reading Support Resources

Name: _____ Date: _____

CHAPTER 3

Lesson 3 Reading Strategy
The Crisis of Confederation

(*A More Perfect Union* pp. 95–99)

Evaluate This reading strategy helps you recognize the difference between facts and opinions. A fact is something that can be proven to be true. An opinion is a belief based on what a person thinks or feels.

1. Read page 95. Which statement below is an opinion? Circle the letter next to your answer.

    a. Daniel Shays was not paid for his military service.

    b. Daniel Shays should have been able to pay his taxes.

    c. The states were taxing the farmers heavily.

2. Read the section "A Critical Period in Finance and Trade." Write a fact about the section.

   _____

3. Read the section "Success in Land Policy." Imagine that you are a settler moving to the Northwest Territory in 1787. Write a sentence stating your opinion of the Northwest Ordinance.

   _____

4. Read the section "Government at a Standstill." Then read the statements below and decide whether each is a fact or an opinion. Write an *O* next to each opinion and an *F* next to each fact.

    a. ___ The Confederation was "little more than the shadow without the substance."

    b. ___ In 1783, Congress suggested a tax based on state populations.

    c. ___ James Madison worked to reform the Articles of Confederation.

Reading Support Resources

CHAPTER 3

Lesson 3 Summary
The Crisis of Confederation

(*A More Perfect Union* pp. 95–99)

Thinking Focus: Why did the Articles of Confederation fail?

A Critical Period in Finance and Trade

Without a strong national government, each state kept as much power as it could for itself. The states would not let Congress be in charge of **commerce** between states and foreign countries. Congress could not collect taxes on goods that came from other countries. Instead, the states kept the money from these taxes. They did not want Congress to do anything that might hurt their state's trade.

The United States was able to develop some foreign trade with France, the Netherlands, Morocco, and China, however. Trade with China would become very important in the 1800s.

? Why did the states refuse to allow the national government to regulate commerce between states and foreign countries?

commerce
(kŏm′ərs)
the buying and selling of large amounts of goods

territory
(tĕr′ĭ-tôr′ē)
an area belonging to the United States that is not a state

Success in Land Policy

Congress was successful in setting up a plan to organize the western **territories** into separate townships.

In 1787, Congress passed the Northwest Ordinance, an important law that spelled out a three-step process for the territories to become states. That process is shown on the chart on the next page. It guaranteed that new states would have the same rights as older states. Congress promised to protect their rights and liberties. It did not allow slavery in the Northwest Territory. It also promised that the government would not take land from American Indians. Sadly, this promise would be broken in less than 10 years. The Northwest Territory included what are today the states of Ohio, Michigan, Indiana, Illinois, Wisconsin, and part of Minnesota.

? Why was the Northwest Ordinance the crowning achievement of the Confederation?

Summary continues on next page

Steps for a Territory to Become a State

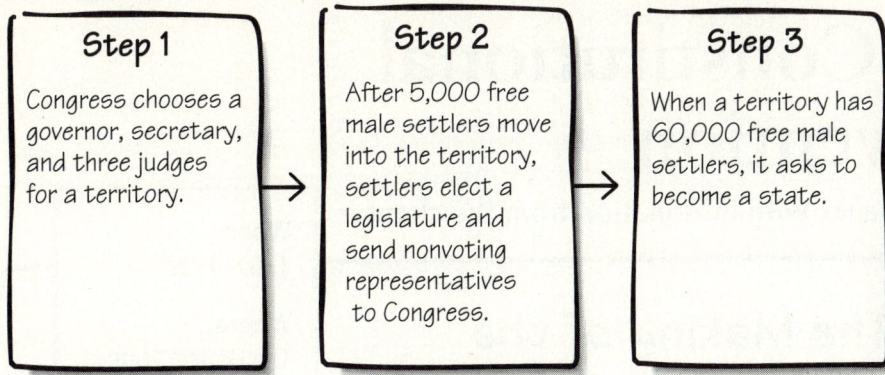

Government at a Standstill

By the 1780s, the Articles of Confederation needed to be changed so that the United States could become a strong nation. But this did not happen immediately.

In 1783, Congress wanted to have a national tax based on the number of people living in each state. In 1784, Congress asked for changes that would give the national government more control over commerce. The states did not give Congress either of these things. The Articles were not made stronger, and so, the central government stayed weak.

James Madison, a member of Congress from Virginia, tried to get some changes made to the Articles. He set up meetings with representatives from all the states. Very few states sent people to the meetings, so nothing was done. Finally in May 1787, Congress called a meeting in Philadelphia in order to work on the problems of the Articles of Confederation.

? Find evidence to support this statement: the Confederation was an inefficient and largely ineffective government.

Use with *A More Perfect Union* Pages 104–129

Chapter Overview
The Constitutional Convention

Fill in the blanks with information from the chapter.

When: 1787–1792

Where: The United States

The Making of the Constitution

- **A New Government Debated**
  - Connecticut Compromise
  - New Jersey Plan
  - _____
  - Three-Fifths Compromise

- **The Ratification Debate**
  - Federalists
  - _____

- **Balancing the Constitution**
  - 12 amendments proposed
  - _____

Name: Date:

CHAPTER 4
Lesson 1 Preview
The Constitutional Convention

(*A More Perfect Union* pp. 106–113)

Compromises Leading to the Constitution

Areas of Conflict
- North vs. South
- large vs. small states
- central vs. state government
- repair Articles of Confederation vs. new document

→ Compromise → **Result** the Constitution

1. **Look at the graphic organizer above. Then read the question below. Circle the letter of the correct answer.**

   Before the Constitution could be written, which conflict had to be resolved?

   a. The large states had to reach an agreement with the small states.

   b. The delegates had to agree whether to include all thirteen colonies.

   c. The delegates had to agree who would be president.

2. **Look at the chart that explains the Connecticut Compromise on page 110 in your text. What part of the New Jersey Plan is part of the Connecticut Compromise?**

   _____

   _____

   _____

Name: _____ Date: _____

CHAPTER 4
Lesson 1 Reading Strategy
The Constitutional Convention

(*A More Perfect Union* pp. 106–113)

Summarize This reading strategy helps you remember key points about what you have read. When you get to a good break in your reading, stop and write down the main ideas of what you have read.

1. Read page 106. Which of the following statements is the best summary of James Madison arriving for the convention? Circle the letter next to the best answer.

    a. Madison was always early.

    b. Madison was well-prepared, but he was worried that the convention would be difficult.

    c. Madison thought that the Articles of Confederation needed a few simple changes.

2. Read the section "A New Government Debated." What is the best summary of the delegates' response to the Virginia Plan? Circle the letter next to the best answer.

    a. The delegates wanted to give complete authority to the national government.

    b. The delegates completely rejected the plan.

    c. The delegates were not ready to give up the independence of the states, but thought that the plan had value.

3. Study the chart on page 110. Write a sentence summarizing the Connecticut Compromise.

    _____

    _____

4. Read the sections "The Slavery Issue" and "The Constitution Is Signed." Then write a sentence or two summarizing what you have learned about each section.

    _____

    _____

    _____

50 Chapter 4, Lesson 1 • Reading Strategy   Reading Support Resources

CHAPTER 4

Lesson 1 Summary
The Constitutional Convention

(*A More Perfect Union* pp. 106–113)

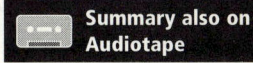

Thinking Focus: What important compromises did delegates to the Constitutional Convention make?

A New Government Debated

In 1787, Congress called for a convention in Philadelphia to solve the new government's many problems. Most of the delegates were men of great wealth and achievement. Many other groups were not present, including African Americans, Native Americans, and women.

The delegates decided that the new government would have three branches: the **legislative branch**, the **executive branch**, and the **judicial branch**. The branches were set up according to a system of **checks and balances**.

The larger states disagreed with the smaller states about how to set up the legislative branch. Delegates from Virginia wanted states with larger populations to have more representatives in the legislature. Delegates from New Jersey wanted each state to have the same number of representatives. The debate ended in the Connecticut Compromise. The legislative branch would be made up of two parts, the House of Representatives and the Senate. The people of each state would elect representatives to the House. The number of representatives would be based on the state's population. Each state would also elect two senators to the Senate.

❓ Find evidence to support this statement: Willingness to compromise helped the delegates settle the issue of how to represent each state in Congress.

legislative branch
(lĕj´ĭ-slā´tĭv brănch)
the division of government that passes laws

executive branch
(ĭg-zĕk´yə-tĭv brănch)
the division of government led by the President

judicial branch
(jōō-dĭsh´əl brănch)
the division of government made up of the federal courts of law

checks and balances
(chĕks ənd băl´ən-səz)
a system in which the branches of government make sure that no single branch has too much power

Summary continues on next page

Reading Support Resources — Lesson Summary • Chapter 4, Lesson 1

Connecticut Compromise

Virginia Plan
- Representation in both houses of Congress based on population.
- Favored by large states.

New Jersey Plan
- One state, one vote; equal representation regardless of size.
- Favored by small states.

Connecticut Compromise
- Allows for the equal representation of each state in the Senate.
- Bases representation of states in the House on population.

The Slavery Issue

The delegates could not agree on how to count each state's population to determine its number of representatives. There were many more slaves in the South than in other regions. The New England delegates wanted to count only the number of free people. Southern delegates wanted to count everyone, including slaves. The delegates finally decided to count the total number of free persons plus three-fifths of all other persons (slaves). They decided to delay a final vote about ending slavery until 1808.

[?] Why did the Northern states agree to postpone a vote on the slave trade, despite their antislavery feelings?

The Constitution Is Signed

By September 17, 1787, the delegates were ready to sign the Constitution. Many delegates still disagreed about some issues. But only three delegates refused to sign the new Constitution. Two of these men objected to the lack of a **bill of rights**.

The Articles of Confederation required the states to approve their work. The delegates could not relax until nine of the thirteen states approved the Constitution.

[?] Why didn't the signing of a document on September 17 finish the business of creating the Constitution?

bill of rights
(bĭl ŭv rīts)
a list of the basic liberties of citizens

Name: _____ Date: _____

CHAPTER 4
Lesson 2 Preview
The Ratification Debate

(*A More Perfect Union* pp. 118–122)

Differences Between Federalists and Antifederalists

	Federalists	Antifederalists
Power balance	wanted strong central government	wanted state sovereignty
Finances	wanted to pay foreign debts	feared taxes
General Concerns	feared struggles between different groups in society	feared power of strong central government

1. Look at the graphic organizer above. Then read the following sentences. Circle the letter next to the sentence that gives accurate information about the Federalists.

   a. The Federalists wanted state sovereignty.
   b. The Federalists feared struggles within sociey and wanted a strong central government.

2. Look at the timeline on page 122 in your text. Then answer the following questions:

   a. In what year did North Carolina ratify the Constitution?
   _____

   b. What happened between February and April of 1789?
   _____
   _____
   _____

Reading Support Resources

Name: _____ Date: _____

CHAPTER 4
Lesson 2 Reading Strategy
The Ratification Debate

(*A More Perfect Union* pp. 118–122)

Using the Visuals This reading strategy asks you to use photographs, maps, charts, and illustrations to help you understand what you read. As you read, be sure to study the visuals and carefully read the captions.

1. Look at the picture on page 118 and read the caption. What can you learn from this picture? Circle the letter next to the best answer.

    a. Patrick Henry is listening to the speech.

    b. Patrick Henry is a strong speaker.

    c. Mr. Parson is giving a speech.

2. Look at the illustration on page 119 and read the caption. Write a sentence explaining what you can learn from this illustration.

   _____

3. Look at the timeline on page 122. Which of the following statements is true? Circle the letter next to the best answer.

    a. Eleven states had ratified the Constitution by July, 1788.

    b. Federalists did not agree to add the Bill of Rights.

    c. North Carolina was one of the first states to ratify the Constitution.

4. Using only the pictures and captions in the lesson, find answers to the questions in the chart below.

Questions	Answers
Why were only 300 copies of *The Federalist* printed?	
How did Patrick Henry win fame as a speaker?	
When did Rhode Island ratify the Consitution?	

CHAPTER 4

Lesson 2 Summary
The Ratification Debate

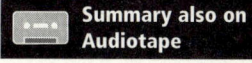

(*A More Perfect Union* pp. 118–122)

Thinking Focus: How did the ratification of the Constitution depend on the debates in each of the states?

The Debate Goes Public

Nine of the thirteen states were needed to approve the Constitution before it could replace the Articles of Confederation. But the Constitution remained the subject of great debate. The American people were divided between the **Federalists** and the **Antifederalists**. The Federalists liked the Constitution. The Antifederalists opposed the Constitution. They were afraid that a national government would have more power than the states. They also wanted a bill of rights. Antifederalists feared that a strong central government could not be trusted. Federalists made fun of these fears. The Antifederalists and the Federalists tried to win public approval by printing their views in pamphlets and newspapers.

? Explain how the Federalists used ridicule to respond to the arguments of the Antifederalists.

Federalist
(fĕd´ər-ə-lĭst)
one who supported the Constitution

Antifederalist
(ăn´tē-fĕd´ər-ə-lĭst)
one who opposed the Constitution

Summary continues on next page

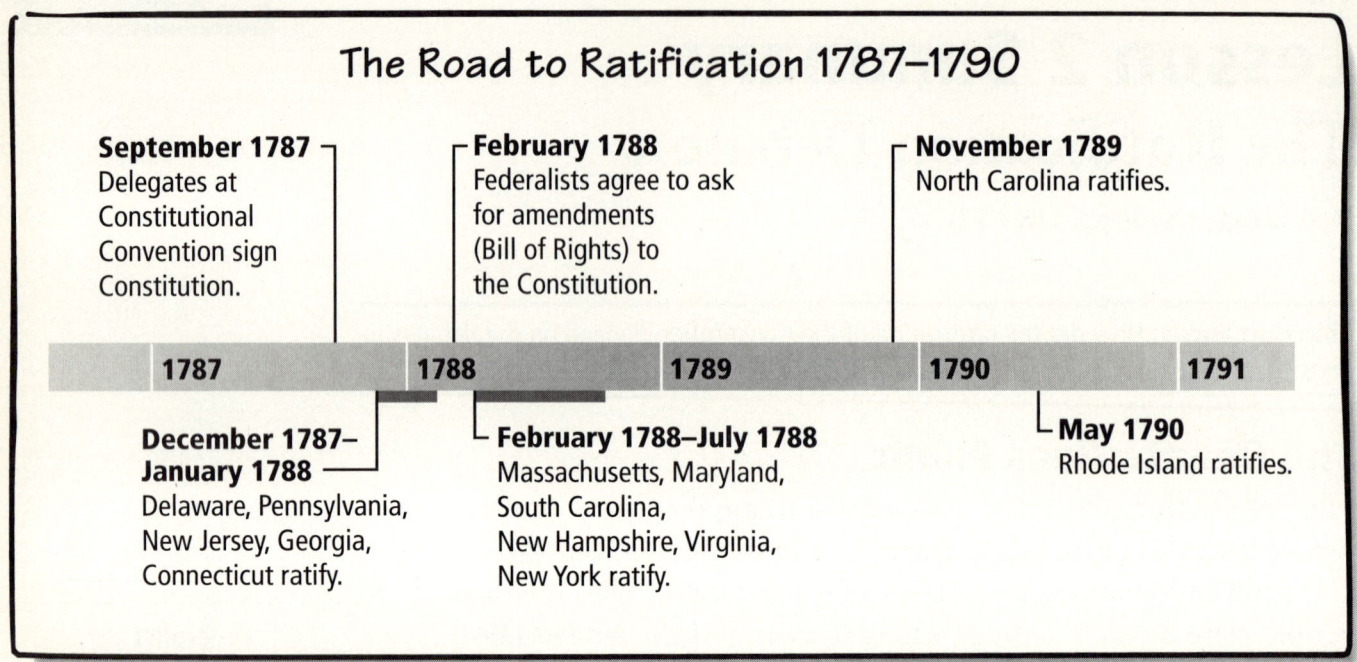

Ratification—Just Barely

On December 7, 1787, Delaware became the first state to **ratify** the Constitution. Pennsylvania was the second. The Antifederalists were upset by how quickly the first two states' conventions were held. They tried to delay the state convention process. But New Jersey, Georgia, and Connecticut followed shortly in approving the Constitution. Massachusetts became the sixth state to approve the Constitution. Maryland, South Carolina, and New Hampshire were the last three states needed to approve the new government.

The Federalists gained public support for four reasons:

- They acted more quickly than the Antifederalists to bring the Constitution to vote in many states.
- They were better organized than the Antifederalists.
- Some of America's best thinkers wrote essays in favor of the Constitution.
- The majority of newspapers favored the Federalists.

In the end, the Antifederalists lost the debate against approving the Constitution. But they convinced the people that the Constitution needed a bill of rights.

? What were the strategies of the Federalists and the Antifederalists for winning votes in the states?

ratify
(răt´ə-fī´)
to approve formally

Name: _____ Date: _____

CHAPTER 4
Lesson 3 Preview
The Bill of Rights

(*A More Perfect Union* pp. 124–127)

1. **Look at the graphic organizer above. Then read the statements below. Circle the letter next to the statements that give correct information.**

   a. The Bill of Rights came about to avoid the central government's potential abuse of power.
   b. The protection of individuals' and states' rights is guaranteed by the Bill of Rights.
   c. The potential abuse of power by central government guarantees individuals and states' rights.

2. **Look at the document shown on page 126 in your text. Then read the caption. Answer the following questions:**

   a. How many amendments were ratified?
   _____

   b. Describe the contents of the two amendments that were <u>not</u> ratified.
   _____
   _____
   _____
   _____

Reading Support Resources

Name: _____ Date: _____

CHAPTER 4
Lesson 3 Reading Strategy
The Bill of Rights

(*A More Perfect Union* pp. 124–127)

Self-Question This reading strategy helps you stay focused on what you read. Ask yourself questions before you read a section. Then read to see if you can find the answer to your questions.

1. Read the lesson title, the red heading on page 124 and the blue headings on pages 125. Which question below do you think you will be able to answer after reading this section? Circle the letter next to the best answer.

    a. Why did some colonists want guaranteed rights?
    b. How does the Bill of Rights affect our lives today?
    c. Who wrote the Articles of Confederation?

2. Read the first paragraph under the heading "Balancing the Constitution." Which question below do you think you will be able to answer after reading this section? Circle the letter next to the best answer.

    a. Where was James Madison born?
    b. How does the bill of rights balance the rights of states and individuals with the powers of a central government?
    c. How are the three branches of government balanced?

3. Look at the picture on page 125 and read the caption. How do you think officials' authority changed with the addition of a bill of rights?

    _____

4. Think of one example of how your rights as an individual are protected by the Bill of Rights. Explain your answer on the lines below.

<u>How Does the Bill of Rights Protect My Rights</u>

_____
_____
_____
_____

CHAPTER 4
Lesson 3 Summary
The Bill of Rights
(*A More Perfect Union* pp. 124–127)

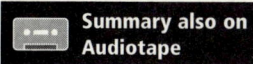
Summary also on Audiotape

Thinking Focus: How does the Bill of Rights balance governmental powers with the rights of individuals?

Why Massachusetts Resisted

Americans had fought hard against the British to earn the right to a **free press** and other freedoms. The Antifederalists wanted to make sure these rights were preserved.

In Massachusetts, several great political thinkers demanded a bill of rights to protect individuals from a strong central government. The Federalists did not see the need for a bill of rights. But they were willing to compromise so that the Constitution could be approved.

In order to compromise, Federalists in Massachusetts wrote **amendments** to the Constitution. With the amendments, the Antifederalists agreed to support the new government. So the Federalists gained enough votes to approve the Constitution. Other states followed this example of compromise, and demanded a Bill of Rights.

[?] What made some Federalists change their minds about including a bill of rights in the Constitution?

free press
(frē prĕs)
the right to publish anything, including criticism of the government

amendment
(ə-mĕnd′mənt)
an addition or change to the Constitution that is made into law

Summary continues on next page

The Bill of Rights (Lesson 3 Summary continued)

Balancing the Constitution

In March 1789, the first Congress under the new Constitution met in New York. The amendments from the state conventions were combined into a list of 12 amendments. This list was sent to all the states for approval.

In December 1791, 10 of the 12 proposed amendments were approved. These 10 amendments became the Bill of Rights. The Bill of Rights protects citizens from abuses of power by the government. With the acceptance of the Bill of Rights, many of the Antifederalists supported the Constitution and even became active in the new government.

The Constitutional Convention of 1787 created a strong but flexible new government. The addition of amendments to the Constitution allows the government to change as the nation grows. For more than two hundred years, the Constitution has been strong because it is flexible.

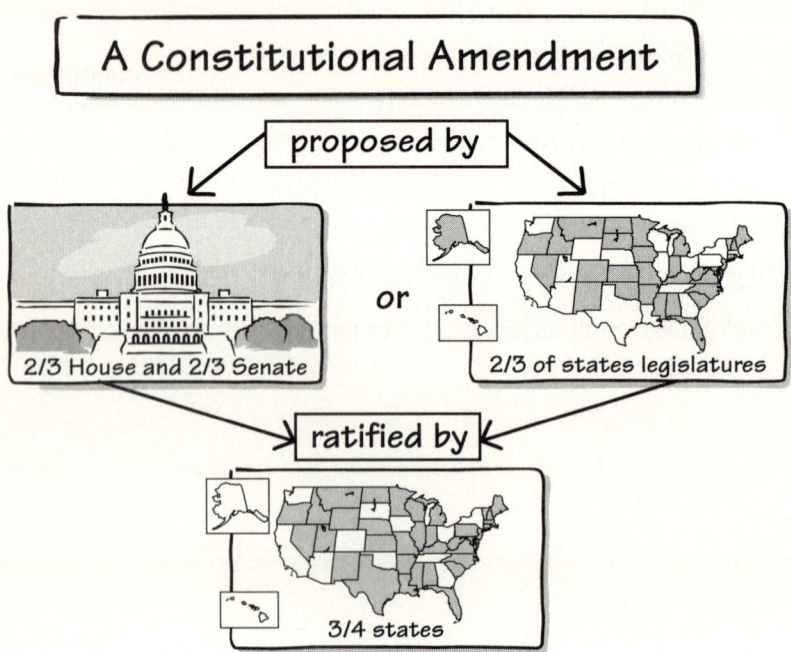

? How did the amendment process provide the flexibility to make the Constitution strong?

Use with *A More Perfect Union* Pages 132–161

Chapter Overview
The Creation of a Party System

Fill in the blanks with information from the chapter.

When: 1789–1823

Who: The Federal Government

Early United States Government Policies

Federalists: John Adams
- Strong Central Government
- Support National Bank
- _____
- _____

Republicans: Thomas Jefferson / James Monroe
- _____
- Support Farmers
- _____
- Neutrality
- War of 1812
- _____

Reading Support Resources   Chapter Overview • Chapter 5   **61**

Name: _____ Date: _____

CHAPTER 5
Lesson 1 Preview
Internal Conflict

(*A More Perfect Union* pp. 134–139)

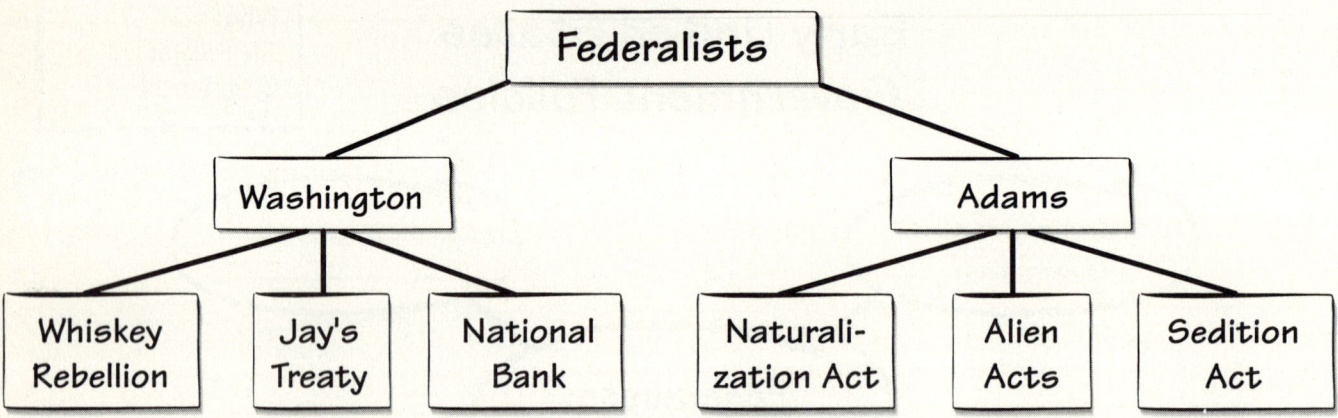

1. **Look at the graphic organizer above. Then circle the letter next to the correct statement.**

    a. The National Bank was created during the term President Washington.

    b. President Adams approved Jay's Treaty.

    c. The Whiskey Rebellion led to the Naturalization Act.

2. **Study the chart, "Two Approaches to Government," at the top of page 136 in your text. Then look at the painting and caption at the bottom of the page. Does the scene in the painting reflect Hamilton's vision or Jefferson's vision of the new nation? Explain your answer.**

    _____
    _____
    _____
    _____
    _____

Name: _____ Date: _____

CHAPTER 5
Lesson 1 Reading Strategy
Internal Conflict

(*A More Perfect Union* pp. 134–139)

Evaluate This reading strategy helps you recognize the difference between facts and opinions. A fact is something that can be proven to be true. An opinion is a belief based on what a person thinks or feels.

1. Read the section "Federalists Shape a Government." Which statement below is an opinion? Circle the letter next to your choice.

   a. The President selected department heads for the new government.

   b. Only men of wealth and education should run the government.

   c. Hamilton wanted to create a national bank.

2. Read the section "Some Oppose Federalist Centralization." Which statement below is a fact? Circle the letter next to your choice.

   a. The power of government should be limited.

   b. By 1791, Congress had approved Hamilton's credit program.

   c. The tax on imported goods was unfair.

3. Read the section "Events in Europe Cause Tension at Home." Write one opinion held by Americans about the French Revolution.

   _____
   _____
   _____

4. Write down one fact about the French Revolution.

   _____
   _____
   _____

5. Write down one fact about the Alien and Sedition Acts.

   _____
   _____
   _____

CHAPTER 5

Lesson 1 Summary
Internal Conflict

(*A More Perfect Union* pp. 134–139)

Thinking Focus: What issues divided Americans so much that they formed separate political parties?

Federalists Shape a Government

In 1789, George Washington became the nation's first President. New York became the nation's first capital. As the first President, Washington had to build a new government. He used the Constitution as his guide. He also chose assistants to run parts of the government. These men became known as the **Cabinet**. Then, as now, the Cabinet's main task is to give advice to the President.

The men in Washington's **administration** were mostly Federalists. They believed in a strong central government. Alexander Hamilton was a very strong Federalist. He wanted to do several things:

- Improve the growth of manufacturing and commerce
- Have the federal government pay off the states' debts from the Revolutionary War
- Create a national bank

Hamilton believed these policies would make the nation financially stronger and more stable.

? Alexander Hamilton favored government by the elite. Why would this make some Americans feel uncomfortable?

Cabinet
(kăb′ə-nĭt)
the advisory group selected by the President to be heads of the executive departments

administration
(ăd-mĭn′ĭ-strā′shən)
the executive branch of the U.S. government, made up of the President, his Cabinet, and the Vice President

Summary continues on next page

Internal Conflict (Lesson 1 Summary continued)

Some Oppose Federalist Centralization

James Madison questioned the fairness of Hamilton's plans to pay off the war debt. He believed they favored Northerners because the North had more debts than the South. He also opposed a national bank because the Constitution did not give the federal government the power to create banks.

Thomas Jefferson led the group that opposed Hamilton's plans. Jefferson and Madison called themselves Republicans. Jefferson believed in an **agrarian** nation with limited government.

Hamilton also passed a tax on whiskey. Many farmers made whiskey from their grain. They felt that this tax was unfair to them. Angry Pennsylvania farmers attacked tax collectors. President Washington sent troops to control the farmers. Many Americans disliked this use of force. So Republicanism, which called for limited government control, grew in popularity.

[?] The policies Hamilton proposed were designed to create national unity. But instead they divided people. Why?

Events in Europe Cause Tension at Home

Events in Europe also divided the new nation. One event was the French Revolution. Federalists were horrified by the beheading of French King Louis XVI in 1793. But Republicans continued to favor France's struggle for liberty.

In addition, during its war with France, Britain refused to allow American ships to travel freely on the seas. The Federalists approved a treaty that allowed Britain to continue with this policy. This treaty angered many Americans and strengthened Republican support.

The Federalists also passed new laws that the Republicans opposed. The Alien Act allowed the President to jail or send home any **alien** he considered dangerous. The **Sedition** Act allowed the government to punish anyone who said things against the government. These new laws made Republicans across the country rally against the Federalists.

[?] What motivated the Federalist Congress to pass the Alien and Sedition Acts—and why did they cause problems?

---

agrarian
(ə-grâr′ē-ən)
having to do with land and farming

alien
(ā′lē-ən)
a foreign resident of a country who has not become a citizen

sedition
(sĭ-dĭsh′ən)
a rebellion against governmental authority

Name: Date:

CHAPTER 5

Lesson 2 Preview

Jefferson and the Republicans

(*A More Perfect Union* pp. 146–151)

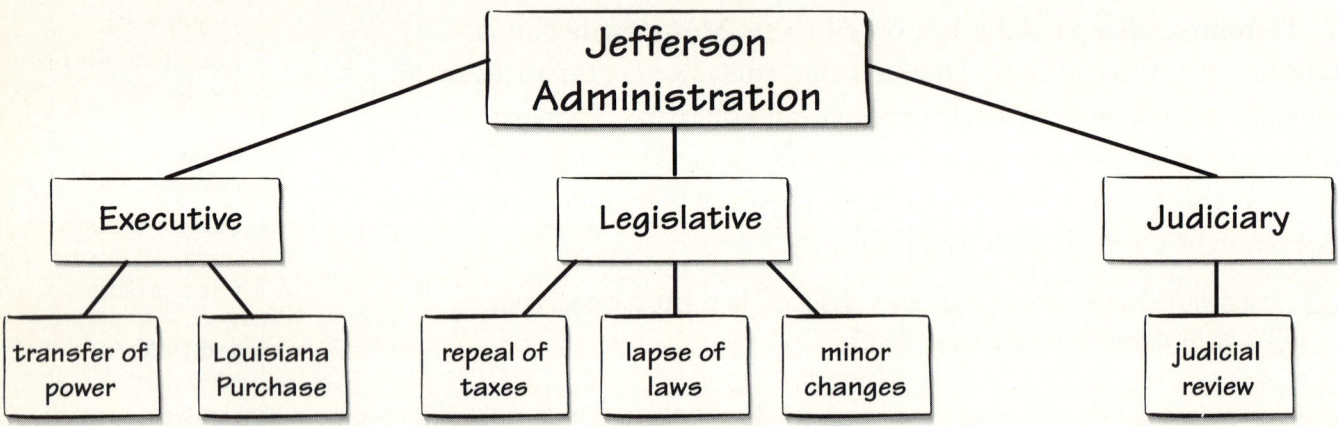

Responsibilities of the Three Branches of Government

1. Look at the graphic organizer above. Then read the following sentences. Circle the letters next to the sentences that are correct.

    a. The Legislative branch is in charge of the Judicial branch.
    b. The Legislative branch can repeal taxes.
    c. The transfer of power was handled by the Executive branch.
    d. The Judicial branch carried out the Louisiana Purchase.

2. Look at the chart on page 151 in your text and read the caption. How do certain laws come up for review by the Supreme Court?

    _____
    _____
    _____
    _____
    _____

Name: _____   Date: _____

CHAPTER 5
Lesson 2 Reading Strategy
Jefferson and the Republicans

(*A More Perfect Union* pp. 146–151)

Sequence This reading strategy helps you follow what is happening in your reading. As you read, pay attention to dates and times, as well as to words such as *before*, *finally*, *after*, and *then*.

1. Read the section "Jefferson Takes the Reins." Place the following events in order by writing *1*, *2*, and *3* in the blanks.

    ___ The House votes in order to break the tie between Jefferson and Burr.

    ___ Jefferson becomes the first President inaugurated in Washington, D.C.

    ___ The Republicans begin to build a national party organization.

2. Read "The Republicans Make Some Changes." Place a *1* next to the event that came first and a *2* next to the event that came second.

    ___ The Alien and Sedition acts ran out.

    ___ The national bank's charter ran out.

3. Read the first sentence of the section "The Nation Matures Under Jefferson." What word helps you understand the sequence of events?

    _____

4. Continue reading the rest of the section "The Nation Matures Under Jefferson." Place the following events in order by writing *1*, *2*, and *3* in the blanks.

    ___ Jefferson sends Livingston and Monroe to Paris.

    ___ France agrees to sell Louisiana to the United States.

    ___ Spain gives Louisiana to France.

CHAPTER 5

Lesson 2 Summary
Jefferson and the Republicans

(*A More Perfect Union* pp. 146–151)

Thinking Focus: How did the transfer of power to the Republicans in 1800 make a difference for the nation?

Jefferson Takes the Reins

Presidents are not elected directly by the people. Instead, people specifically chosen in each state cast **electoral votes**. Electoral votes determine who gets elected.

In the election of 1800, Americans wanted a change from the Federalists. The most electoral votes went to two Republicans, Thomas Jefferson and Aaron Burr. Both men had the same number of votes. So the House of Representatives had to decide who would be President. They took many votes. At last, Jefferson was elected President.

Jefferson thought it was important that a new political party was gaining power. Many feared that the change of power from the Federalists to the Republicans would be violent. But this change of power happened in an orderly and peaceful way.

? Why did Jefferson think of his election as the Revolution of 1800?

electoral vote
(ĭ-lĕk′tər-əl vōt)
the vote cast by the persons chosen by each state to elect the President

The Republicans Make Some Changes

The Federalists were afraid that the Republican President would make big changes. Instead, Jefferson allowed many things to go on as they did before. He tried to bring the Federalists into the Republican Party and focused on the similarities between the two parties. Slowly, Jefferson and his people made the government fit Republican goals.

Summary continues on next page

Jefferson and the Republicans *(Lesson 2 Summary continued)*

Jefferson selected Republican judges. He shortened the amount of time needed for immigrants to become citizens. He also reduced the amount of taxes Americans had to pay. In general, he created a simpler, more relaxed form of government.

? How did Jefferson earn the cooperation of the Federalists?

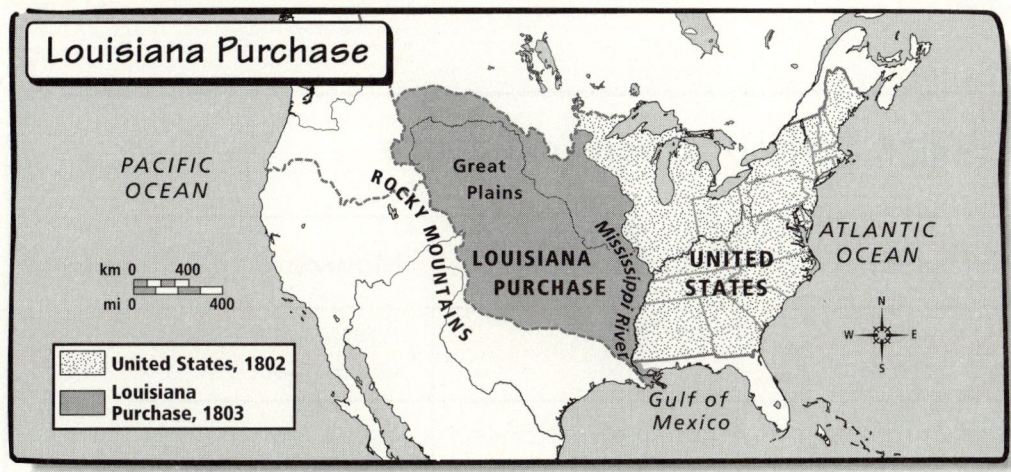

The Nation Matures Under Jefferson

Jefferson's greatest accomplishment was the Louisiana Purchase. His presidency is also remembered for an important Supreme Court case, *Marbury* v. *Madison*.

Jefferson wanted all Americans to have an equal chance to own farmland. Fortunately, there was land available to meet this goal. France owned Louisiana, a huge area west of the Mississippi River. The French agreed to sell Louisiana to the Americans. The Louisiana Purchase doubled the amount of American land. It also gave Americans control of the Mississippi River, an important transportation route for western farmers.

The case of *Marbury* v. *Madison* said that the Supreme Court had the power to order the President to obey a law as long as the law was **constitutional**. This decision established the principle of **judicial review**. This means that the Court could review the actions of the other branches of government and overturn them if these actions were unconstitutional. With this decision, the Supreme Court became an independent and equal part of the United States government.

? Why did Americans consider control of the Mississippi River so important?

constitutional
(kŏn'stĭ-tōō'shən)
in agreement with the principles of the Constitution

judicial review
(jōō-dĭsh'əl rĭ-vyōō')
the power of a court, especially the Supreme Court, to decide if a law or an executive act agrees with the Constitution

Reading Support Resources　　　　　　　　　　　　　Lesson Summary • **Chapter 5, Lesson 2**　　**69**

Name: _____ Date: _____

CHAPTER 5
Lesson 3 Preview
The United States and the World

(*A More Perfect Union* pp. 153–159)

Foreign Policy of Three Presidents

	Jefferson	Madison	Monroe
Action	Embargo Act Non-Intercourse Act	War of 1812	Adams-Onís Treaty Monroe Doctrine
Evaluation	ineffective against France and Britain	increased nationalistic pride	gained new territory, earned respect

1. Look at the graphic organizer above. Then read the following sentences and fill in the blanks.

   During the Jefferson presidency, the _____ and _____ were not very effective. Later, during the Madison and Monroe presidencies, the _____ helped increase national pride.
   The Adams-Onís Treaty and the Monroe Doctrine gained new _____ and earned _____.

2. Look at the map on page 159 in your text. Then answer the following questions:

   a. What is the title of the map?
   _____

   b. What was the largest of the British territories?
   _____

   c. What areas were disputed lands?
   _____

Chapter 5, Lesson 3 • Lesson Preview   Reading Support Resources

Name: _____ Date: _____

CHAPTER 5
Lesson 3 Reading Strategy
The United States and the World

(*A More Perfect Union* pp. 153–159)

Cause and Effect This reading strategy helps you understand events and why they occur. As you read, think about the factors that caused an event. Then think about what the effects of that event may be.

1. Read the section "Jefferson's Foreign Policy Is Challenged." What caused Congress to pass the Embargo Act?

    a. U.S. ships were being attacked by France and Great Britain.

    b. The United States wanted to begin a policy of neutrality.

    c. France and Great Britain were unable to buy American goods.

2. What were two effects of the Embargo Act?

    _____

    _____

3. Read the section "Madison Pressured into War." Then fill in the chart below.

Cause	Effect
	Anti-British feeling increases.
	Madison asks Congress to declare war on Great Britain.
The Hartford Convention is held after the Battle of New Orleans and the Treaty of Ghent.	
	Americans feel a sense of national pride.

4. Read the section "American Influence Expands." What policy was the effect of Americans' fears that Spain would regain control of Latin America?

    _____

    _____

Reading Support Resources   Reading Strategy • Chapter 5, Lesson 3   **71**

CHAPTER 5

Lesson 3 Summary
The United States and the World

(*A More Perfect Union* pp. 153–159)

Thinking Focus: How well did the United States handle international conflicts?

Jefferson's Foreign Policy Is Challenged

Under Jefferson, trade with Europe was very important. The United States was mostly a farming nation. Europeans bought American farm products. Americans bought European manufactured goods. Jefferson tried to protect this trade with a policy of **neutrality**. Jefferson wanted to keep America out of European wars and keep the seas free.

In 1803, Britain and France entered into another war. They each captured ships that tried to enter the enemy's port. Many American ships were captured. The sailors were taken from their ships under Britain's policy of **impressment**.

In 1807, Jefferson passed the Embargo Act. He would not allow American ships to trade with Europe. This law hurt the British and the French. They needed American supplies. But it also hurt American farmers and merchants. So Congress passed a new law called the Non-Intercourse Act. This law said that America could trade with all countries except Britain and France. This law did not work. The Americans were still hurt by less trade with Europe.

neutrality
(noo-trăl´ĭ-tē)
the state of not participating in a war or other conflict

impressment
(ĭm-prĕs´mənt)
forcing someone into naval service

[?] Why was the war between Great Britain and France so harmful to the United States?

Madison Pressured into War

President James Madison faced many of the same problems as Jefferson. In addition, Indians in the Northwest Territory were attacking white settlers who were taking their land. The Americans believed that the British were helping the Indians. The problems on land and at sea made many people want to fight the British. In 1812, Madison declared war on Britain.

Summary continues on next page

The United States and the World (Lesson 3 Summary continued)

The British army was very strong in the War of 1812. But Americans won a great victory in the Battle of New Orleans. This battle was fought, however, after the United States and Britain had signed a peace treaty in Ghent, Belgium. News traveled so slowly in those days that the armies had not yet heard that the war was over.

The news was also slow to reach a group of Federalists in New England. These Federalists were planning how to weaken Republican power. Once Americans learned the good news about the peace treaty and their army's victory, they were filled with national pride. No one was interested in the Federalist plan. Federalism collapsed soon after.

? How did the War of 1812 help to bring Americans together?

American Influence Expands

James Monroe became President in 1816. The country was strong and at peace. During Monroe's presidency, the Spanish agreed to sell Florida to the United States and to give up its claim to the Oregon country. This treaty greatly increased American land.

During the early 1800s, Spain's empire in the Americas had fallen apart. In 1822, the British asked America to help it stop Spain from regaining control of Latin America. President John Quincy Adams did not want to work with the British. He decided that it was time for America to act as an independent nation. The Monroe Doctrine stated Adams's ideas. The doctrine said European countries could not set up colonies in the Western Hemisphere. It also said Europe could not try to control Latin America. In return, the United States would stay out of Europe's affairs.

? Why was John Quincy Adams determined not to form a joint foreign policy with Great Britain?

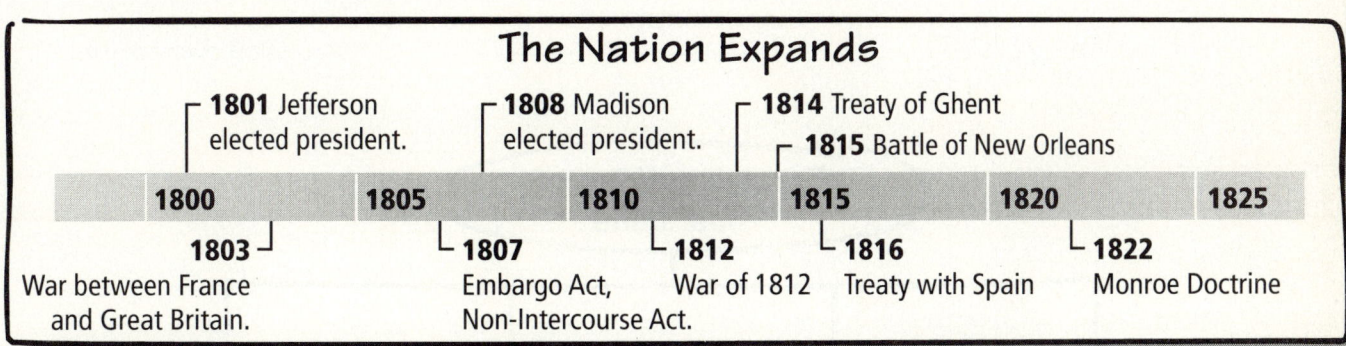

Reading Support Resources — Lesson Summary • Chapter 5, Lesson 3 — 73

Use with *A More Perfect Union* Pages 162–187

Chapter Overview
The Maturing Republic

Fill in the blank spaces below with information from the chapter.

When: 1782–1840

Where: The United States

Who: Americans

America in the Early 1800s

- **Republican Culture**
  - _____
  - The new individualism
  - The Second Great Awakening

- **Jackson's Presidency**
  - more democratic politics
  - _____
  - struggles over tariffs

- **Europeans' View of Americans**
  - What is an American?
  - more equality than in Europe
  - _____
  - criticism about manners

74 Chapter 6 • Chapter Overview

Name: _____   Date: _____

CHAPTER 6
Lesson 1 Preview
Republicanism and Culture

(*A More Perfect Union* pp. 164–169)

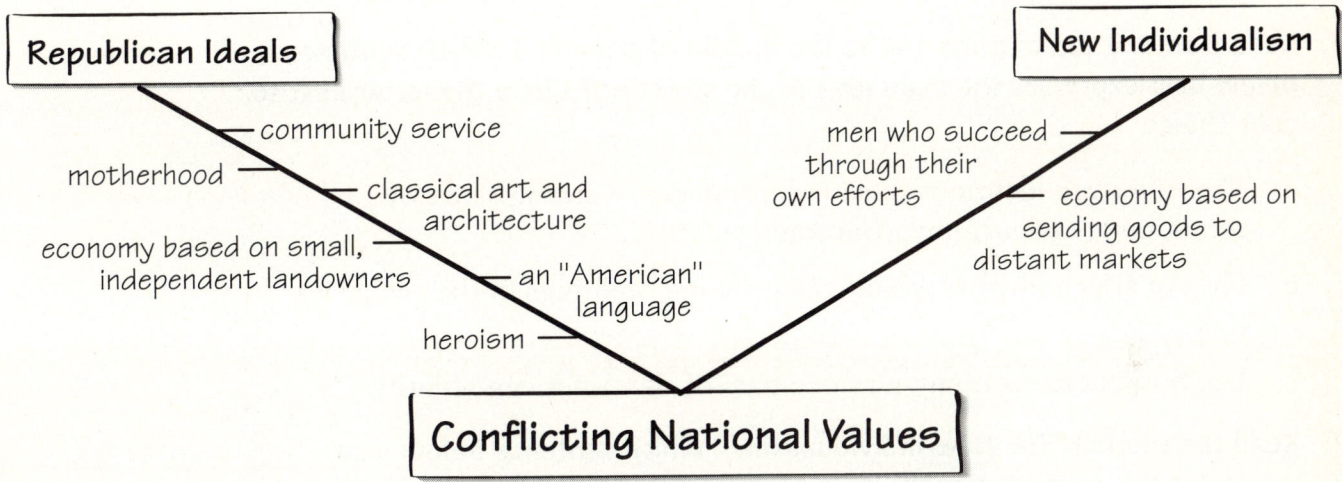

1. **Look at the graphic organizer above. Then read the following sentences and fill in the blanks.**

   a. The graphic organizer contrasts Republican Ideals and the
   _____.

   b. Two kinds of economies shown in the graphic organizer are
   _____
   _____.

2. **Study the map and legend on page 167 of your text. Then fill in the blanks below.**

   The purple parts of the map show the _____.
   The pink parts show the _____.
   The orange parts show the _____.
   The Florida Territory is one of the _____.
   New York is one of the _____.
   Tennessee is one of the _____.

Reading Support Resources   Lesson Preview • Chapter 6, Lesson 1   **75**

Name: _____   Date: _____

CHAPTER 6
Lesson 1 Reading Strategy
Republicanism and Culture

(*A More Perfect Union* pp. 164–169)

Finding the Main Idea This reading strategy helps you organize and remember what you read. When you finish a selection, jot down the main idea and its supporting details.

1. Read from the top of page 164 to the middle of page 166. Which sentence below best expresses the main idea of the selection? Circle the letter next to your choice.

   a. The American identity valued independence, a strong sense of community, and wealthy, educated leaders.

   b. The American identity meant constructing buildings in the classical style.

   c. The household economy was one part of the American identity.

2. Read the section "The New Individualism." Which sentence below best expresses the main idea of the section? Write an *M* next to your choice. Put a *D* next to the supporting details.

   ___ People began to send goods to distant markets.

   ___ Better transportation networks helped the nation grow.

   ___ The U.S. government began to build the national road.

3. Read the section "Values in Conflict." Then fill in the chart below with the section's main idea and at least two supporting ideas.

Main Idea	Supporting Details

CHAPTER 6

Lesson 1 Summary
Republicanism and Culture

(*A More Perfect Union* pp. 164–169)

Thinking Focus: How did Americans define their own national values in their new nation?

Creation of an American Identity

In the early 1800s, Americans were building their country's identity. They talked about republican ideals for their republic, such as independence and placing the public good above selfish concerns. The **household economy** was also a republican ideal. Farmers grew enough food to feed their families. But there was also enough left over to trade with others in the community. In this way, the farmers' desire profit was balanced with their responsibility to their neighbors.

At the same time, Americans began seeing their country's leaders as heroes. Many people compared George Washington to great Greek and Roman leaders of the past. Americans made buildings that looked like those from old Greece and Rome. This kind of building was in the **neoclassical** style.

? How did Americans use classical models at the beginning of the 1800s?

household economy
(hous'hōld' ĭ-kŏn'ə-mē)

the production of food by a family for use in the household or for trade with the community

neoclassical
(nē'ō-klăs'ĭ-kəl)

relating to classical Greek and Roman art forms

Summary continues on next page

Republicanism and Culture *(Lesson 1 Summary continued)*

The New Individualism

Americans also began moving west. Many settled in Kentucky and Tennessee. Others explored the territories that would become today's Midwest. Southern settlers moved into what would later be Alabama, Mississippi, and Louisiana.

Better transportation allowed people to move from place to place and helped the nation grow. The U.S. government started work on a national road. Steamboats carried goods from one place to another quickly and cheaply.

These changes led to a great increase in trade. People could now send their goods to markets many miles away. Most of the time they did not even see the people who bought their goods. Farmers could sell their crops for cash. This new **market economy** began to replace the household economy. People began to care more about their own lives and less about what was good for their communities.

[?] Summarize the economic changes that led to the weakening of people's ties to their communities.

market economy
(mär′kĭt ĭ-kŏn′ə-mē)
the production of food and other things for cash sale

suffrage
(sŭf′rĭj)
the right to vote

Values in Conflict

Church membership had gone down during the Revolution. Now church leaders wanted to bring people back. They held big meetings. They asked the people to renew their faith and be useful to society. Many black churches also started up around the country. Now blacks and whites came back to their churches. This renewed interest in religion was called the Second Great Awakening.

America was also becoming more democratic. Barriers to **suffrage** were done away with, at least for white males. Some states no longer required voters to own land. Men without wealth began to seek power.

[?] What national values did the preachers of the Second Great Awakening draw on to revive their ministries?

Name: _____   Date: _____

CHAPTER 6
Lesson 2 Preview
The First Western President
(*A More Perfect Union* pp. 172–178)

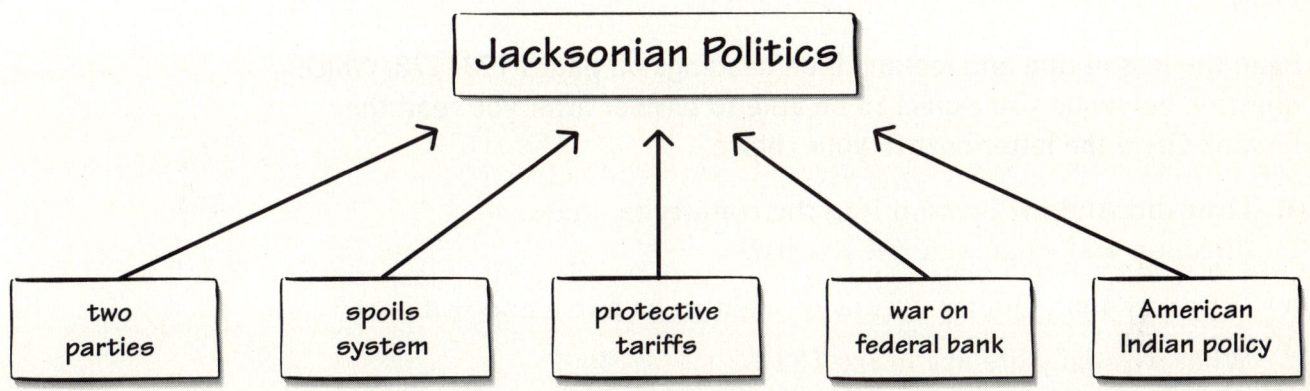

1. Look at the graphic organizer above. The word *Jacksonian* means "related to Andrew Jackson's presidency." Then read the following sentences and fill in the blanks.

   a. How many political parties were there during the time of Jackson's presidency?

   _____

   b. How did President Jackson feel about the federal bank?

   _____

2. Look at the map on page 175 in your text. What percentage of the electoral vote did Andrew Jackson get in the 1828 election? _____

3. What percentage of the electoral vote did John Quincy Adams get? _____

Reading Support Resources   Lesson Preview • Chapter 6, Lesson 2   **79**

Name: _____   Date: _____

CHAPTER 6

Lesson 2 Reading Strategy
The First Western President

(*A More Perfect Union* pp. 172–178)

Self-Question This reading strategy helps you stay focused on what you read. Ask yourself questions before you read a section. Then read to see if you can find the answer to your questions.

1. Read the lesson title and red and blue headings on pages 173–178. Which question below do you expect to be able to answer after you read the lesson? Circle the letter next to your choice.

    a. How did Andrew Jackson lead the country in a new direction and what were the results?

    b. Why was John Quincy Adams thought to be harsh and stubborn?

    c. What was daily life like in the 1820s?

2. Look at the map on page 175. Which question below does the map help you answer? Circle the letter next to your choice.

    a. Why did so many people support Jackson in the 1828 election?

    b. When did the U.S. territories become states?

    c. Which states supported Jackson in the 1828 presidential election?

3. Read the heading "A Strong Presidency." Write a question you would expect to be able to answer after you read the section.

    _____

4. Read the red and blue headings on pages 177 and 178. Fill in the left-hand column of the chart below with two questions you would expect to have answered in the section. As you read, fill in the right-hand column.

My Questions	What I Learned by Reading

80   Chapter 6, Lesson 2 • Reading Strategy   Reading Support Resources

CHAPTER 6
Lesson 2 Summary
The First Western Presidency
(*A More Perfect Union* pp. 172–178)

Summary also on Audiotape

Thinking Focus: How did Andrew Jackson's presidency reflect the politics of his time?

The Rise of Jacksonian Politics

Andrew Jackson ran for President in 1824, but lost the election to John Quincy Adams. Although Jackson had won more electoral votes, the House of Representatives chose Adams for President. This choice angered many Americans.

Adams wanted a high **tariff,** or tax, on imported goods. He wanted to use this tax money to build roads and canals. Adams had many new ideas, but he was not a strong leader because the American people did not support him.

Andrew Jackson took the side of the common people. He wanted to give power to the American people, not to big businesses. Americans liked these ideas and elected Jackson in 1828. Jackson won more than 56 percent of the **popular vote.** Before Jackson was elected, a small group of men known as a **caucus** had decided who would run for President. During Jackson's presidency, this practice ended and elections became more democratic. In addition, the Republican party split into two branches, the Democrats and the Whigs.

tariff
(tăr′ĭf)
a government tax on imports or exports

popular vote
(pŏp′yə-lər vōt)
all the votes by people in each state

caucus
(kô′kəs)
a meeting of a group of leaders to decide on candidates for office

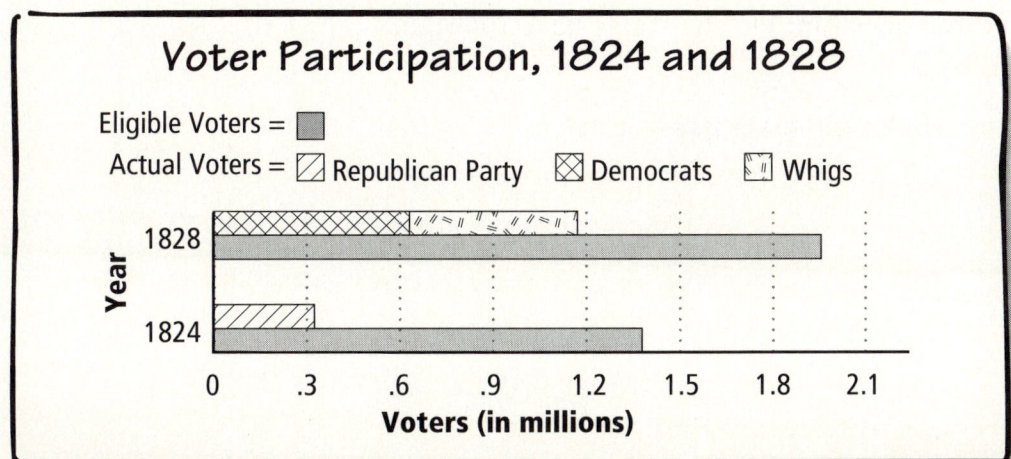

❓ Find evidence to support this statement: The American people were ready for Jacksonian politics.

Summary continues on next page

The First Western Presidency *(Lesson 2 Summary continued)*

A Strong Presidency

As President, Jackson chose men who had supported him before he was elected to help him run the country. He gave them important jobs. This was called the **spoils system**. Jackson had strong views. He wanted to move all Indians east of the Mississippi River. He wanted their land for American farmers. He did not care about the Indians' rights. He told some states to ignore treaties they had signed with the Indians. Jackson also fought against the federal bank. He felt the bank was not fair to the common people.

? What specific attitudes serve to identify Jackson as a Western President?

The Federal Union Put to the Test

When John Quincy Adams was President, Congress passed a tariff, which was a law that taxed imported goods. Congress wanted Americans to buy American goods instead. But the South had few factories and wanted to import goods. Because of this debate, the idea of **states' rights** gained strength. People who supported states' rights believed that:

- the power of the federal government came from the states;
- each state had the right to **nullify** laws of Congress;
- the tariff should be lowered.

Vice President John Calhoun supported states' rights. But Jackson did not think the states should be able to refuse federal laws. Jackson agreed to lower the tariff. But he also got Congress to pass the Force Bill. This law said that the President could use the army and navy to make states follow federal laws. This conflict was known as the nullification crisis. It asked the question: Do the states have the right to nullify the laws of Congress?

? How did the nullification crisis test the doctrine of states' rights?

---

spoils system
(spoilz sĭs'təm)
a system in which people who supported the winning candidate are given government jobs after the election

states' rights
(stāts rīts)
the power of states to govern themselves

nullify
(nŭl'ə-fī')
to refuse to enforce a law

Name: _____ Date: _____

CHAPTER 6
Lesson 3 Preview
How Others Saw Us

(*A More Perfect Union* pp. 179–183)

Comparing Others' Views of the United States

	Behavior	Social Equality	Beliefs
Trollope	rude manners		
Crèvecoeur	lawless on the frontier	lack of social class	respect for law
Martineau	too talkative	hypocritical attitude about slavery	"worship of opinion"
Tocqueville	struggle for perfection	social mobility	reign of the people

1. Look at the graphic organizer above. Then read the following sentences and fill in the blanks.

    a. What did Frances Trollope think about the American people?
    _____
    _____

    b. What did Harriet Martineau think about the American idea of equality?
    _____
    _____

2. Read the lesson title and skim the headings. Write one sentence describing what you think this lesson will be about.
    _____
    _____
    _____

Reading Support Resources   Lesson Preview • Chapter 6, Lesson 3   83

Name: _____   Date: _____

CHAPTER 6
Lesson 3 Reading Strategy
How Others Saw Us

(*A More Perfect Union* pp. 179–183)

Think About Words This reading strategy helps you figure out the meaning of new words. When you come to an unfamiliar word, look for word parts you already know and use clues such as context and pictures.

1. Read the section "The American Defined." Then reread the second paragraph and find the word *fictional*. What part of the word *fictional* is a word that you already know?

   _____

2. What does *fictional* mean?

   _____

3. Read the section "Criticism of America" on page 181. Find three words that tell you what Harriet Martineau thought about American society.

   _____
   _____
   _____

4. Read the section "Tocqueville's America." Then choose one of the following words and fill in as much of the chart below as you can to figure out what the word means.

   aristocratic   perfection   loftier
   observation   distinctions   insights

   WORD: _____

clues from the reading:	
clues from the pictures:	
similar words I already know:	
parts of words I already know:	
the word means	

84   Chapter 6, Lesson 2 • Reading Strategy   Reading Support Resources

CHAPTER 6
Lesson 3 Summary
How Others Saw Us

(*A More Perfect Union* pp. 179–183)

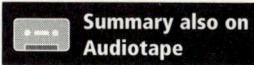

Thinking Focus: What can we learn about our history from Europeans who visited the young United States?

The American Defined

The rest of the world was interested in the new nation called the United States. People from other countries came to visit. Some wrote books about what they thought of the United States. Americans did not like to have bad things written about themselves. Often they got even by writing nasty cartoons and **satires** about their European visitors.

A Frenchman named Michel-Guillaume Jean de Crèvecoeur tried to answer the question "What is an American?" Crèvecoeur liked many American ways. He felt America was fair to its people. He said **social class** was less important in the United States than in Europe. Americans could work and be successful even if they had been born poor. But he also said that American slavery was bad. He thought the American frontier was a place with no laws. And he feared Americans would become selfish.

[?] Summarize Crèvecoeur's definition of the new American.

satire
(săt'īr')
a cartoon or piece of writing that makes fun of human faults

social class
(sō'shəl klăs)
a part of society that has certain cultural and economic traits

Summary continues on next page

Criticism of America

In 1834, an English author named Harriet Martineau visited the United States. She thought Americans talked too much. She felt they tried too hard to get her to like them. Martineau also opposed American slavery. She could not understand how Americans could call themselves free and still let people own slaves.

[?] In what ways was Martineau critical of American society?

Tocqueville's America

In 1831, a Frenchman named Alexis de Tocqueville came to the United States. He wrote a lot about the United States and its people. He too was against American slavery. But he admired how the free people in the United States lived in equality. Even a poor person could get rich. Americans were always looking for a better way to do things. Tocqueville also admired how American women were treated. They received greater respect than in England. He wrote that in America the people ruled themselves. The writings of Tocqueville and others showed the world what Americans were like. These writings also helped Americans to see themselves.

[?] List four features that Tocqueville chose to describe as characteristic of American democracy.

Use with *A More Perfect Union* Pages 188–217

Chapter Overview
People of the New Nation

Fill in the blank spaces below with information from the chapter.

When: 1790–1840
Where: The United States

Americans in the Early 1800s

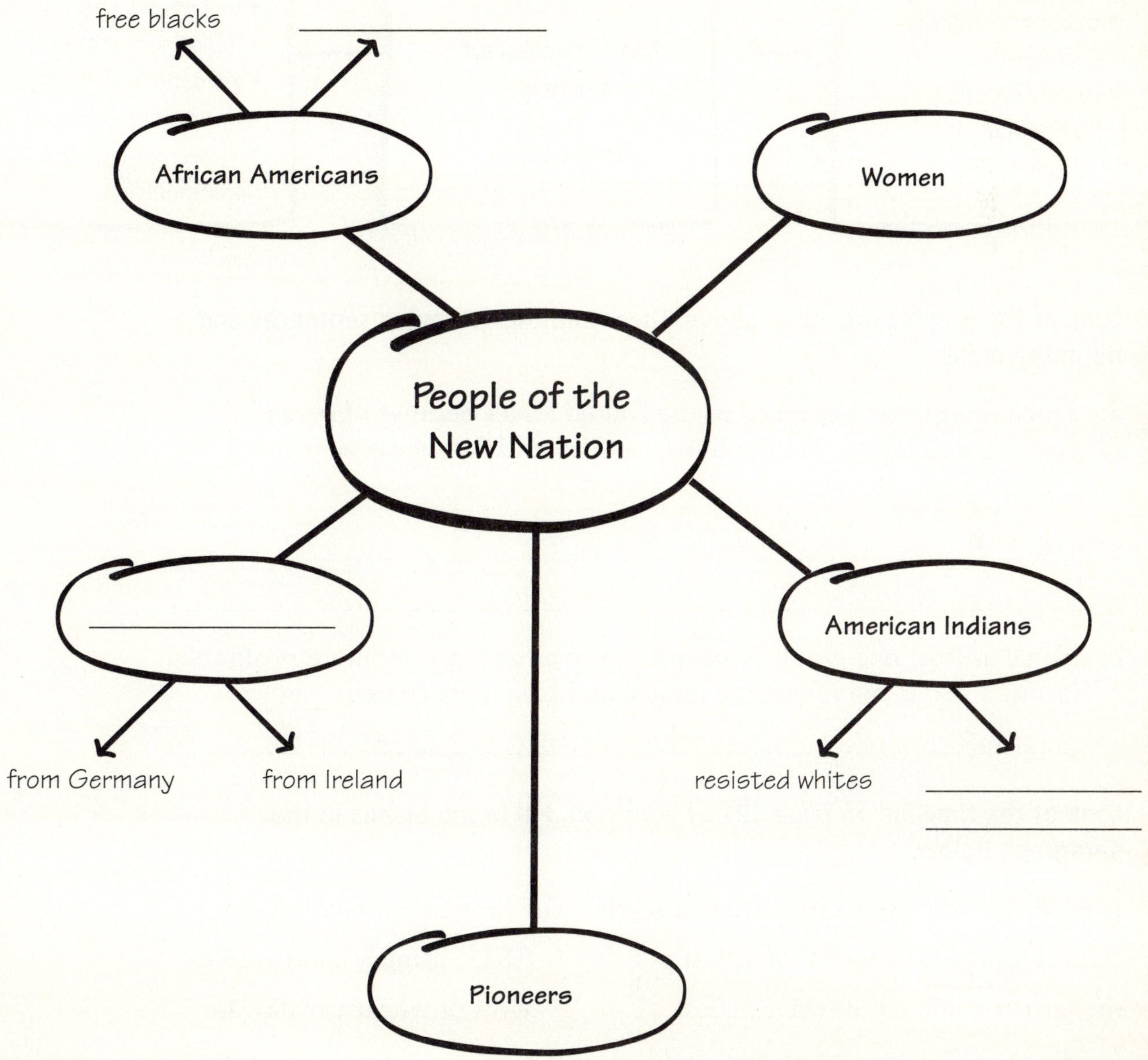

- **African Americans**
  - free blacks
  - _____
- **Women**
- **_____**
  - from Germany
  - from Ireland
- **American Indians**
  - resisted whites
  - _____
- **Pioneers**

People of the New Nation

Reading Support Resources · Chapter Overview · Chapter 7 · 87

CHAPTER 7
Lesson 1 Preview
Life Changes Along the Atlantic Seaboard

(*A More Perfect Union* pp. 190–195)

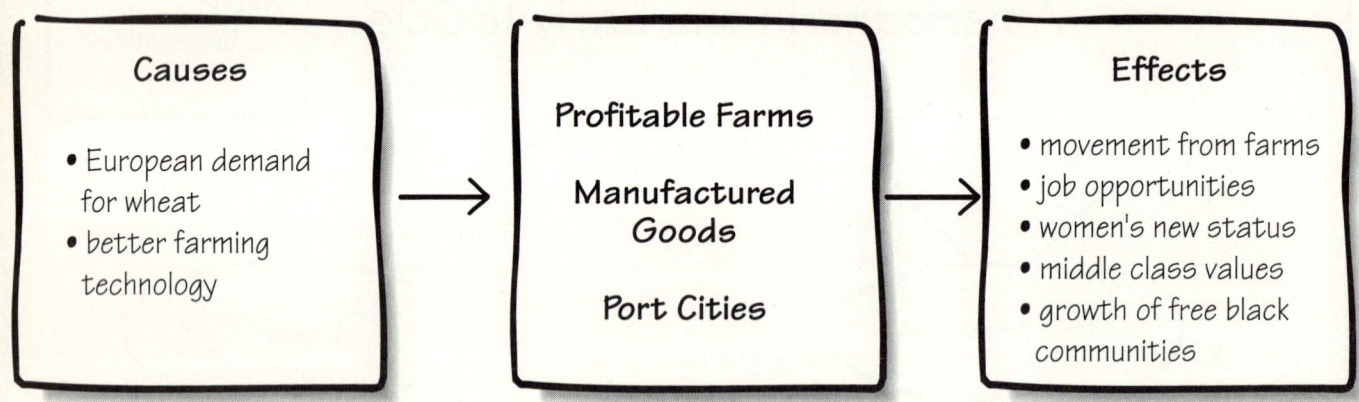

1. **Look at the graphic organizer above. Then read the following sentences and fill in the blanks.**

   a. Three things that happened in the United States because of better farming technology and the European demand for wheat were

   _____

   _____

   _____.

   b. Name at least one group of people that was changed by more profitable farms, a rise in manufactured goods, and busy port cities.

   _____

2. **Look at the timeline on page 191 of your text. Fill in the blanks in the paragraph below.**

   In 1790 farmers used a tool called a scythe. The farmer could cut down _____ acre(s) of wheat per day. In 1815, using a hand cradle, the farmer could cut down _____ acres of wheat per day. In 1834, using a reaper, the farmer could cut down _____ acres of wheat a day.

Name: _____ Date: _____

CHAPTER 7
Lesson 1 Reading Strategy
Life Changes Along the Atlantic Seaboard

(*A More Perfect Union* pp. 190–195)

Sequence This reading strategy helps you follow what is happening in your reading. As you read, pay attention to dates and times, as well as to words such as *before*, *finally*, *after*, and *then*.

1. Read the section "Family Farms Become More Profitable" on pages 190–191. Write at least two words or phrases that help you sequence the events.

   _____

2. Now place the following events from the section "Improved Farming Methods" on page 191 in order by writing *1*, *2*, and *3* in the blanks.

   ___ The steel-bladed plow was invented.

   ___ Most farmers used a scythe to cut down their wheat.

   ___ The mechanical reaper was invented.

3. Read the sections "The American Economy Matures" and "Port Cities Provide Economic Opportunity." Put the following events in order by writing *1*, *2*, and *3* in the blanks.

   ___ The book *A Treatise on Domestic Economy* is published.

   ___ The home-based economy begins to change.

   ___ Buying manufactured goods gives women more free time.

4. Read the section "Some African Americans Experience Change." Then fill in the timeline below.

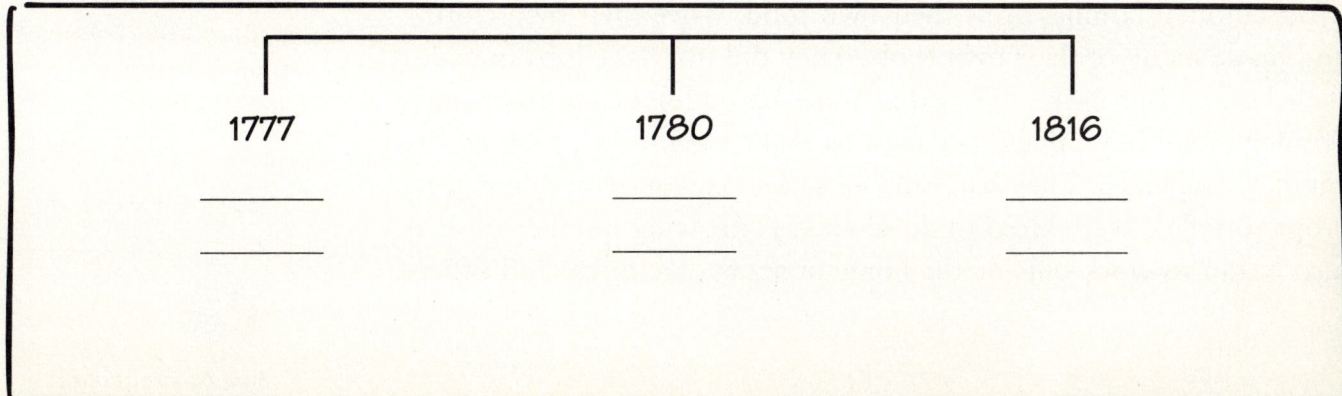

Reading Support Resources

CHAPTER 7
Lesson 1 Summary
Life Changes Along the Atlantic Seaboard

(*A More Perfect Union* pp. 190–195)

Summary also on Audiotape

Thinking Focus: How did economic growth in the new nation change family and community life?

Family Farms Become More Profitable

Two developments changed life for American farmers in the early 1800s. These developments were:

- the growing demand for wheat
- the invention of new farming tools

During the 1800s, Europe's population was growing. But wars in Europe had destroyed the wheat crop. So the United States began exporting huge shipments of wheat to Europe. As a result, many American farmers planted wheat in order to profit from the booming wheat trade. New tools made farm work faster and easier. For example, the mechanical reaper helped farmers cut and tie stacks of wheat faster than ever before. The new steel-bladed plow could cut through even hard, rocky soil. With the new tools, farmers were able to make more money.

[?] How did wars in Europe and new farming tools help American farms become more profitable?

The American Economy Matures

Most colonial families grew their own food, wove their own cloth, and made many of their own tools. They did not have jobs outside their homes. But in the 1790s this home-based life began to change. Women could buy things they used to make themselves, such as soap, candles, and cloth. They had time to make extra money. Some grew crops to sell or were hired to do sewing. A growing number of men also began to work outside the home in shops, factories, and offices.

Summary continues on next page

Life Changes Along the Atlantic Seaboard *(Lesson 1 Summary continued)*

Work began to be seen as separate from the home. The home was seen as a sheltered place away from the world of work.

The rise in manufacturing helped create a growing **middle class**—people with a better-than-average education and income. Many people also belonged to the **working class**—those who labored in mills or workshops for hourly wages.

[?] How were women and the American home affected by economic changes?

middle class
(mĭd′l klăs)
people who have more education and income than most and share common ideas

working class
(wûr′kĭng klăs)
people who are employed for wages, usually in manual labor

Port Cities Provide Economic Opportunity

American port cities like Baltimore, New York, and Philadelphia thrived during the early 1800s. Traditionally, master craftsmen made most of the goods people bought in these and other American cities. But in the early 1800s, these skilled artisans could not keep up with the demand. So city merchants opened up factories that could make goods more quickly than the craftspeople could. The factory goods were also much cheaper. Soon the craftspeople were unable to compete.

[?] How were master craftsmen affected by the booming economy in the port cities?

Some African Americans Experience Changes

Because northern textile and shoe industries could hire workers cheaply, slavery was economically less important in the North than in the South. In addition, many of the people who wanted to do away with slavery lived in the North. Several New England states ended slavery in the late 1700s. Pennsylvania passed a law in 1780 to free slaves slowly. Slaves born before March 1, 1780, would remain slaves for life. Slaves born after that date would work as slaves until age 28. New York and New Jersey passed similar laws. At the same time, communities of free blacks grew. Free blacks formed their own organizations. They built their own schools and churches. Many decided to go west, hoping for better opportunities.

[?] Describe the process, as in the 1780 Pennsylvania law, by which slaves in some Northern states were freed.

CHAPTER 7
Lesson 2 Preview
The Trans-Appalachian Frontier

(*A More Perfect Union* pp. 196–200)

Stages of Settling the Frontier

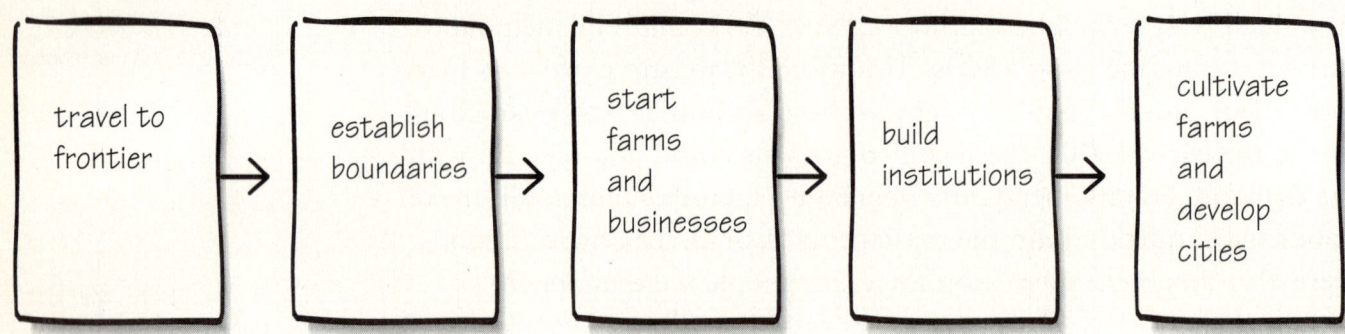

1. **Look at the graphic organizer above. Then read the following sentences and fill in the blanks.**

   a. Name two things the pioneers did once they arrived at the frontier.
   _____
   _____

   b. What did property owners on the frontier have to do before they started their farms or businesses?
   _____

2. **Look at the map on page 198 of your text. What do these roads tell you about the pioneers?**
   _____
   _____
   _____

Name: _____ Date: _____

CHAPTER 7
Lesson 2 Reading Strategy
The Trans-Appalachian Frontier

(*A More Perfect Union* pp. 196–200)

Finding the Main Idea This reading strategy helps you organize and remember what you read. When you finish a selection, jot down the main idea and its supporting details.

1. Read the section "People Move Westward for New Opportunities." Which sentence below best expresses the main idea of the selection? Circle the letter next to your choice.

    a. Most pioneers went west looking for land and opportunities.

    b. Free blacks went west to farm or work as cowhands or miners.

    c. Men who had served in the Revolutionary War were given land by the government.

2. Read the section "Mapping and Planning Towns" on page 199. Which sentence below best expresses the main idea of the section? Circle the letter next to your choice.

    a. Boundaries in colonial times were often unclear.

    b. The new township system allowed pioneers to buy land with clearly defined boundaries.

    c. The Lincoln family lost their Kentucky farm because of a boundary dispute.

3. Read the section "Building Schools and Churches." Then fill in the chart below with the main idea and details from the section.

Main Idea	Supporting Details

Reading Support Resources · Reading Strategy · Chapter 7, Lesson 2

CHAPTER 7

Lesson 2 Summary
The Trans-Appalachian Frontier

(*A More Perfect Union* pp. 196–200)

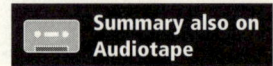

Thinking Focus: What was the sequence of events leading to established, settled communities in the trans-Appalachian frontier?

The First Roads West, 1755-1838

- ❶ Braddock's Road–1755
- ❷ Forbes Road–1758
- ❸ Wilderness Road–1780
- ❹ Nashville Road–1780
- ❺ Hudson Mohawk Route–1793-1803
- ❻ Lancaster Turnpike–1794
- ❼ Cumberland Road–1811
- ❽ National Road–1818-1838

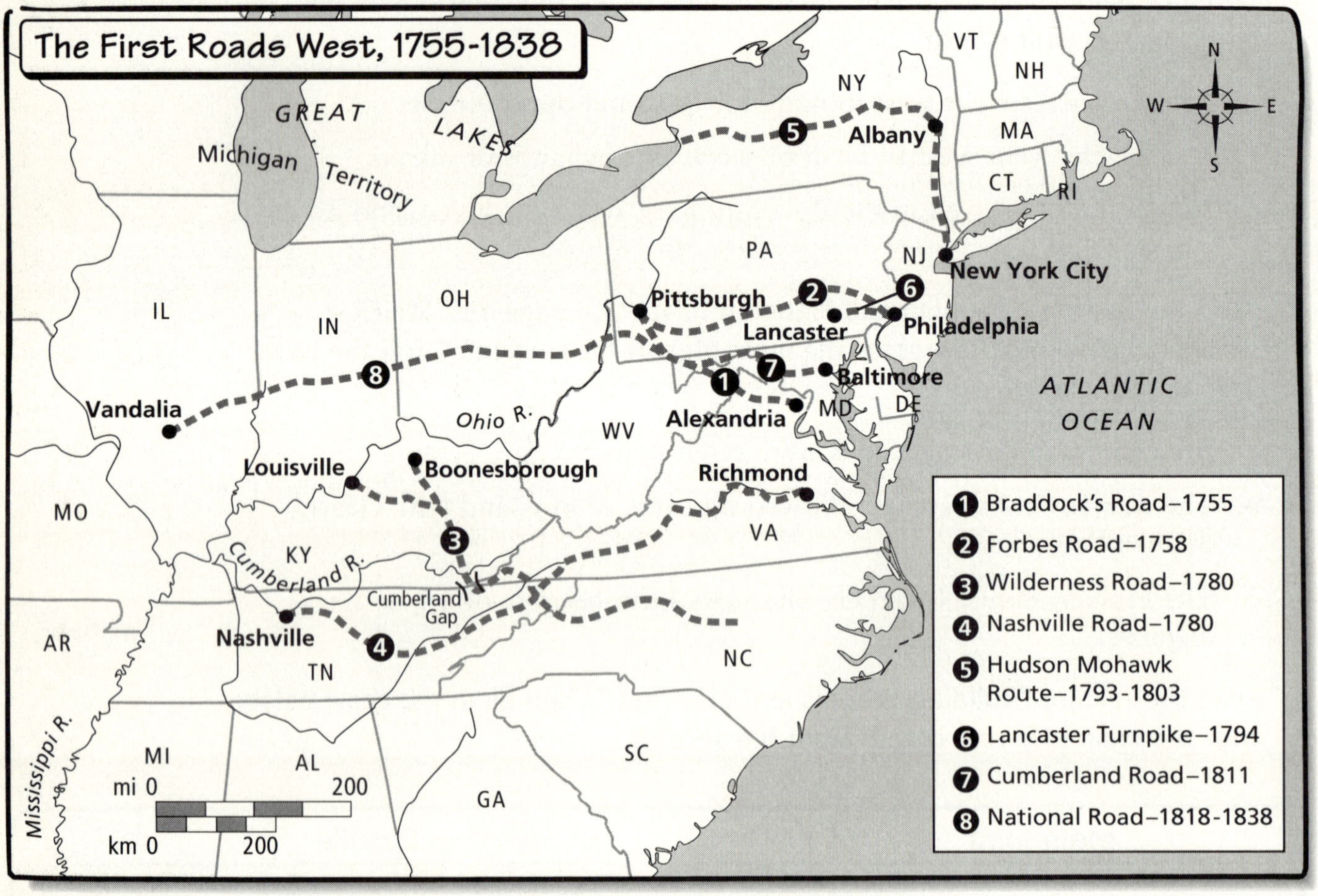

People Move Westward for New Opportunities

The area between the Appalachian Mountains and the Mississippi River was known as the trans-Appalachian frontier. Two million pioneers **migrated** there between 1790 and 1815. Most of these people came looking for land and a better life.

migrate
(mī'grāt')
to come from one place to settle somewhere else

Summary continues on next page

94 Chapter 7, Lesson 2 • Lesson Summary

Reading Support Resources

The Trans-Appalachian Frontier *(Lesson 2 Summary continued)*

Some left small family farms where there was not enough land to divide among the members of the family. Southern planters came to grow cotton in the fertile lower Mississippi River Valley. They brought tens of thousands of slaves. Other people had fought in the Revolutionary War. The government gave these people land in Tennessee and Kentucky as a reward for their war service. Many free blacks moved to the frontier, too. It was a hard trip. But soon people built roads to make the trip easier.

[?] List four reasons for the migration of Americans into the trans-Appalachian frontier.

Pioneers Settle the West

In 1785, pioneers in the trans-Appalachian frontier began to use a new system of land boundaries. The old system used landmarks like trees and rivers. The new system used straight lines to divide pieces of land. It marked out fields and townships on a grid made up of squares. Each township had 36 sections. These sections could be divided up and sold. People could look on a map and see just where their land began and ended. So there were fewer arguments about who owned the land.

In the early days, there were no schools, churches, or other **institutions** on the frontier. The settlers had to build them. But the Land Ordinance of 1787 set aside one piece of land in every township for a public school. By the 1840s, the pioneers had turned the frontier into rich farms and bustling cities. They also had the same services and organizations they used to have back East.

institution
(ĭn'stĭ-tōō'shən)
an organization that provides important social services

[?] How did the township system benefit the pioneers who moved west?

Name: _____ Date: _____

CHAPTER 7
Lesson 3 Preview
The Changing World of American Indians

(*A More Perfect Union* pp. 201–207)

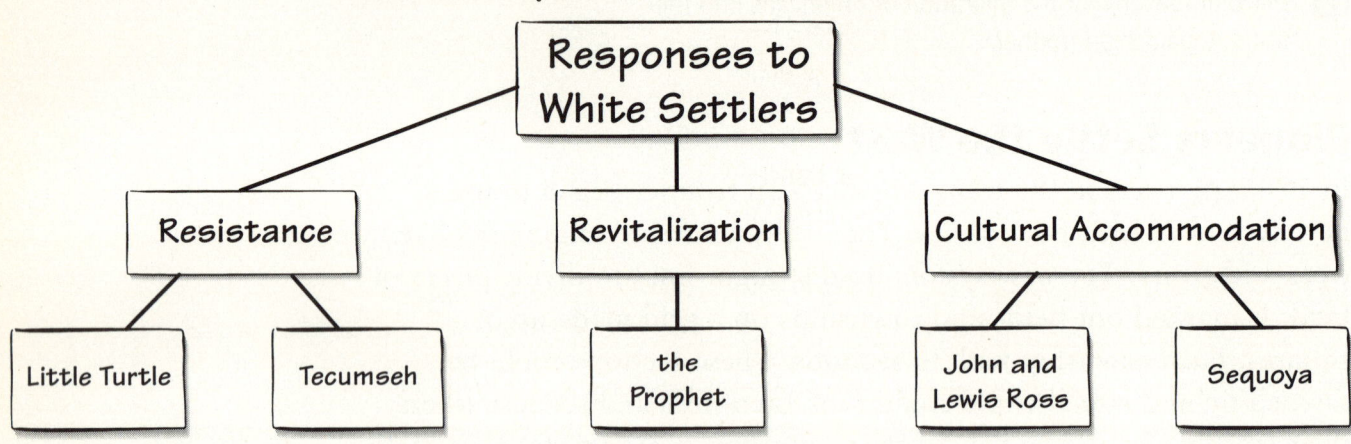

1. Look at the graphic organizer above. Then read the following sentences and fill in the blanks.

   a. What were the three ways American Indians responded to the white settlers?
   _____
   _____
   _____

   b. One of the Indians who used resistance against the white settlers was _____.

2. Look at the two pictures on pages 204 and 205 in your text and read the captions. On the lines below write at least two differences between the Prophet and Sequoya.
   _____
   _____
   _____
   _____

Name: _____   Date: _____

CHAPTER 7
Lesson 3 Reading Strategy
The Changing World of American Indians
(*A More Perfect Union* pp. 201–207)

Predict/Infer This reading strategy helps you understand what you have read and what you will read next. Before you read a section, think about the titles, pictures, and captions. Then think about what will happen in the selection.

1. Read the section "Indian Territories Invaded by the Push Westward" on page 202 up to the section "Hunger for Land." What do you predict will happen next? Circle the letter next to the best answer.

    a. The government will give land back to the Indians.

    b. The government will take more land from the Indians.

    c. The Treaty of Greenville will solve the problems between whites and Indians.

2. Name one clue from your reading that helped you make your prediction.
   _____

3. Read the heading "Various Indian Responses" and look at the illustrations and captions on pages 204 and 205. What do you predict will be two Native American responses to the problems with white settlers?
   _____
   _____

4. Read the red and blue headings on pages 205 and 207 and the illustration on page 206. What can you infer about why the Cherokees' journey to Indian Territory was called the Trail of Tears?
   _____
   _____
   _____
   _____

Reading Support Resources   Reading Strategy • Chapter 7, Lesson 3

CHAPTER 7

Lesson 3 Summary
The Changing World of American Indians

(*A More Perfect Union* pp. 201–207)

Thinking Focus: What were the different responses of the various American Indian peoples when their ancestral lands were threatened?

Indian Territories Invaded by the Push Westward

By the 1780s, most Indian tribes that had lived on the Atlantic coast had been killed by disease, hunger, or war with the settlers. But farther inland, in the Old Northwest, there were still many Indians. Then in 1793, troops sent by President Washington forced Indians in the Old Northwest to give away much of their land. The U.S. government also made the Indians sign treaties that forced them to give away their land.

The government often obtained these treaties unfairly. Sometimes the Indians who signed did not represent their whole tribe. Or they did not have the authority to give away the land. Other times the government used violence to get the Indians to sign. By the end of the War of 1812, most tribes had been forced to move west to distant, undesirable land.

? Find evidence to support this statement: The U.S. government did not deal fairly when signing land cession treaties with American Indians.

Various Indian Responses

When Indian groups were forced off their land, they had to give up their traditional way of life. A Shawnee called the Prophet worked to bring back the old beliefs. His movement was called **revitalization**. He told Indians to stay away from whites. Other Indians, like the Prophet's brother Tecumseh, wanted to keep fighting whites. By 1813, both of their movements failed.

revitalization
(rē-vī´tl-ĭ-zā´shən)
the effort to bring new life and strength to a people or culture

Summary continues on next page

The Changing World of American Indians (Lesson 3 Summary continued)

The Cherokee, on the other hand, wanted **cultural accommodation.** They wanted the best parts of both Indian and European culture. An Indian named Sequoya made a Cherokee alphabet. Cherokee people could then read and write in their own language. Some became successful farmers. They worked hard to make their lives better.

cultural accommodation (kŭl′chər-əl ə-kŏm′ə-dā′shən) compromise of opposing cultures

[?] Compare and contrast the attitudes of the Prophet and Sequoya toward American society.

Defeat of the Cherokee

Many white people did not like the idea of the Cherokee owning land. The white settlers wanted the land for themselves. They asked the government to make the Cherokee leave. The Cherokee went to court to fight to keep their land. But in 1835, all Cherokee were forced to give up their land rights. Some refused to leave. But the U.S. Army forced more than 15,000 Cherokee to move to Indian Territory, 600 miles away. It was winter and they had to walk. More than 4,000 Cherokee died along the way. This sad trip was called the "Trail of Tears."

[?] How was the Cherokee civilization finally destroyed?

CHAPTER 7
Lesson 4 Preview
The Next Wave of Immigrants

(*A More Perfect Union* pp. 210–215)

Comparing German and Irish Immigrants

	German	Irish
Background	artisans, middle class	tenant farmers, unskilled workers
Motivation	wanted political, economic freedom	fled poverty
U.S. Settlement	East and Midwest	Eastern cities
Life in U.S.	some economic success	remained poor, faced nativism

1. Look at the graphic organizer above. Then read the following sentences and fill in the blanks.

   a. What were the main reasons Germans immigrated to the United States?
   _____
   _____

   b. What was the background of most Irish immigrants who came to the United States?
   _____

2. Look at the two maps on page 213 of your text. Then fill in the blanks in the following paragraph.

   In the mid-1800s many _____ and _____ immigrants came to the United States. More than 10 percent of the state population in northeastern cities such as Boston and New York were _____ immigrants. More than 8 percent of the state populations in the midwestern states were _____ immigrants.

Name: _____ Date: _____

CHAPTER 7
Lesson 4 Reading Strategy
The Next Wave of Immigrants

(*A More Perfect Union* pp. 210–215)

Compare and Contrast This reading strategy helps you understand how events are similar and different. As you read about historical events, think about how they compare and contrast with events you already know.

1. Read the section "Germans Seek Democracy." Write a sentence describing the reasons Germans left their homeland.

   _____

2. Read the section "Irish Flee Potato Famine." Write a sentence describing the reasons the Irish left their homeland.

   _____

3. Read the section "Immigrants Establish Themselves in the New Country." Then fill in the chart below to compare and contrast German and Irish immigrants.

German and Irish Immigration

	German Immigrants	Irish Immigrants
What kinds of skills did they have?		
Where did they settle?		
How much money did they have when they arrived?		

4. Read the section "New Americans Perceived as a Threat." Write a sentence or two comparing attitudes toward immigration today with attitudes toward immigration in the mid-1800s.

   _____
   _____
   _____

CHAPTER 7
Lesson 4 Summary
The Next Wave of Immigrants

(*A More Perfect Union* pp. 210–215)

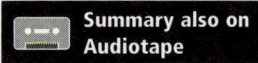
Summary also on Audiotape

Thinking Focus: What experiences characterized German and Irish immigration to the United States in the 1840s and 1850s?

A New Generation of Europeans Arrives

In the 1850s, almost three million people **emigrated** from Europe to the United States. Most came from Ireland or Germany. German people came looking for freedom and a better way of life. Many were trying to escape the harsh German government. They wanted to live in a democracy. The Irish came because their own country was having a **famine**. Many people in Ireland ate almost nothing but potatoes and milk. But in the 1840s, a plant disease wiped out Ireland's potato crop. This left many people with nothing to eat. Millions of people left Ireland and came to America.

emigrate
(ĕm′ĭ-grāt′)
to leave one country forever and settle in another

famine
(făm′ĭn)
a time of starvation

[?] What kind of hardships drove people from Europe to the United States?

Immigrants Establish Themselves in the New Country

Many of the Germans who came to America had skills and money. They wanted to buy land. Many moved to the American frontier. Most of the Irish people who came to America had no money and few skills. Most of them stayed in cities. They took whatever jobs they could get and worked very hard. Over time many Irish immigrants made a better life for themselves.

[?] Why did most Germans find it easier to establish themselves in America than did most Irish?

Summary continues on next page

The Next Wave of Immigrants (Lesson 4 Summary continued)

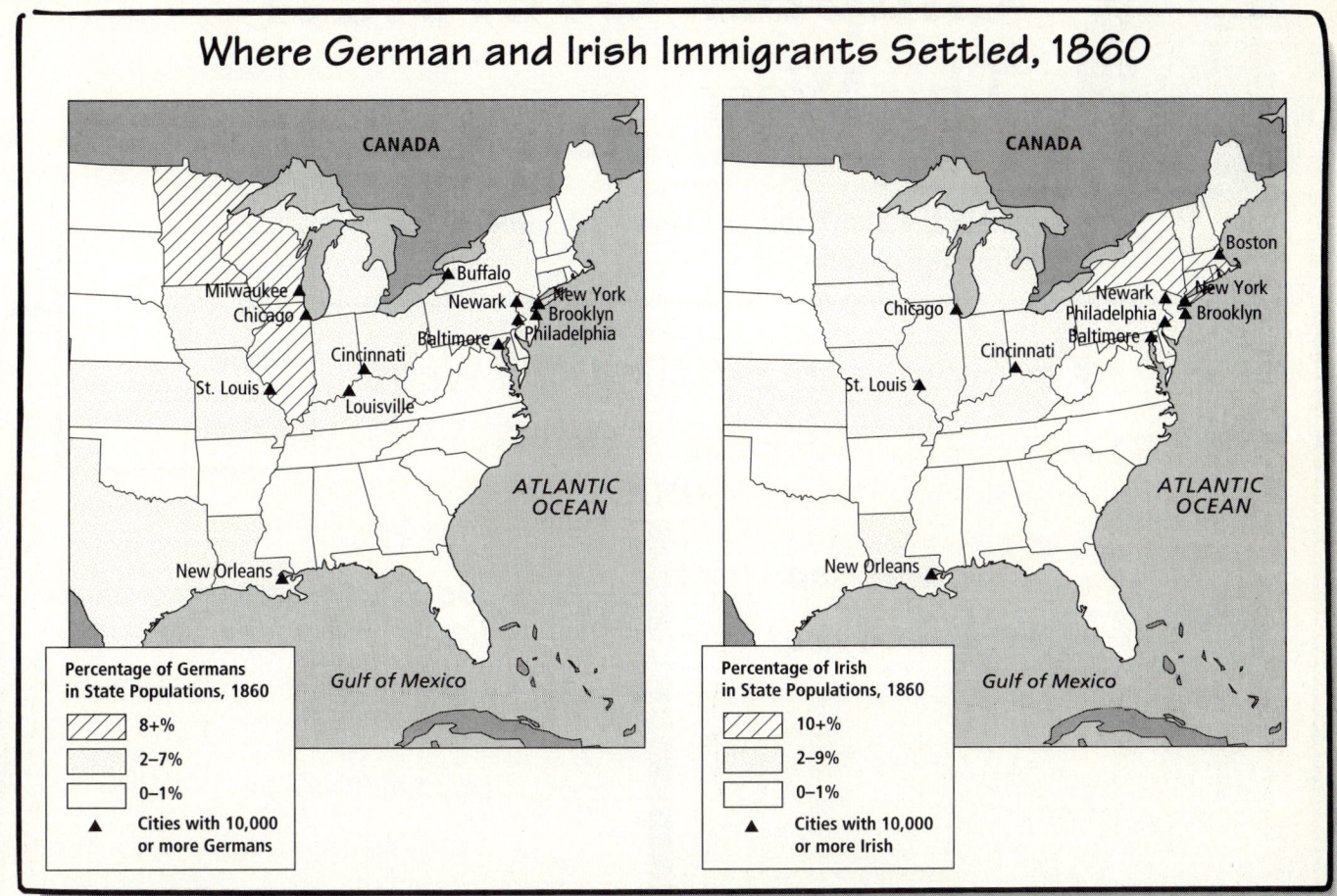

New Americans Perceived as a Threat

Many Americans feared they might lose their jobs to Irish or German workers. Some feared that the immigrants would gain power in government. These fears led to a social movement called **nativism**. Nativists formed anti-immigration groups. One of these groups was called the "Know-Nothings" because they answered "I don't know" when asked about their policies. The Know-Nothings wanted to cut down on immigration. They also wanted to limit immigrants' right to vote. By the late 1850s, the Know-Nothings had lost most of their power.

nativism
(nā′tĭ-vĭz′əm)
a policy that favors native-born people over immigrants

[?] Why did some Americans feel economically and politically threatened by the large immigrant population?

Use with *A More Perfect Union* Pages 220–251

Chapter Overview
The West

Fill in the blank spaces below with information from the chapter.

When: 1790–1860

Where: Western North America

Key Events in Settling the West

1800

_____ 1803

1804–1806 Lewis and Clark expedition

Pike's expedition 1806–1807

1823–1828 _____

Missionaries sent to the Northwest 1835

1836 Texas declares independence from Mexico

Frémont's expedition 1842–1845

_____ 1846–1848

1848 Treaty of Guadalupe Hidalgo

Gold discovered in California; Mormon state established in Utah 1849

1850 California becomes a state

1860

104 Chapter 8 • Chapter Overview

Reading Support Resources

Name: _____   Date: _____

CHAPTER 8
Lesson 1 Preview
Exploring Beyond the Mississippi
(*A More Perfect Union* pp. 222–227)

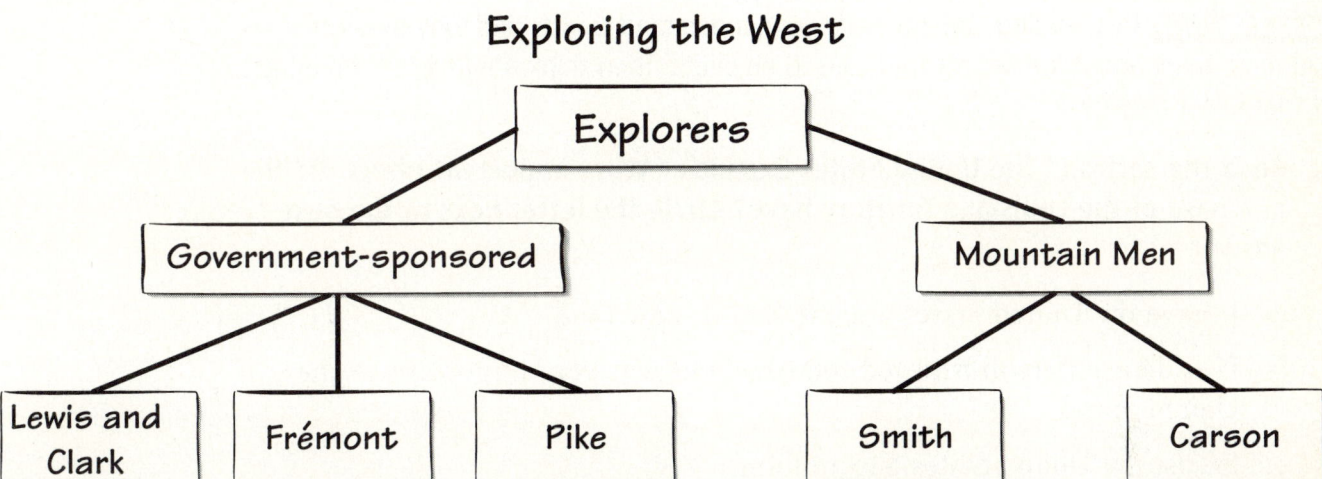

1. According to the graphic organizer above, the two main types of explorers were _____ and _____.

2. The routes of four of the five explorers shown in the graphic organizer appear on the map on page 227 of your text. Look carefully at this map. List the explorers shown on the map and describe how far west each one went.

_____
_____
_____
_____
_____
_____
_____
_____
_____
_____

Name: _____   Date: _____

CHAPTER 8
Lesson 1 Reading Strategy
Exploring Beyond the Mississippi

(*A More Perfect Union* pp. 222–227)

Cause and Effect This reading strategy helps you understand events and why they occur. As you read, think about the factors that caused an event. Then think about what the effects of that event may be.

1. Read the section "The United States Expands." What important effect did the purchase of the Louisiana Territory have? Circle the letter next to the best answer.

    a. It gave the United States a great deal of new land.

    b. President Jefferson believed that the land was very important to the United States.

    c. It cost the United States $15 million.

2. What did the purchase cause President Jefferson to do?
    _____
    _____

3. Read the section "Lewis and Clark Explore the West" on pages 224–225. List two effects of their expedition.
    _____
    _____

4. Read the section "Mountain Men Blaze Trails" on pages 226–227. Fill in the following chart.

Cause	Effect
	Trappers went to the Rockies.
Trappers found and made trails.	
The government sent expeditions.	
More of the West became known.	

106 Chapter 8, Lesson 1 • Reading Strategy   Reading Support Resources

CHAPTER 8
Lesson 1 Summary
Exploring Beyond the Mississippi
(*A More Perfect Union* pp. 222–227)

Summary also on Audiotape

Thinking Focus: Why did the U.S. government call for exploration west of the Mississippi?

The United States Expands

The Louisiana Territory was a huge piece of land west of the Mississippi River. President Thomas Jefferson knew that it would be important to the growing United States. So in 1803, Jefferson bought the land from France. Then he chose Captain Meriwether Lewis to lead an expedition to explore the region. Lewis chose William Clark to be his co-leader. Jefferson told them that their main goal was to explore the Missouri River. Jefferson also hoped they would find the Northwest Passage, a water route that would take people west to the Pacific Ocean. He also wanted Lewis and Clark to make detailed maps and records of the geography, climate, plants, and animals of the region.

What instructions did Jefferson give Lewis and Clark?

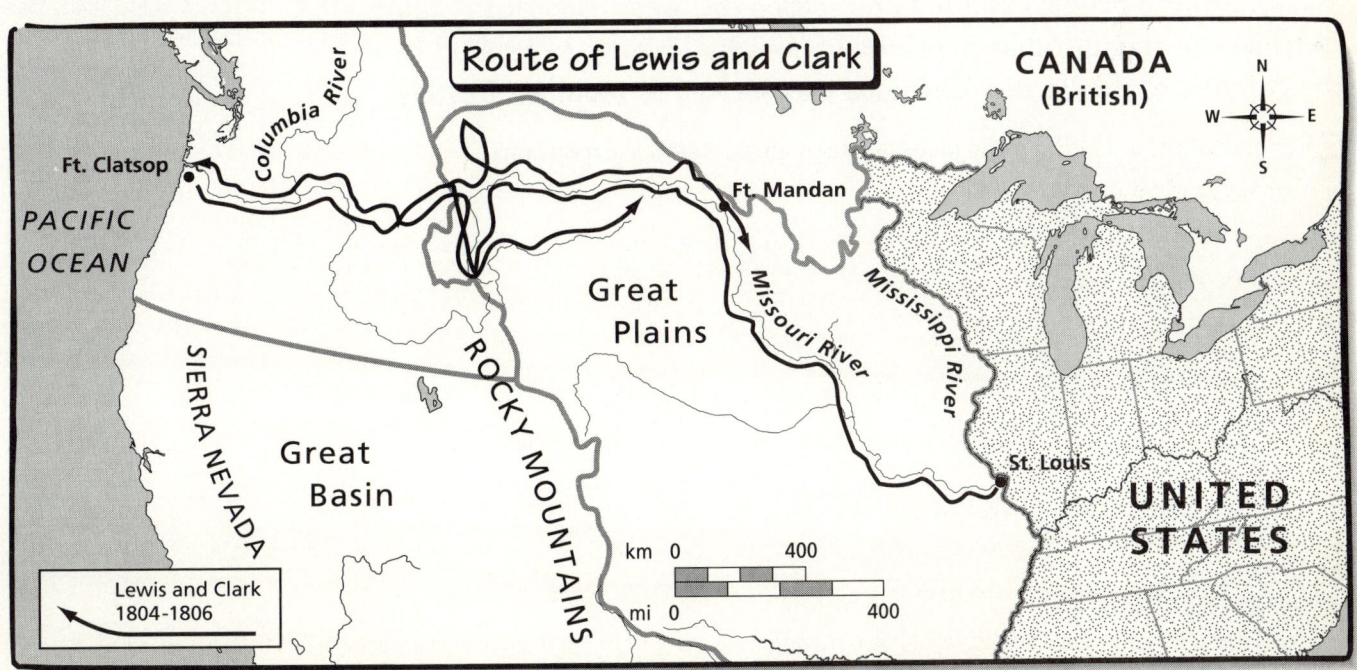

Reading Support Resources

Lesson Summary • Chapter 8, Lesson 1 **107**

Exploring Beyond the Mississippi (Lesson 1 Summary continued)

Lewis and Clark Explore the West

Lewis and Clark left St. Louis on May 14, 1804. They returned on September 23, 1806. Lewis was in charge of all scientific discoveries. Clark drew maps and kept the detailed records that Jefferson ordered. They hired the fur trader Toussaint Charbonneau as an interpreter. Charbonneau brought along his Shoshone wife, Sacajawea. The expedition traveled over the Rockies to the Pacific Ocean. They did not find the Northwest Passage. But they mapped the area of the Columbia River, which helped the United States claim Oregon. They also got to know many American Indians. Clark's careful maps and descriptions of animals inspired many fur trappers to move west. The expedition also increased interest in westward expansion.

[?] What were the achievements of the Lewis and Clark expedition?

Mountain Men Blaze Trails

Other explorers traveled west after Lewis and Clark. Many of them hunted and trapped animals for their fur. These trappers were called **mountain men**. Every spring, mountain men like Jedediah Smith gathered at a **rendezvous** with other trappers, traders, and Indians. There they traded their furs for supplies and visited with each other. They also found routes through the wilderness and across the **continental divide**. Later government expeditions used these routes, and they often used mountain men for their guides. Zebulon Pike and John Frémont led several of these government expeditions to explore the West. As more people explored and settled the West, Americans came to believe in the idea that the United States had a duty to expand from the Atlantic to the Pacific. This idea was known as **Manifest Destiny**.

[?] How did the activities of the mountain men encourage U.S. expansion?

---

mountain man
(moun′tən măn)
a fur trapper of the West during the 1800s

rendezvous
(rän′dā-vōō′)
a French word meaning "meeting place"; a place where mountain men, traders, and Indians met once a year to trade furs

continental divide
(kŏn′tə-nĕn′tl dĭ-vīd′)
an imaginary line that divides the rivers that flow west in the United States from those that flow east

Manifest Destiny
(măn′ə-fĕst′ dĕst′tə-nē)
a belief held by some people in the 1840s that the United States must expand from the Atlantic Ocean to the Pacific Ocean

Name: _____ Date: _____

CHAPTER 8
Lesson 2 Preview
Achieving Manifest Destiny

(*A More Perfect Union* pp. 230–235)

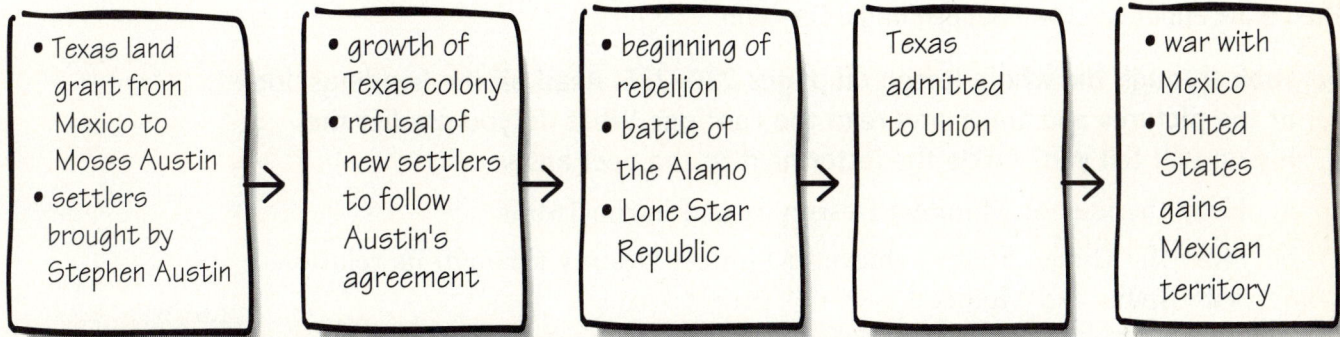

1. Look at the graphic organizer above. Then read the following list of events. Number the events in order according to which happened first, second, and so on.

   ___ Texas is admitted to the Union.

   ___ New settlers in the Texas colony do not follow Austin's agreement.

   ___ A land grant is given to Moses Austin by Mexico.

   ___ The rebellion begins; the battle of the Alamo takes place.

2. Look at the two pictures on page 231 in your text. Read the caption and the descriptions of the two towns. List two ways the towns are different.

   _____
   _____
   _____
   _____

Reading Support Resources   Lesson Preview • Chapter 8, Lesson 2 **109**

Name: Date:

CHAPTER 8
Lesson 2 Reading Strategy
Achieving Manifest Destiny

(*A More Perfect Union* pp. 230–235)

Predict/Infer This reading strategy helps you understand what you have read and what you will read next. Before you read a section, think about the titles, pictures, and captions. Then think about what will happen in the selection.

1. Look through the whole lesson on pages 230–235. Read all the headings, look at the pictures and maps, and read the captions. What do you predict the lesson will tell you? Circle the letter next to the best answer.

    a. How the idea of Manifest Destiny began in the 1600s.

    b. How the United States achieved Manifest Destiny through its relations with Spain and Mexico.

    c. Why white Americans thought they had a duty to expand their culture.

2. List two clues from the headings and visuals that helped you make your prediction.

    _____

    _____

3. Read the first column of page 232 down to the head "Independence Proclaimed." How do you think the battle of the Alamo will affect Texans? Circle the letter next to the best answer.

    a. It will make them want to have a war.

    b. It will make them want to have peace.

    c. It will inspire them to want to be independent of Mexico.

4. Read the first paragraph on page 234 under "War with Mexico." Then read the blue headings that follow. Fill in the chart below.

What I Know	What I Predict

CHAPTER 8

Lesson 2 Summary
Achieving Manifest Destiny

(*A More Perfect Union* pp. 230–235)

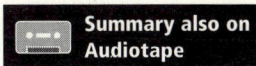
Summary also on Audiotape

Thinking Focus: How did Texas become the center of a conflict that gave the United States vast new lands?

Development of Texas

In the early 1800s, Spain claimed a huge area of western North America, including Texas. As Spain watched **expansionists** from the United States move westward, it worried that the Americans might invade its territory. So Moses Austin offered a plan to bring a limited number of U.S. settlers to Texas. In return for cheap land, the settlers would promise to be loyal to Spain and to accept the Catholic religion. Spain agreed, hoping that Texas would be a **buffer zone**.

When Mexico became independent from Spain, Texas became part of Mexico. U.S. settlers continued to arrive, and soon they outnumbered the Mexicans. Many refused to honor Austin's agreement. The settlers did not want to be Catholics. They wanted the government to be like the government in the United States. The new settlers also wanted to keep slaves, even though slavery was outlawed. Some wanted independence. Mexico sent troops to keep order. More settlers kept coming even after laws were passed to stop them.

[?] How did the white settlers' disregard for Mexican law and religion contribute to tension in Texas?

Texas Gains Independence

In 1835, a small band of Texas settlers drove 1,100 Mexican troops out of San Antonio. This made the Mexican leader, General Santa Anna, angry. He put together a large army and surrounded another group of rebels who were inside the Alamo, an old Spanish mission. Their leader, William Barrett, promised he would never surrender. As this battle was fought, another group of Texas settlers declared independence from Mexico.

expansionist
(ĭk-spăn′shən-ĭst)
a person who thinks a nation should increase the size of its land

buffer zone
(bŭf′ər zōn)
an area that separates two enemies and lessens the danger of conflict

Summary continues on next page

Achieving Manifest Destiny (Lesson 2 Summary continued)

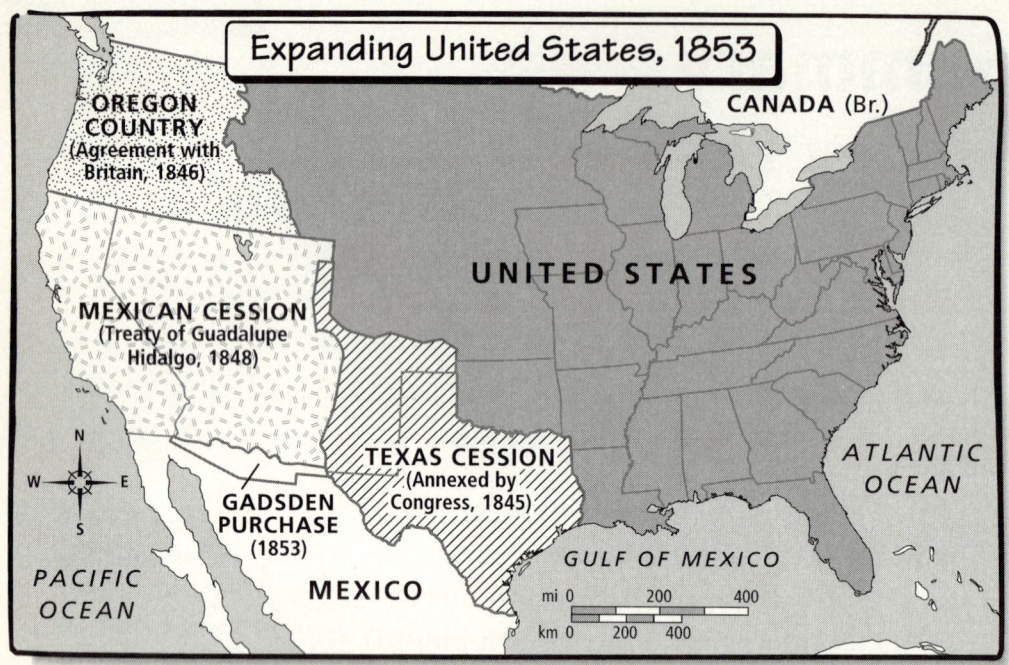

Santa Anna won the battle of the Alamo, and ordered everyone inside killed. He continued to fight anyone resisting his rule. But Sam Houston, commander of the Texas army, defeated Santa Anna in a surprise attack in 1836. As a result, Mexico surrendered, and Texas became an independent Republic. It was called the Lone Star Republic. The United States did not want to **annex** Texas, and it stayed independent for almost 10 years.

? What events made Texas the Lone Star Republic?

> **annex**
> (ə-nĕks′)
>
> to increase the size of a country by making other land a part of it

War with Mexico

In 1845, Congress voted to add Texas to the Union. President Polk wanted to extend the territory of the United States to the Pacific Ocean. But Mexico owned much of this land and refused to sell it to the United States. After a small battle at the Mexican border, Congress declared war on Mexico in 1846. After two years of fighting, Mexico was defeated. Mexico and the United States signed the Treaty of Guadalupe Hidalgo in 1848. The United States paid Mexico $15 million for most of its land north of the Rio Grande and west to the Pacific Ocean. The United States had finally achieved its Manifest Destiny—a dream to settle the land from the Atlantic Ocean to the Pacific Ocean.

? How did the United States achieve Manifest Destiny through war with Mexico?

Name: _____ Date: _____

CHAPTER 8

Lesson 3 Preview
Settling the West

(*A More Perfect Union* pp. 236–240)

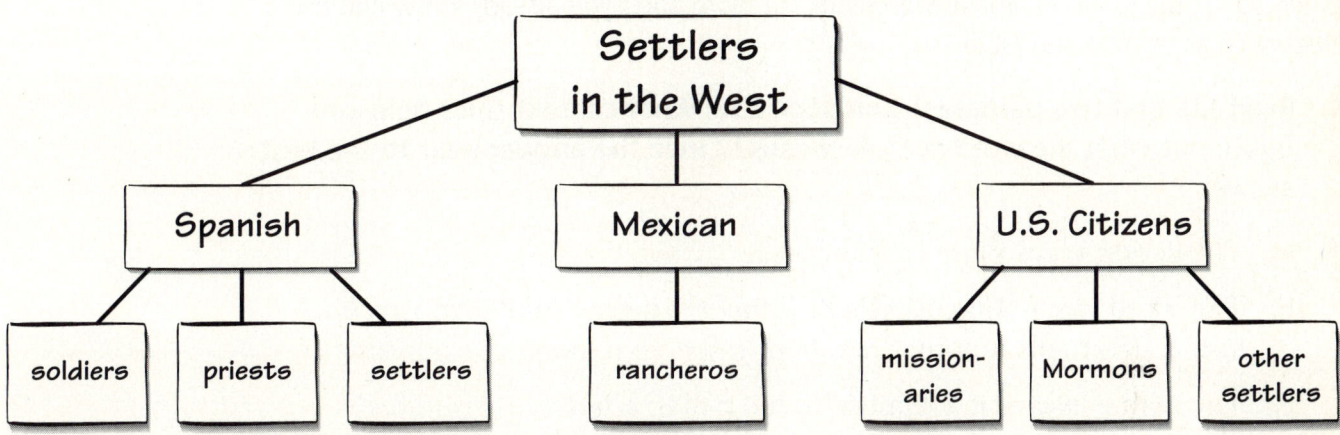

1. Look at the graphic organizer above. Who were the three main groups of settlers in the West?

   _____

   _____

   _____

2. Read the red and blue headings on pages 236–240 in your text. The names of two states are mentioned in the headings. What are they?

   _____

   _____

Reading Support Resources   Lesson Preview • **Chapter 8, Lesson 3** **113**

Name: _____ Date: _____

CHAPTER 8
Lesson 3 Reading Strategy
Settling the West

(*A More Perfect Union* pp. 236–240)

Think About Words This reading strategy helps you figure out the meaning of new words. When you come to an unfamiliar word, look for word parts you already know and use clues such as context and pictures.

1. Read the first two paragraphs on page 236. What context clues help you figure out what the word *ranchero* means? Circle the answer next to the best answer.

    a. The action takes place in California.

    b. The word *rancho* means ranch. *Ranchero* seems similar to *rancho*, and context tells you that *ranchero* refers to a man.

    c. The man is wearing a sombrero and riding a horse.

2. Look at the picture on page 236 and read its caption. What do you think a *veranda* is? Write your answer below.

   _____

3. Read the second paragraph at the top of page 238. Use context clues to help you know what a *vaquero* is. Write your answer below.

   _____

4. Choose a word from the lesson that is unfamiliar to you. Then fill in as much as you can of the chart below to help you understand the meaning of the word.

   WORD: _____

clues from the reading:
clues from the pictures:
similar words I already know:
parts of words I already know:
the word means

114 Chapter 8, Lesson 3 • *Reading Stategy*   Reading Support Resources

CHAPTER 8
Lesson 3 Summary
Settling the West

(*A More Perfect Union* pp. 236–240)

Thinking Focus: Why did U.S. citizens begin to settle in the lands west of the Mississippi River?

Spaniards Settle in California

In the 1700s, Spain set up colonies in California and Texas. Settlers came to these colonies for different reasons:

- Priests went to establish churches and convert Indians to Christianity.
- Soldiers went to build forts and protect others.
- Settlers went to grow food for the soldiers and start their own ranches.

Priests established missions that supported themselves. Each included a church, workshops, and rooms for the priests. Indians lived on these missions, too. They farmed and raised livestock. But the Indians found it hard to live there, and many ran away.

After Mexico became independent from Spain, it took over control of California and began to **secularize** the missions. The mission lands were supposed to be given to the Indians. Instead, the government gave huge areas to rancheros. Rancheros were Mexican landowners who raised cattle for meat, hides, and other products on their ranchos. On the wealthier ranchos, skilled horsemen, called vaqueros, did most of the work. Yankee traders sailed to California ports to buy cattle products for eastern shoe factories, and for the manufacture of candles and soap.

secularize
(sĕk´yə-lə-rīz´)
to change something from religious use or ownership to civil use or ownership

[?] How did taking the missions away from the church change life in California?

Summary continues on next page

Settling the West *(Lesson 3 Summary continued)*

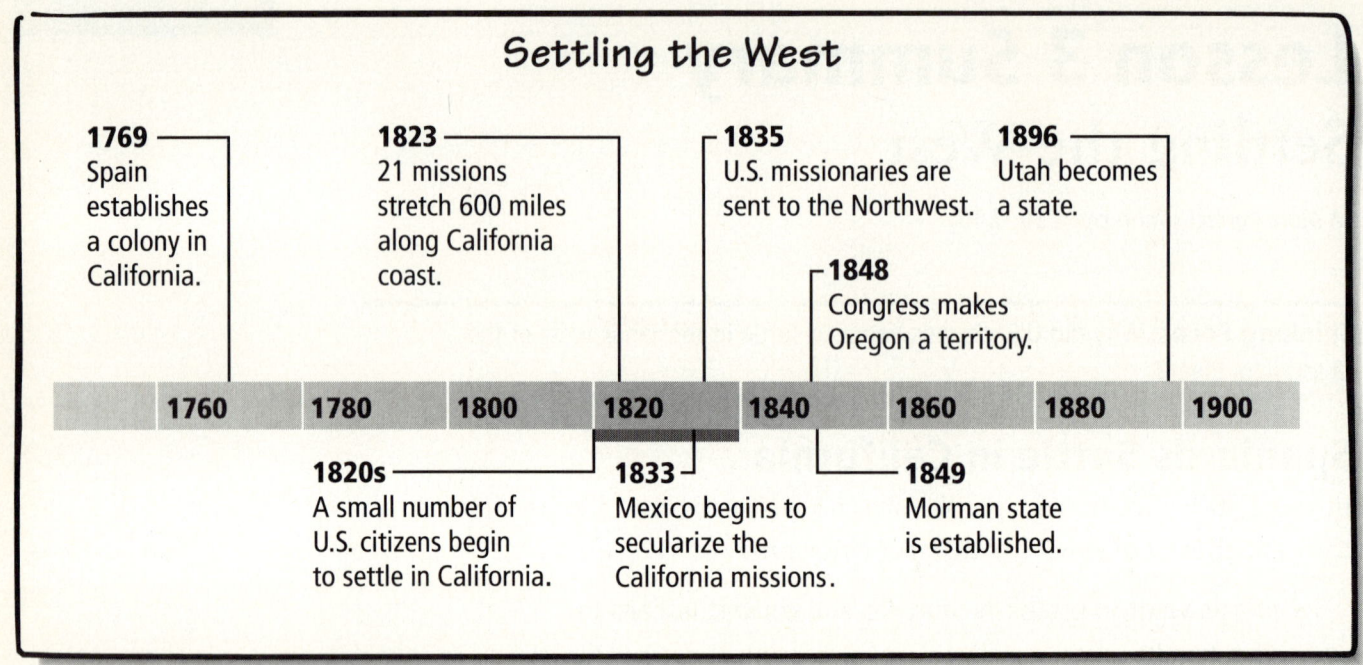

U.S. Citizens Go West

Because California was part of Mexico until 1848, most U.S. citizens who went west went to the Oregon Country. In 1835, the American Board for Foreign Missions began to send missionaries to settle the area. By 1845, more than 5,000 Americans lived there. As the number of settlers increased, there were conflicts between the Indians and the whites. To protect the settlers, Congress made Oregon a territory in 1848.

A group of Mormons led by Brigham Young also moved west to an area outside the United States called the Great Basin. There they created a Mormon state named Desert in 1849. Mormons are members of the Church of Jesus Christ of Latter-day Saints. Many Americans were upset that Mormon religious leaders also ran the government. This concern prevented Congress from admitting Utah into the Union until 1896.

? Briefly describe how U.S. settlements developed in Oregon.

Name: _____ Date: _____

CHAPTER 8
Lesson 4 Preview
Surviving on the Frontier

(*A More Perfect Union* pp. 241–247)

1. According to the graphic organizer above, what caused increased U.S. settlement in the West?

   _____

2. Look at the pictures on pages 242, 243, and 245 in your text and read the captions. What do they tell you about living conditions in the West and on the way there?

   _____
   _____
   _____
   _____
   _____

Name: _____   Date: _____

CHAPTER 8
Lesson 4 Reading Strategy
Surviving on the Frontier

(*A More Perfect Union* pp. 241–247)

Using the Visuals This reading strategy helps you use photographs, maps, charts, and illustrations to help you understand what you read. As you read, be sure to study the visuals and carefully read the captions.

1. Look at the picture on page 241. What does it tell you about the miners who came to California? Circle the letter next to your answer.

   a. Some miners came from China, as well as from many other parts of the world.

   b. People had to travel from China to California by boat.

   c. The gold miners were called forty-niners.

2. Look at the photographs on page 242 and read the caption. What do they tell you about mining during the gold rush? Circle the letter next to your answer.

   a. Miners used advanced technology to mine gold.

   b. Working a claim was probably difficult even with a Long Tom.

   c. Most miners became rich.

3. Study the map on page 244 and read the captions. Write a sentence describing V.E. Geiger's journey.

   _____

4. Look at the pictures of pioneer families on pages 243 and 245. Suppose you were a pioneer. Write a brief description of your journey west in the space below.

   My Journey West
   _____
   _____
   _____
   _____

CHAPTER 8

Lesson 4 Summary
Surviving on the Frontier

(*A More Perfect Union* pp. 241–247)

Thinking Focus: What impact did the discovery of gold have on the West?

The Gold Fields

Gold was discovered at Sutter's sawmill in California on January 24, 1848. Thousands of people soon came to California from all over the world. They were called forty-niners. Americans and Mexicans traveled to California by horse or by wagon. Others came by sea from places like China and Chile. Americans from the East Coast traveled on uncomfortable but expensive ships. Many Indians joined the gold rush, too. They were often forced into slavery or even killed.

A few miners did get rich, but most did not. They usually lived in camps full of single men. Life there was rough and violent. Supplies were expensive. Miners would often leave town when they heard of a richer strike somewhere else. This left behind many **ghost towns**.

? Why did few mining towns become permanent settlements?

ghost town
(gōst toun)
a town that has been completely abandoned

Hardships of the Overland Trail

More than 145,000 people had moved west by 1860. The journey was hard. The settlers traveled by wagon train. But the wagons mostly carried supplies. People walked or rode horses. The Overland Trail from Missouri to California was 2,000 miles long. The wagons could only travel about two miles an hour, and so the trip took months. The pioneers worked very hard to keep themselves, the wagons, and the animals moving. Bad weather could flood rivers and upset and scatter the animals. Steep mountain trails forced people to leave their belongings behind.

Summary continues on next page

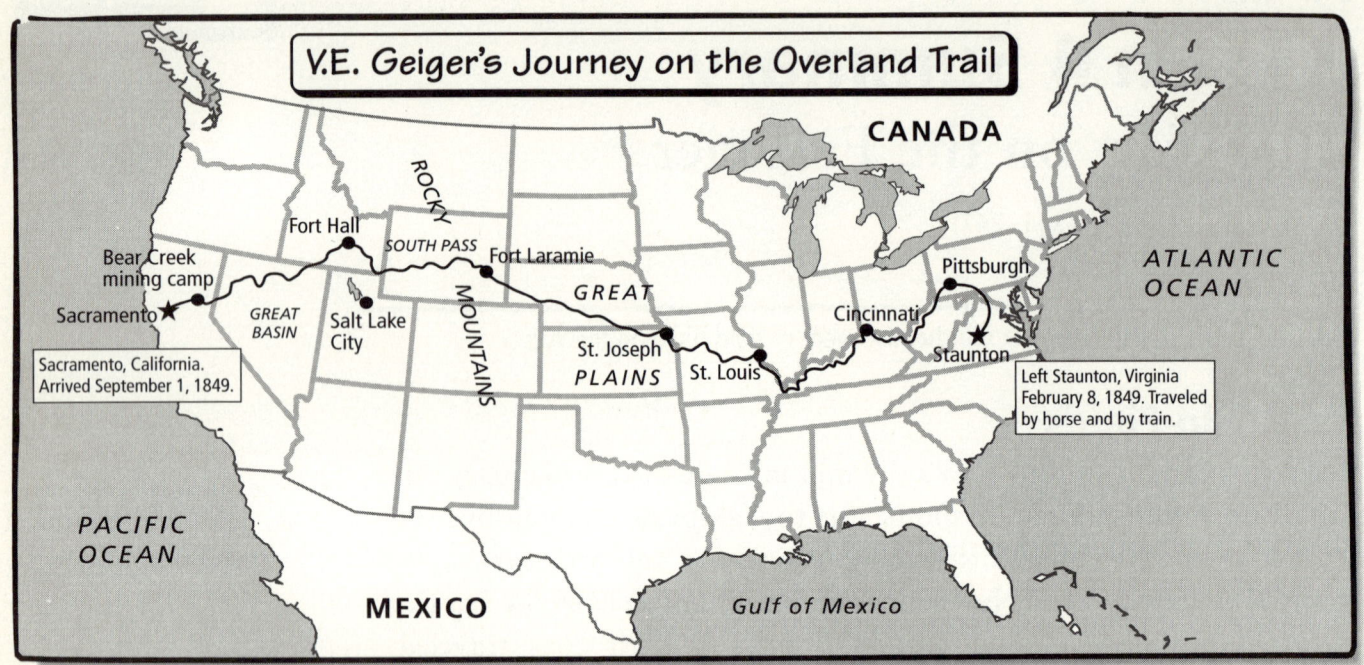

Some people died in the desert because of the lack of water. Others died because of disease and poor diet. After reaching the West, settlers still faced the work of building homes and getting the land ready for planting.

[?] What problems of weather and geography did the pioneers face?

Impact of the Westward Movement

The journey west gave settlers a sense of **regionalism** and community. They had worked together to reach their goal and were proud of what they had done. But the effect of westward movement on the people who already lived in the region was not so positive. Many Mexicans had stayed in California after it became a U.S. territory and became American citizens. The forty-niners and pioneers often just took over the Mexicans' land, even though there was a law protecting the Mexicans. Most of the rancheros lost their land grants because the boundaries and titles to ownership were not clear. And even though most settlers passed through the Great Plains, the Indian tribes in that area began to worry about the safety and security of their lands.

regionalism
(rē′jə-nəl-ĭz′əm)
a sense of belonging to a separate region or area

[?] How did the westward movement affect those who already lived there?

Use with *A More Perfect Union* Pages 252–281

Chapter Overview
The North

Fill in the blank spaces below with information from the chapter.

When: 1790–1860

Where: Northern United States

Changes in the North

CHANGES

- Industrial Revolution
  - new machines
  - _____
  - growth of factories

- City Life
  - _____
  - new social classes
  - new problems, especially for poor

- Reform Movements
  - education
  - _____
  - workers
  - _____

Reading Support Resources — Chapter Overview • Chapter 9 — 121

Name: _____ Date: _____

CHAPTER 9
Lesson 1 Preview
The Industrial Revolution

(*A More Perfect Union* pp. 254–260)

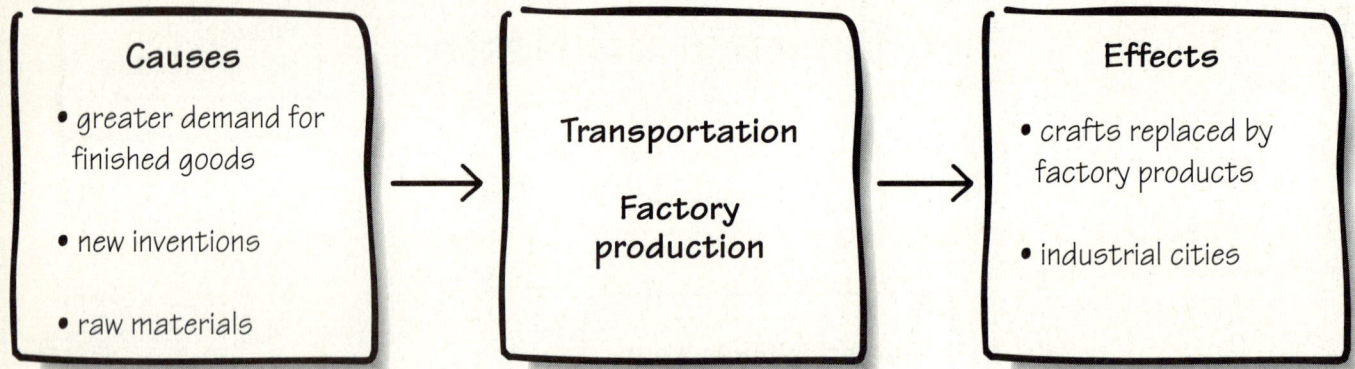

Causes and Effects of the Industrial Revolution

Causes
- greater demand for finished goods
- new inventions
- raw materials

→ Transportation

Factory production →

Effects
- crafts replaced by factory products
- industrial cities

1. **Look at the graphic organizer above. Then read the following sentences and fill in the blanks.**

   a. What brought about the changes in transportation and factory production in the first half of the 1800s?
   _____
   _____

   b. What happened as a result of the changes in transportation and factory production?
   _____
   _____

2. **Look at the timeline on pages 256–257 in your text and answer the following questions:**

   a. In 1807 what happened that changed transportation in America?
   _____

   b. What happened in 1816 that showed that new inventions were becoming available to more people?
   _____

   c. What happened in 1825 that made transporting goods easier?
   _____

Name: Date:

CHAPTER 9
Lesson 1 Reading Strategy
The Industrial Revolution

(*A More Perfect Union* pp. 254–260)

Self-Question This reading strategy helps you stay focused on what you read. Ask yourself questions before you read a section. Then read to see if you can find the answers.

1. **Read the heading "Revolution in Industry" on page 255. Which question below do you expect to have answered in the section that follows? Circle the letter next to the best answer.**

   a. How did new farming methods help farmers grow more crops?

   b. What led to the revolution in industry in the United States?

   c. Who helped build the railroads?

2. **Look at the timeline on pages 256–257. Which question asks about the events and pictures shown there? Circle the letter next to the best answer.**

   a. How did people feel about all the changes in American industry from 1790 to 1860?

   b. What were some of the things that were invented during the Industrial Revolution?

   c. What was happening in Europe during the Industrial Revolution?

3. **Read the red heading "Building a Transportation Network" on page 256 and the blue headings that follow. Write a question that you think this section will answer.**

   _____

4. **Read the red heading on page 258 and the blue headings that follow. Fill out the left hand side of the chart with questions you expect will be answered in the section. Then read the section and fill out the right-hand side of the chart.**

My Questions	What I Learned by Reading

Reading Support Resources   Reading Strategy • Chapter 9, Lesson 1 **123**

CHAPTER 9
Lesson 1 Summary
The Industrial Revolution

(*A More Perfect Union* pp. 254–260)

 Summary also on Audiotape

Thinking Focus: How did inventions of the Industrial Revolution change the way people lived, worked, and traveled?

Revolution in Industry

In the mid-1800s, factories started to replace craftspeople. This change occurred because of some new inventions in England. Two of these inventions, the spinning jenny and the power loom, were used to make cloth. These machines were large and expensive. So cloth manufacturing moved from people's homes to factory buildings. This change is known as the **Industrial Revolution**. The United States copied British factories. New machines and factories helped U.S. businesses. Americans invented other helpful machines, such as the cotton gin. The United States became a leader of industry.

Industrial Revolution (ĭn-dŭs′trē-əl rĕv′ə-lōō′shən) social and economic change that happened when factories replaced skilled crafts workers

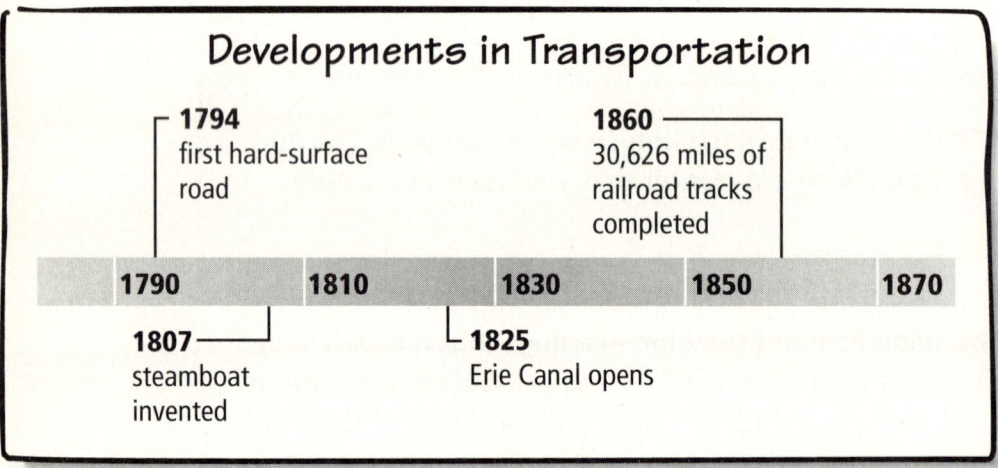

? How did British industry influence American industrialization?

Summary continues on next page

124 Chapter 9, Lesson 1 • Lesson Summary

The Industrial Revolution *(Lesson 1 Summary continued)*

Building a Transportation Network

The young United States needed easier, quicker, cheaper ways to transport people and goods. It solved the challenge in the following ways:

- By building more roads
- By building canals to ship **raw materials** like iron ore from place to place
- By Robert Fulton's invention of the steamboat
- By dramatically increasing railroad travel

raw materials
(rô mə-tĭr′ē-əls)
natural products used in manufacturing

[?] What changes occurred in transportation in the 1800s?

Production Revolutionized

Most factories were located in New England. There were several reasons for this:

- New England was a center of trade.
- New England had rivers and streams that could be used to power factories and mills.
- The land was not good for farming, so many people left farms to live in cities and work in factories.

Huge textile factories opened up in Massachusetts. Around 1820, these factories began hiring young women as well as men. Most of the women came from farm families. They worked an average of twelve hours a day, six days a week for low wages. In the mid-1800s, the factories began to hire more immigrant workers. These changes in American industry happened quickly. Old traditions ended as Americans faced the challenges of adjusting to a new way of life.

[?] What made New England the center of the textile industry?

Name: Date:

CHAPTER 9
Lesson 2 Preview
The Urban North

(*A More Perfect Union* pp. 261–266)

Factors Contributing to the Growth of Cities

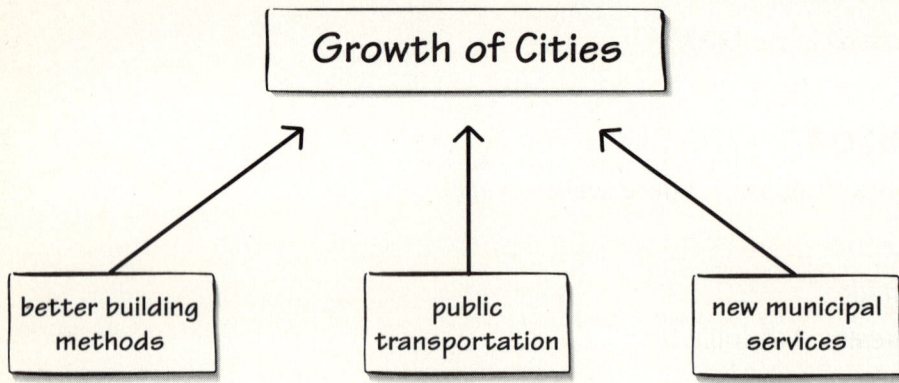

1. Look at the graphic organizer above. Then read the following sentences and fill in the blanks.

   a. Name one change that contributed to the growth of cities.

   _____

   b. Fill in the blanks in the short paragraph below.

   American cities grew quickly in the 1840s. Better _____ methods gave people better houses. And _____ services, such as garbage collection, kept the cities cleaner. People could take public _____ to move around the city.

2. Look at the maps on page 262 in your text. Which city had 30,000–125,000 people in 1800?

   _____

3. How many people did it have in 1860?

   _____

Name: _____ Date: _____

CHAPTER 9
Lesson 2 Reading Strategy
The Urban North

(*A More Perfect Union* pp. 261–266)

Cause and Effect This reading strategy helps you understand events and why they occur. As you read, think about the factors that caused an event. Then think about what the effects of that event may be.

1. Read the section "Urban Growth." What caused the shift from trade to industry in the U.S. economy? Circle the letter next to the best answer.

    a. major colonial cities in the North

    b. advances in technology and transportation

    c. trade with other countries

2. Study the two maps on page 262. What do these maps show was the effect of better transportation and new industry? Circle the letter next to the best answer.

    a. There was a huge increase in the populations of many cities.

    b. New York was no longer the biggest city.

    c. Most of the largest cities were near Lake Erie.

3. Read the section "Protecting People" on pages 263–264. What caused the need for a police force in New York City in 1845?

    _____

4. Read the section "People in the Cities" on pages 264 and 266. Then fill in the chart below.

Cause	Effect
Over four million immigrants enter the United States.	
	The gap between social classes increased.
	Reform movements developed.
Dorothea Dix visited a women's prison in 1841.	

Reading Support Resources

Reading Strategy • Chapter 9, Lesson 2

CHAPTER 9
Lesson 2 Summary
The Urban North

(*A More Perfect Union* pp. 261–266)

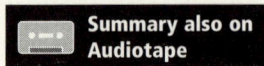
Summary also on Audiotape

Thinking Focus: How did the growth of cities affect American society?

Urban Growth

During the 1800s, the American economy changed from a trade economy to an industrial one. Many people moved to cities to work in the factories there. Cities grew. People needed a place to live, and so buildings became taller. Crowded streets, and the need for people to travel longer distances from home to work forced cities to create new transportation systems. In New York City, for example, a **municipal** or city-run horse-car system was developed. With more people came higher crime rates. In 1845, New York City set up the first police force. Many of the new city buildings were made of wood and heated with wood stoves or fireplaces. Fire was a danger and often spread quickly in the crowded neighborhoods. As a result, cities had to hire firemen. They also hired people to build sewer and garbage systems to protect citizens from disease.

municipal
(myoo-nĭs′ə-pəl)
of a city or urban political unit

[?] What types of services did the growing cities need?

People in the Cities

Wealthy factory owners and bankers, middle-class shopkeepers, and poor workers all lived in the city. For some, life in the city was good. The rich got richer. The middle class grew larger. But others stayed poor. Many of these people were unskilled workers. They came from the farms. Some were free blacks. Others were immigrants. They lived in crowded buildings near the factories where they worked.

Summary continues on next page

128 Chapter 9, Lesson 2 • Lesson Summary

Reading Support Resources

The Urban North *(Lesson 2 Summary continued)*

Working conditions could be harsh in cities. If people wanted to keep their jobs, they had to put in 10 to 12 hours a day plus six hours on Saturday. If they got sick, they could not work. And if they could not work, they lost their jobs. The factory owners did little to help protect their workers. Sometimes they might get help from a church or a charity. Many years later, the government and other groups would try to solve the problems of the poor.

? How did industrialization change the relationship between social classes?

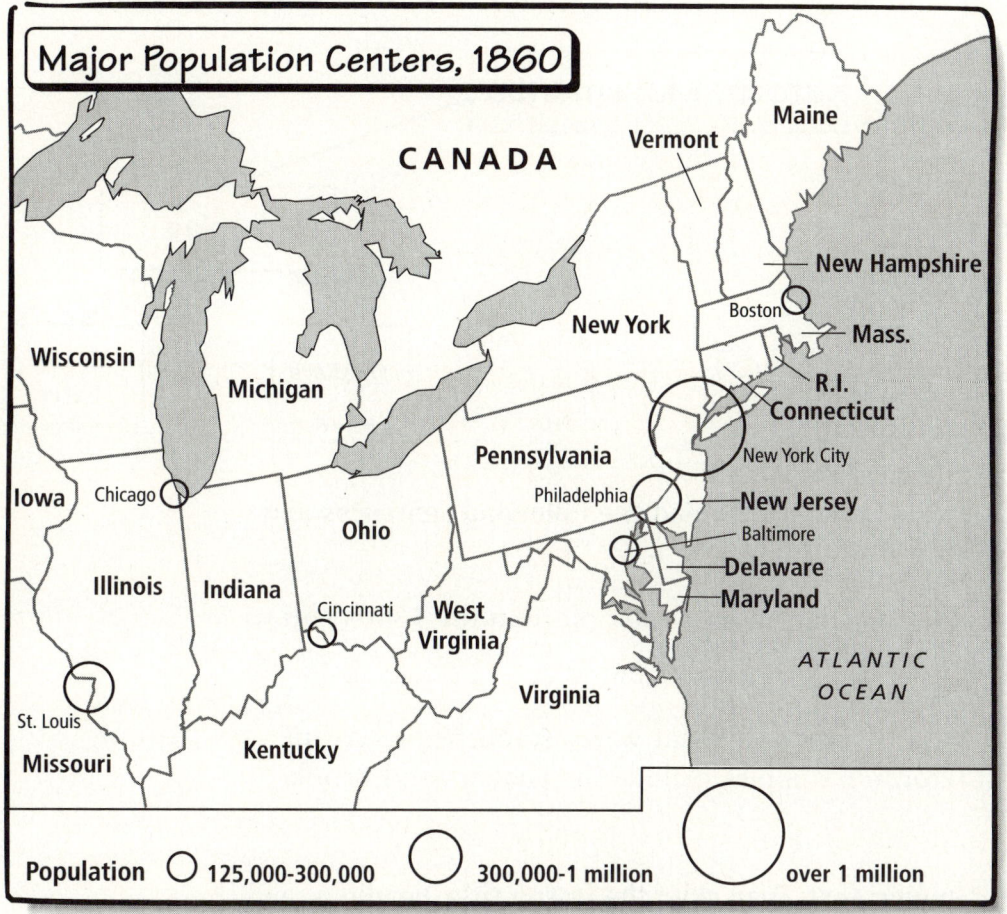

Lesson Summary • Chapter 9, Lesson 2 **129**

Name: _____ Date: _____

CHAPTER 9
Lesson 3 Preview
Seeking a Better Way

(*A More Perfect Union* pp. 267–273)

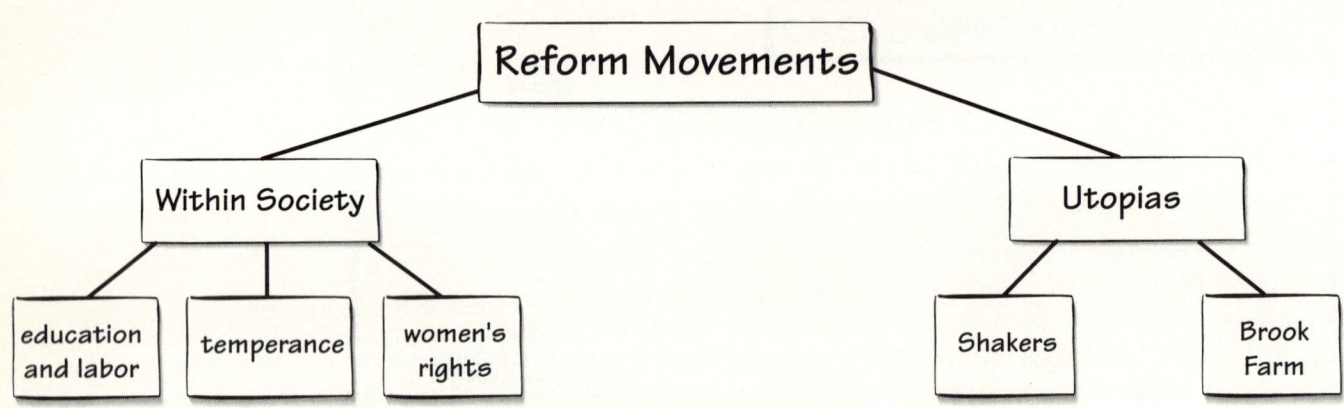

1. Look at the graphic organizer above. Then read the following sentences and fill in the blanks.

   a. Within society, some of the changes that took place in the 1800s had to do with education and labor, temperance, and _____.

   b. _____ were communities that were established to create social and political reform. Examples include the Shakers and Brook Farm.

2. Look at pages 267–273 in your text. Then skim the lesson title, headings, and subheadings. What do you think the term *reform movement* means?

   _____

   _____

   _____

Name: _____ Date: _____

CHAPTER 9
Lesson 3 Reading Strategy
Seeking a Better Way

(*A More Perfect Union* pp. 267–273)

Sequence This reading strategy helps you follow what is happening in your reading. As your read, pay attention to dates and times, as well as to words such as *before*, *finally*, *after*, and *then*.

1. **Read the section "The Temperance Movement." Place the following events in order by writing *1*, *2*, and *3* in the blanks.**

   ___ Alcoholism drops off sharply.

   ___ Reformers call for temperance.

   ___ There are 5,000 local temperance societies.

2. **Read the first two paragraphs in the section "Establishing Public Education" on page 269. What words help you understand the sequence of events?**

   _____

3. **Read the sections "Men Protest Working Conditions" and "Woman Workers Organize." Place the following events in order by writing *1*, *2*, and *3* in the blanks.**

   ___ New York seamstresses form a union.

   ___ Philadelphia trade workers strike.

   ___ Women workers strike in Dover, New Hampshire.

4. **Read the section "Utopian Societies." Then complete the timeline below.**

   1774 _____   _____

   _____   Brook Farm is established.   The number of Shakers reaches 6,000.

CHAPTER 9

Lesson 3 Summary
Seeking a Better Way

(*A More Perfect Union* pp. 267–273)

Thinking Focus: What types of social reform movements developed in the 1800s?

Reform Takes Many Shapes

The Industrial Revolution brought Americans many opportunities. But it also brought problems. People joined together in reform movements to help solve social problems. One such movement was the **temperance** movement. Its goal was to have everyone stop drinking alcohol. Many of the women interested in this movement understood the problems that alcohol caused in families and in the work place. Other women worked for changes in education. They wanted women to have the same education as men had. People like Horace Mann worked for free public education for all children. He set up the first school to train teachers. Other men led a movement to make working conditions better. They wanted to be paid more and to have a shorter workday. They went on strike—that is, they stopped work until their demands were met. Women workers wanted the same things. They organized, too, and went on strike. These groups wanted change. They worked to make the lives of all Americans better.

temperance
(tĕm´pər-əns)
giving up the drinking of alcohol

? What part did women play in the reform movements of the 19th century?

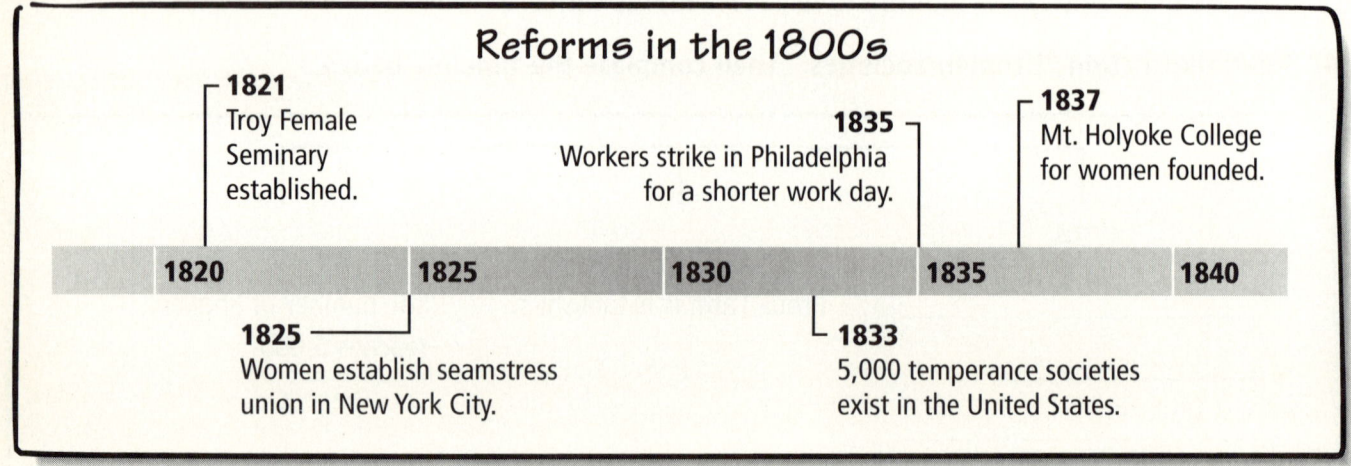

Seeking a Better Way (Lesson 3 Summary continued)

Utopian Societies

Some people felt America's problems were too big and too many to fix. They thought that a whole new society needed to be set up. These people formed communities called **utopias**. They hoped to create a perfect society. They believed it was not good to work only for one's self-interest. They thought everyone should work for the common good. The Shakers were one utopian society. They first settled in New York State. They did not believe in marriage or having children. Everything they had was owned by the community. The Shakers had many followers.

Another utopian society was Brook Farm in West Roxbury, Massachusetts. The community started in 1841. Like the Shakers, the people of Brook Farm owned the land as a group. They believed in hard work and study. One of their goals was to learn as much as they could. They had a very good school. But after six years, Brook Farm closed. Some members said that a utopian community had as many problems as the city.

? What were the goals of utopian societies?

---

utopia
(yōō-tō′pē-ə)
a community that is set up to be better than the rest of society

Use with *A More Perfect Union* Pages 282–309

Chapter Overview
The South

Fill in the blank spaces below with information from the chapter.

When: 1790–1860

Where: Southern United States

People of the South

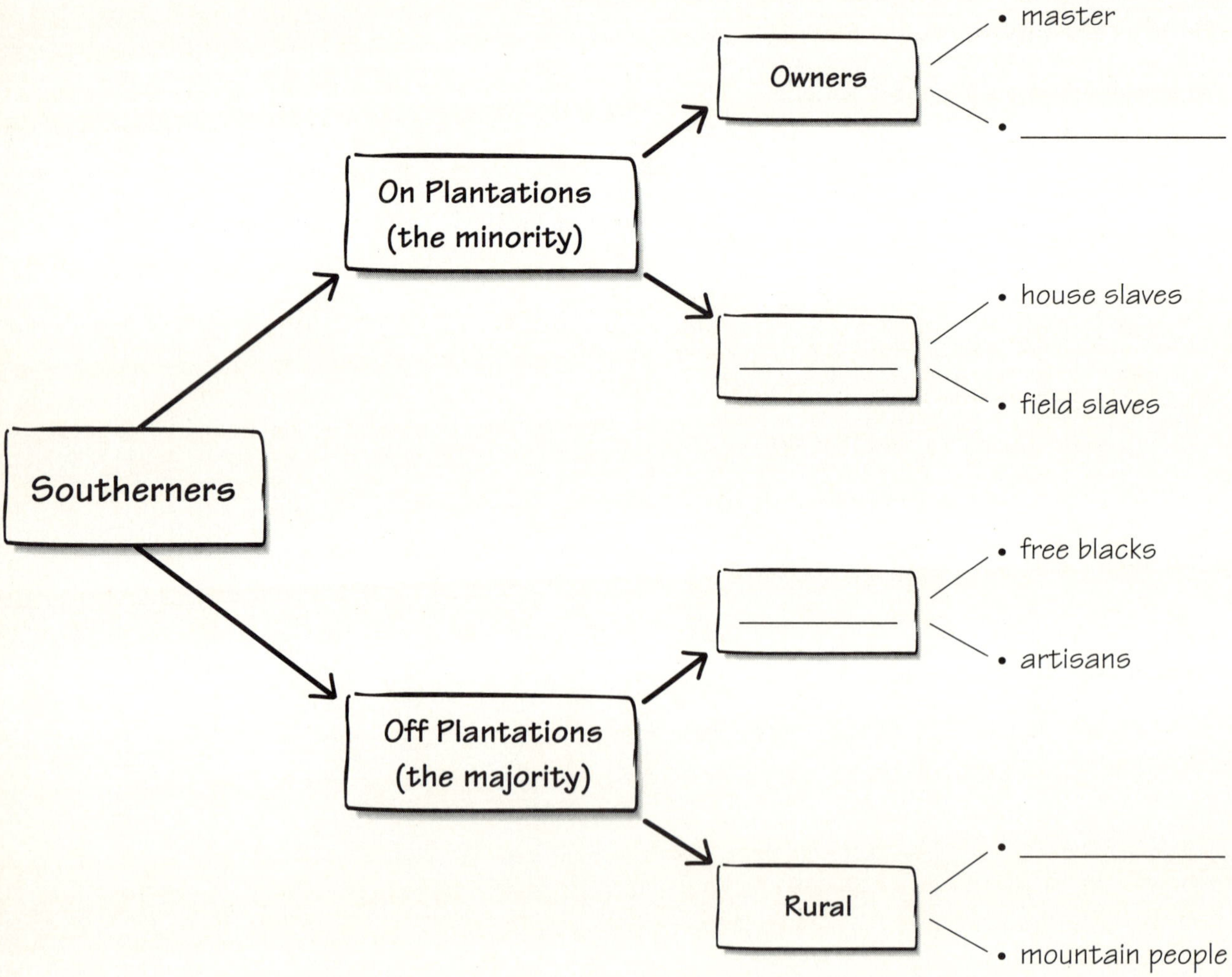

Southerners
- On Plantations (the minority)
  - Owners
    - master
    - _____
  - _____
    - house slaves
    - field slaves
- Off Plantations (the majority)
  - _____
    - free blacks
    - artisans
  - Rural
    - _____
    - mountain people

134 Chapter 10 • Chapter Overview

Reading Support Resources

Name: _____ Date: _____

CHAPTER 10
Lesson 1 Preview
The Cotton Kingdom

(*A More Perfect Union* pp. 284–289)

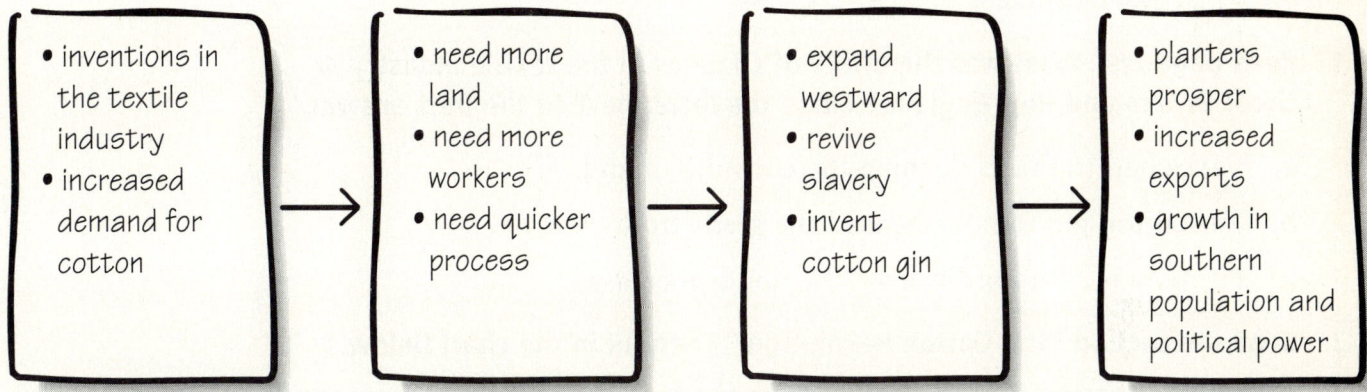

Steps in the Growth of the Cotton Industry

- inventions in the textile industry
- increased demand for cotton

→

- need more land
- need more workers
- need quicker process

→

- expand westward
- revive slavery
- invent cotton gin

→

- planters prosper
- increased exports
- growth in southern population and political power

1. **Look at the graphic organizer above. Then read the following sentences and fill in the blanks.**

   a. Inventions in the textile industry and increased demand for cotton led to the need for more _____, more _____, and a _____ process.

   b. Name one effect of the growth of the cotton industry on the South.
   _____

2. **Study the map on page 288 of your text. Then answer the following questions:**

   a. What crop covered the most land?
   _____

   b. What crops were grown in Tennessee?
   _____

Reading Support Resources   Lesson Preview • Chapter 10, Lesson 1   **135**

Name: _____   Date: _____

CHAPTER 10
Lesson 1 Reading Strategy
The Cotton Kingdom

(*A More Perfect Union* pp. 284–289)

Cause and Effect This reading strategy helps you understand events and why they occur. As you read, think about the factors that caused an event. Then think about what the effects of that event may be.

1. Read page 284. What was the effect of changes in the textile industry in Great Britain and New England? Circle the letter next to the best answer.

    a. Slaves had to finish cleaning the cotton by hand.

    b. The cotton gin rapidly cleaned the seeds from cotton.

    c. The demand for cotton from the South increased.

2. Read the section "The Cotton Revolution." Then fill in the chart below.

Cause	Effect
Cotton growers use the cotton gin.	
	Slavery is revived.
Plantations produce increasing amounts of cotton.	
	Few cities develop in the South.

3. Read the section "Proslavery Movement." What caused an increase in the antislavery feeling in the North?

   _____
   _____
   _____
   _____

CHAPTER 10

Lesson 1 Summary
The Cotton Kingdom

(*A More Perfect Union* pp. 284–289)

Thinking Focus: How did the cotton gin change the economy and the landscape of the South between 1790 and 1860?

The Cotton Revolution

In 1792, Eli Whitney invented the cotton gin. This machine took the seeds out of the cotton and sped up cotton production. One person using a cotton gin could do the work of 50 workers. With the cotton gin, cotton production in the South soared.

Southern farmers grew cotton on large farms called **plantations**. They used slaves to do the hard work of growing, picking, and processing the cotton.

- Slaves planted the cotton in April and watched over the fields.
- When the cotton was ready to pick, the slaves picked it all day in the hot summer sun.
- After they picked the cotton, they loaded it onto wagons and took it to the cotton gin.
- Once the cotton was ginned, the slaves pressed it into bales.

Cotton was a **cash crop** for farmers in the **antebellum**, or pre–Civil War, South.

While Southerners were farming and growing cotton, Northerners were building factories and railroads. The Southern economy remained agricultural. The North built an industrial economy based on a variety of manufactured products and goods.

? Why did cotton cultivation require back-breaking field work during most of the year?

plantation
(plăn-tā′shən)
a large farm that uses slaves as workers

cash crop
(kăsh krŏp)
a crop grown in large amounts for sale

antebellum
(ăn′tē-bĕl′əm)
referring to the time period before the Civil War

Summary continues on next page

The Cotton Kingdom (Lesson 1 Summary continued)

Comparing the North and South, around 1850

The North	The South
• Transportation by railroads and canals	• Transportation by steamboats on natural inland rivers
• Industrial economy	• Agricultural economy, centered on plantations
• Variety of manufactured products, textiles, and steel goods	• Major crop concetration on cotton
• Voluntary labor force, many immigrants	• Slave labor force
• Few large cities; many mill towns	• Few cities; river towns busy during harvest

Proslavery Movement

Even people in the South who did not own slaves supported slavery. Cotton had made the South rich. Almost no one wanted to change that. And cotton plantations depended on slaves. Southerners used many arguments to defend slavery. They argued that slavery was mentioned in the Bible and had existed for thousands of years. Some Southerners said that slaves were lucky because they had learned from their owners how to be Christians. Other Southerners said that some white workers in the North were treated just as badly as slaves.

But people who opposed slavery questioned these arguments. Quakers and others said slavery was a sin. They also said that slavery shouldn't exist in a democratic country that was founded on the Declaration of Independence. A few Southerners were against slavery. But the antislavery movement was strongest in the North.

[?] List two arguments people gave opposing slavery.

Name: _____ Date: _____

CHAPTER 10
Lesson 2 Preview
Life on the Plantation

(*A More Perfect Union* pp. 290–295)

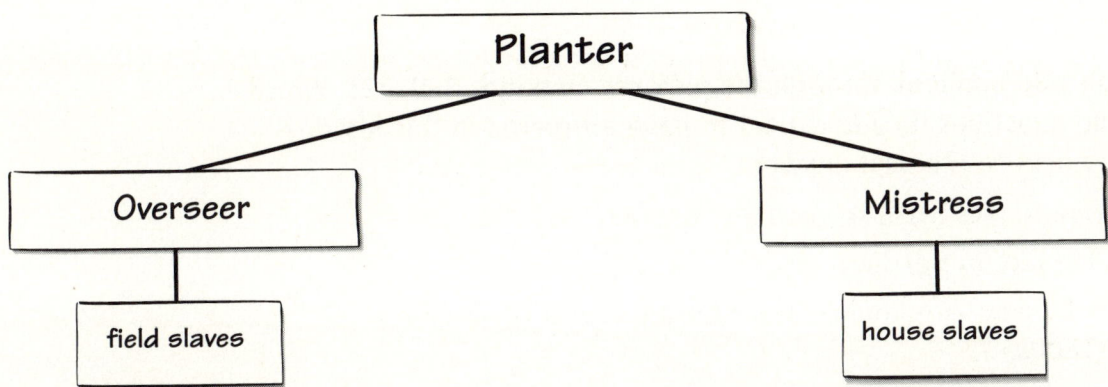

Plantation Responsibilities

1. **Look at the graphic organizer above. Then read the following sentences and fill in the blanks.**

   a. On Southern plantations the plantation mistress was in charge of the _____.

   b. The person in charge of the whole plantation, including the mistress, overseer, house slaves, and field slaves was the _____.

2. **Look at the diagram on page 291 in your text. What can you tell about the people who lived on this plantation?**

   _____
   _____
   _____
   _____

Reading Support Resources   Lesson Preview • **Chapter 10, Lesson 2** **139**

Name: _____ Date: _____

CHAPTER 10
Lesson 2 Reading Strategy
Life on the Plantation

(*A More Perfect Union* pp. 290–295)

Self-Question This reading strategy helps you stay focused on what you read. Ask yourself questions before you read a section. Then read to see if you can find the answer to your questions.

1. Read the lesson title and look through the pictures on pages 290–295. Which of the following questions do you expect to have answered in this lesson? Circle the letter next to the best answer.

    a. Why did some slaves learn to read and write?

    b. What was life like in northern cities?

    c. What were the lives of planters, their families, and their slaves like in the 1800s?

2. Read the red heading on page 290 and the two blue headings that follow. Write a question that you think the section will answer.

    _____

3. Read the section title "The Slave Community" on page 293 and the first paragraph under the heading. What question do you expect the rest of the section will answer? Circle the letter next to the best answer.

    a. What were some of the things white plantation owners enjoyed doing?

    b. How did the South differ from the North on the issue of slavery?

    c. What was life like in the slave community?

4. Look at the headings and the pictures in the section "Resistance to Slavery." Then write two questions in the chart below. After you read the section, fill in the chart with the answers to your questions.

My Questions	What I Learned by Reading

CHAPTER 10

Lesson 2 Summary
Life on the Plantation

(*A More Perfect Union* pp. 290–295)

Thinking Focus: Describe the responsibilities of the plantation owner, his wife, and the slaves they controlled.

The Slave South

Each person who lived on the plantation had a carefully assigned role. The master of the plantation had final say in all matters of plantation life and business. Most plantation owners thought of their slaves as possessions, not people. They sometimes treated the slaves just well enough so that they could work hard. Sometimes the plantation owner hired a white overseer. His job was to be sure the slaves did their work. The plantation mistress ran the "Big House" and took charge of the plantation when her husband was away. She was also responsible for all food preparation. The mistress had to be sure that the slaves had food, clothing, housing, and medical care. She might also offer advice and teach them religion. Slave women, however, had even more work to do. They had to take care of their own families' needs. As a result, they had little time for themselves.

❓ What were some of the skills a woman needed to learn when she became mistress of the plantation?

The Slave Community

There were different groups within the slave community. Some slaves were the house slaves. Most of the year they waited on the whites in the "Big House." Some house slaves got better food and clothing than the other slaves. Often, however, they were separated from their families. Other slaves were field hands. They worked taking care of the crops.

Summary continues on next page

Life on the Plantation *(Lesson 2 Summary continued)*

When slaves were captured in Africa, they were often separated from their families. The slaves found ways to hold onto their **cultural heritage**. For example, they adapted the African custom of "jumping the broom" to unite a couple in marriage. Many slaves had two names: one that their white owners gave them, and African names that they called each other. The slaves used natural plant medicines when they were sick rather than the white owner's treatments. They mixed African rhythms and music with American religious songs to create new musical forms.

cultural heritage
(kŭl´chər-əl hĕr´ĭ-tĭj)
the customs, language, and beliefs of one's culture

[?] Give three examples of cultural activities, separate from the white culture, in which plantation slaves participated.

Resistance to Slavery

Many slaves worked against slavery in ways that were not violent and that the whites did not notice. They might use the words of a song to tell a secret message. Sometimes they pretended to be sick. Some broke tools on purpose. Others worked as slowly as they could. Some slaves ran away even though they knew they would be caught. Sometimes plantation owners were afraid of their slaves. They thought the slaves might poison their food or revolt. There were also a few slave rebellions over the years. The most terrifying revolt was led by Nat Turner in 1831. It lasted three days and 57 whites were killed.

[?] Describe nonviolent methods slaves used to resist the master's authority.

Name: _____ Date: _____

CHAPTER 10
Lesson 3 Preview
The Other Souths

(*A More Perfect Union* pp. 298–305)

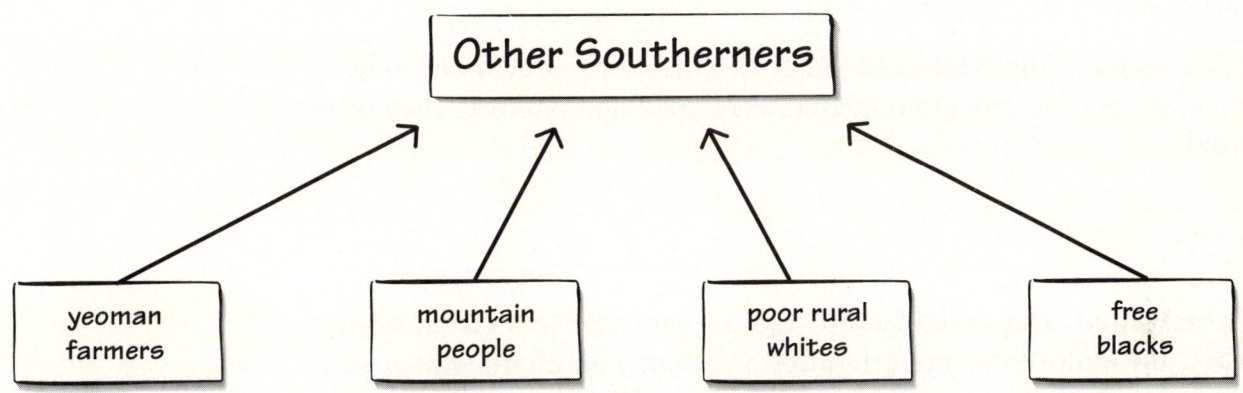

1. Look at the graphic organizer above. Then read the following sentences and fill in the blanks.

   a. Name two groups of Southerners who who did not live on plantations.
   _____
   _____

   b. In what ways do you think the people shown in the graphic organizer were different from the wealthy plantation owners?
   _____
   _____

2. Look at the headings, subheadings, and pictures on pages 298–305 in your text. What are some of the things you expect to learn about in this chapter?
   _____
   _____
   _____
   _____

Reading Support Resources   Lesson Preview • Chapter 10, Lesson 3   **143**

Name: _____ Date: _____

CHAPTER 10
Lesson 3 Reading Strategy
The Other Souths

(*A More Perfect Union* pp. 298–305)

Compare and Contrast This reading strategy helps you understand how events are similar and different. As you read about historical events, think about how they compare with events you already know.

1. Read the section "The Neglected Majority." Then write down one way yeoman farmers and mountain people were alike and one way they were different.

   Alike: _____

   Different: _____

2. Read the section "The Urban South." Write a sentence that compares and contrasts the educational opportunities of wealthy Southern whites with those of slaves.

   _____
   _____

3. Read the section "Free Blacks." Then choose one of the other groups you read about in the lesson. Write a short paragraph comparing and contrasting free blacks with the group you chose.

   _____
   _____
   _____
   _____
   _____

CHAPTER 10
Lesson 3 Summary
The Other Souths

(*A More Perfect Union* pp. 298–305)

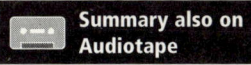

Thinking Focus: What groups made up the majority of Southerners who lived outside the plantation system?

The Neglected Majority

Most people in the South did not own slaves. Some were **yeoman farmers**. Others were mountain people who lived in and around the Appalachian Mountains. The yeoman farmers grew crops for their families. Some also raised a few cash crops. During planting and harvesting, the farmers sometimes borrowed slaves from plantations near them. Although they did not own slaves, these farmers supported slavery. The mountain people were mostly hunters and grew just enough crops to feed their families. Cut off from the rest of society, they had a rich culture and a strong sense of community.

yeoman farmer
(yō′mən fär′mər)
the owner of a small farm

artisan
(är′tĭ-zən)
people in skilled trades

[?] How did the lives of yeoman farmers and mountain settlers differ from life on the plantations?

The Urban South

The cities of the South were small and grew slowly. Only the larger cities had theaters and hotels. **Artisans** in the cities were skilled in trades like printing and woodworking. Most plantation families spent part of the year in the city.

Much of the early South had been settled by the French and the Spanish. In cities like New Orleans, these cultures blended with those of black Americans, southern whites, and German and Irish

Summary continues on next page

immigrants. Many rich Southerners were well educated. But most Southerners could not read because of the poor public schools. Slaves were not allowed to learn to read or write. Some, like Frederick Douglass, were able to teach themselves. He escaped slavery and became one of the greatest African American leaders in the antislavery movement.

[?] What made most southern cities different from cities in the North during the antebellum period?

Where Southerners Lived	
In the Country	In the Cities
Yeoman farmers	Plantation owners (part of the year)
Plantation owners	Artisans
Slaves	Various immigrant groups
Mountain people	Free blacks

Free Blacks

Many free blacks—slaves who had been given or bought their freedom—lived in southern cities. They were able to earn a living in many different trades. Often, these were trades that they had learned on the plantation. Most free blacks in cities and towns were women. The freedom of both men and women, however, was limited by law. Free blacks could not vote. They had to sit in special blacks-only areas in public places. State laws limited their travel. The homes of free blacks could be searched for runaway slaves. These laws existed because white Southerners were afraid of free blacks. They didn't want free blacks to help slaves escape or threaten the slave system in any way. This made it dangerous for blacks to socialize with one another.

[?] In what ways were free blacks' rights limited?

Use with *A More Perfect Union* Pages 312–339

Chapter Overview
Causes of the Civil War

Fill in the blank spaces below with information from the chapter.

When: 1820–1861

Where: The North, the South, territories

Events Leading to the Civil War

- **Balancing North and South**
  - Missouri Compromise
  - _____

- **The Antislavery Movement**
  - _____
  - former slaves
  - _____
  - women

- **The Kansas-Nebraska Act**
  - Republican opposition
  - Popular sovereignty
  - illegal voting
  - _____

- **_____**
  - Dred Scott case
  - Underground Railroad
  - Harpers Ferry
  - election of Abraham Lincoln

Name: _____ Date: _____

CHAPTER 11
Lesson 1 Preview
The Sectional Conflict

(*A More Perfect Union* pp. 314–319)

Differences Between North and South

	South	North
Labor System	slave and free labor	free labor
Fugitive Slave Law	supported law	opposed law
Economic Direction	expanded farming/limited industry	expanded industry/ limited farming
Slavery in Territories	supported slavery	opposed slavery

1. Look at the graphic organizer above. Then decide whether each statement that follows is true or false. Write *T* or *F* on the line. If a statement is false, rewrite the statement to make it true.

   a. People in the North supported the Fugitive Slave Law but opposed slavery.

   _____

   b. The South used slave labor and supported the Fugitive Slave Law.

   _____

   c. The North had a free labor system and wanted to expand industry.

   _____

   d. The North wanted to expand farming by using slave labor.

   _____

2. Look at the chart on page 315 in your text. Then fill in the blanks in the following sentences.

   Before the Missouri Compromise, there were _____ states in the Union. _____ were free states. After the Missouri Compromise, _____ more states joined the Union.

Name: _____   Date: _____

CHAPTER 11
Lesson 1 Reading Strategy
The Sectional Conflict

(*A More Perfect Union* pp. 314–319)

Think About Words This reading strategy helps you figure out the meaning of new words. When you come to an unfamiliar word, look for word parts you already know and use clues such as context and pictures.

1. Read the section "A Delicate Balance." This section describes the Missouri Compromise. Write two clues from the section that help you understand the meaning of the word *compromise*.

   _____
   _____

2. Read the section "South Eyes Texas for Slavery." Then look at the word *annex*. Based on the context of the paragraph, what do you think *annex* means?

   _____
   _____

3. Read the first three paragraphs on page 318. Then look at the map and read the picture. Based on the context, what do you think *sectionalism* means?

   _____
   _____

4. Read the rest of the section. Choose a word from the section that is new to you. Then fill in as much of the chart below as you can to help you figure out what the word means.

   WORD: _____

   clues from the reading: _____

   clues from the pictures: _____

   similar words I already know: _____

   parts of words I already know: _____

   the word means _____

Reading Support Resources   Reading Strategy • Chapter 11, Lesson 1

CHAPTER 11
Lesson 1 Summary
The Sectional Conflict

(*A More Perfect Union* pp. 314–319)

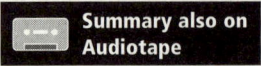

Thinking Focus: Why was the compromise necessary between the North and the South as the United States expanded into western territories?

Different Regions, Different Needs

In the early 1800s, the North and South were very different. In the North, most people worked in business and industry. Workers enjoyed a system of work called **free labor** in which they had the right to leave their jobs. In the South, the main occupation was farming. The cotton economy depended on slave labor, not free labor. Southerners made money from this system and did not want to change it. The South also wanted to get more new land to grow cotton and make their economy stronger. As the United States grew westward, the different interests of the two regions clashed.

free labor
(frē lā′ bər)
a system of work in which employees have the right to leave their employers and their jobs.

? Why did white Southerners resist the system of work called free labor?

A Delicate Balance

In 1819, the U.S. government tried to balance the interests of both the North and South in balance. But certain events caused disagreements. For example, admitting new states to the Union would change the number of free and slave states. The North wanted to let in free states to get control of Congress. The South wanted to let in slave states for the same reason. In 1819, Missouri wanted to join the Union as a slave state. Maine wanted to join the Union as a free state. If Missouri was admitted as a slave state, the South would gain control of the Senate.

The Missouri Compromise let Missouri enter the Union as a slave state. It let Maine enter as a free state. The Compromise also did not allow slavery in the region that was west of the Mississippi River and north of the Missouri River.

This Missouri Compromise seemed to keep the balance of power between the North and South. But the South was afraid that the North would gain control of the Senate if free states were added north and west of Missouri.

? The Missouri Compromise ensured a senatorial balance between North and South. Why then did the Compromise frustrate and anger Southerners?

Summary continues on next page

The Sectional Conflict (Lesson 1 Summary continued)

Missouri Compromise

Free States or Territories		Slave States or Territories	
Maine	New Jersey	Delaware	South Carolina
Vermont	Pennsylvania	Maryland	Georgia
New Hampshire	Ohio	Virginia	Alabama
Connecticut	Indiana	Kentucky	Mississippi
Rhode Island	Illinois	Missouri	Louisiana
New York	Michigan Territory	Tennessee	Arkansas Territory
Massachusetts		North Carolina	Florida Territory

Unorganized Territories closed to slavery

Sectionalism Deepens

Mexico and America went to war after the United States annexed Texas. As result of the war, the United States won a great deal of new land from Mexico. The North didn't want this new land open to slavery, but the South did.

The North and South also disagreed about runaway slaves. About 1,000 slaves escaped from their owners each year. Slave holders wanted a stronger federal law to get back their "property." Northerners did not want runaway slaves given back to their owners.

The Compromise of 1850 tried to solve the problem. Instead, it made things worse. The law said people in the North had to help capture runaway slaves. It also made Utah and New Mexico slave territories. California was offered as a free state. Now there were more free states than slave states.

[?] The Compromise of 1850 gave the South a tougher fugitive slave law and two new territories. The North gained a free state. Why did both sides feel the Compromise was unacceptable?

Name: _____ Date: _____

CHAPTER 11
Lesson 2 Preview
The Antislavery Movement

(*A More Perfect Union* pp. 320–324)

Who Took Part in the Antislavery Movement?

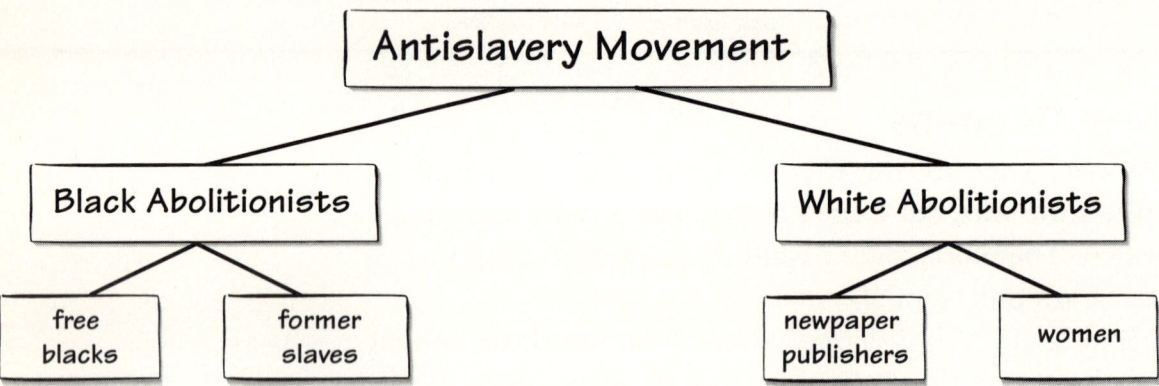

1. Look at the graphic organizer above. Then read the following sentences and fill in the blanks.

   Both white and black _____ took part in the antislavery movement. Many black abolitionists were free blacks and _____. Many white abolitionists were newspaper publishers and _____.

2. Look at the picture of the Quaker Abolitionist on page 323 in your text. What things does she carry to the meeting that will help her in the fight to end slavery?

   _____
   _____
   _____
   _____

Name: _____ Date: _____

CHAPTER 11
Lesson 2 Reading Strategy
The Antislavery Movement

(A *More Perfect Union* pp. 320–324)

Finding the Main Idea This reading strategy helps you organize and remember what you read. When you finish a selection, jot down the main idea and its supporting details.

1. Read the section "Antislavery Movement Speaks with Many Voices." Which sentence below best expresses the main idea of the section? Circle the letter next to your answer.

    a. Sojourner Truth helped hundreds of slaves escape.

    b. Slaves, free blacks, and white abolitionists fought against slavery.

    c. Frederick Douglass devoted his life to fighting slavery.

2. Now write three details from the section that support the main idea.

    _____
    _____
    _____

3. Read the section "Women Play a Crucial Role." Then fill in the chart below.

Main Idea	Supporting Details

Reading Support Resources   Reading Strategy • Chapter 11, Lesson 2   **153**

CHAPTER 11
Lesson 2 Summary
The Antislavery Movement

(*A More Perfect Union* pp. 320–324)

Thinking Focus: How did the abolitionist movement contribute to the ongoing conflict between the North and the South?

Antislavery Movement Speaks with Many Voices

Slaves tried to escape from their owners whenever they could. Free blacks in the North, such as Sojourner Truth, helped hundreds of slaves to escape. In 1831, William Lloyd Garrison started a newspaper called the *Liberator,* which supported **abolitionism**. In 1834, he helped found the American Antislavery Society, which supported the abolition movement. This group spread their ideas through the mail, lectures, and by asking Congress to support their ideas.

Fredrick Douglass also spoke against slavery. In 1845, he started giving speeches describing his experiences as a slave. He spoke against the segregation, or separation, of blacks and whites in public places. He also went to England and spoke against slavery in the United States. In 1845, he published a book about his experiences. He started a newspaper, the *North Star,* to also help him spread his antislavery views.

[?] What techniques did abolitionists Sojourner Truth, William Lloyd Garrison, and Frederick Douglass use to gain support for the antislavery movement?

abolitionism
(ăb´-ə-lĭsh´ə-nĭz´əm)
the support of the end of slavery in the United States

Summary continues on next page

The Antislavery Movement *(Lesson 2 Summary continued)*

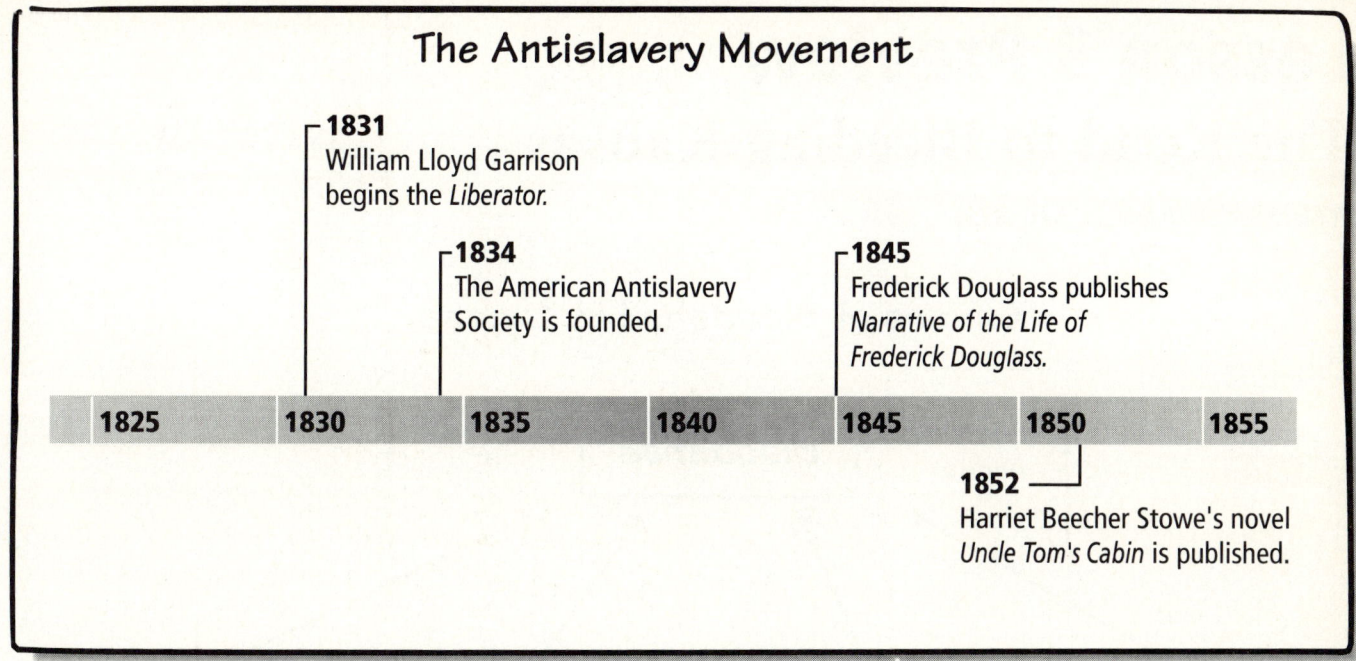

Women Play a Crucial Role

Women were very active in the abolition movement. They saw slavery as sinful and unChristian. At first, they worked separately from men. Over time, women came to believe that the abolition movement could lead to equal rights for them too. Angelina and Sarah Grimké spoke against slavery to groups of men and women. They believed that what was right for men was also right for women.

In 1852, Harriet Beecher Stowe published the classic book *Uncle Tom's Cabin*. Stowe wrote this book because she was very much against slavery. She wanted to show the horrible suffering of the slaves. Through her book, millions of people learned about what it was like to be a slave.

? Why did women join the abolitionist movement? How did their reasons change in time?

Name: Date:

CHAPTER 11
Lesson 3 Preview
The Road to Bleeding Kansas

(*A More Perfect Union* pp. 325–329)

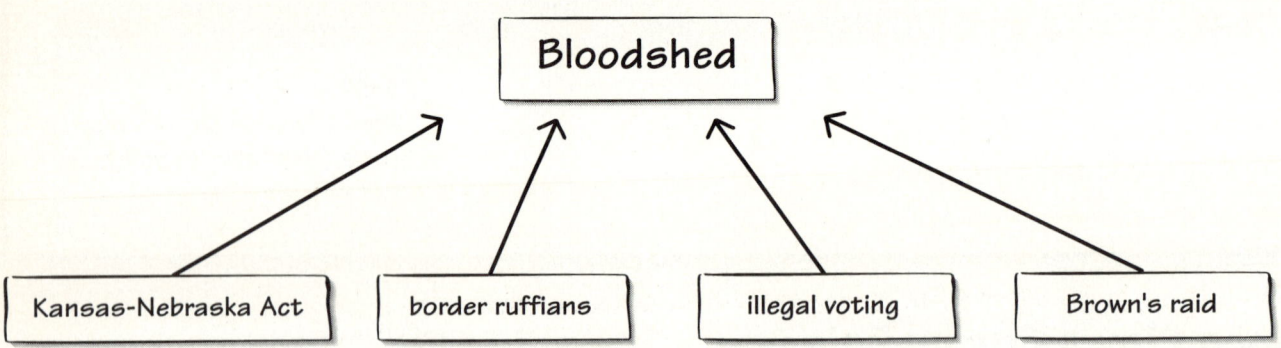

1. Look at the graphic organizer above. From the information in the organizer, decide whether each statement that follows is true or false. Write *T* or *F* on the line.

   a. Brown's raid helped ease tensions about slavery. ___

   b. Illegal voting was one of causes of bloodshed. ___

   c. Bloodshed was the cause of illegal voting. ___

   d. Brown's raid and the Kansas-Nebraska Act led to bloodshed. ___

2. Look at the chart of political parties on page 326 in your text. Read the following sentences and fill in the blanks.

   During the mid-1800s, there were _____ political parties. The _____ Party was popular in the North and was against slavery. The Whigs were popular in the _____ and were opposed to the _____ and _____.

156 Chapter 11, Lesson 3 • Lesson Preview Reading Support Resources

Name: _____ Date: _____

CHAPTER 11
Lesson 3 Reading Strategy
The Road to Bleeding Kansas

(*A More Perfect Union* pp. 325–329)

Sequence This reading strategy helps you follow what is happening in your reading. As you read, pay attention to dates and time, as well as to words such as *before, finally, after,* and *then.*

1. Read the section "The Kansas-Nebraska Act Paves the Way." Place the following events in order by writing *1, 2,* and *3* in the blanks.

    ___ The Missouri Compromise closes Kansas and Nebraska to slavery.

    ___ The Kansas-Nebraska Act is passed.

    ___ Republicans meet in Ripon, Wisconsin.

2. Read the sections "Kansas Bleeds Under Western Expansion" and "Buchanan Gains a Narrow Victory." Then fill in the timeline below.

    _____   _____   May, 1856

    Kansas holds its first   The majority of settlers in   _____
    territorial election.   Kansas are from the North.   _____

3. Write three words or phrases on the lines below that helped you understand the sequence of events in the lesson. Include the page numbers where you found these words or phrases.

    _____
    _____
    _____

Reading Support Resources   Reading Strategy • **Chapter 11, Lesson 2** **157**

CHAPTER 11
Lesson 3 Summary
The Road to Bleeding Kansas

(*A More Perfect Union* pp. 325–329)

Thinking Focus: In what ways did the slavery issue continue to affect the American political process?

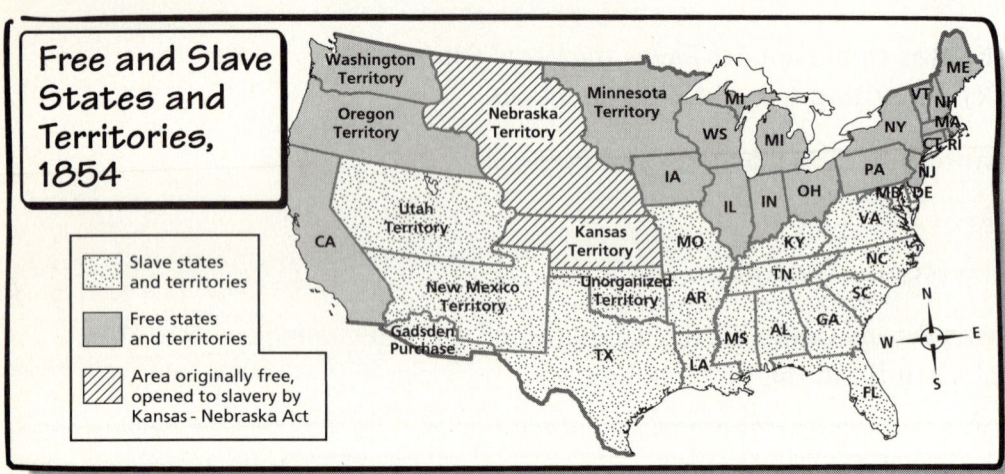

Free and Slave States and Territories, 1854

- Slave states and territories
- Free states and territories
- Area originally free, opened to slavery by Kansas - Nebraska Act

The Kansas-Nebraska Act Paves the Way

Thousands of Americans raced to settle the area west of the Mississippi. Farmers settled in Kansas and Nebraska where the rich prairie land was good for farming. Others moved to California to mine gold. The government wanted to build a railroad to connect the country from Chicago to California. Land in the territories had to be set aside for the railroad.

The Missouri Compromise had said that Kansas and Nebraska would become free states. The Compromise did not allow slavery in the western territories, which the Southern states wanted. They would not support the railroad unless the Missouri Compromise was undone. So a new compromise was reached. This was the Kansas-Nebraska Act, which was based on the idea of **popular sovereignty**, or letting voters decide.

? The Kansas-Nebraska Act implied that Congress could no longer decide whether or not a state or territory would allow slavery. How did this Act conflict with the earlier Missouri Compromise?

popular sovereignty
(pŏp′yə-lər sŏv′-ər-ĭn-tē)
voters in each territory choose whether to be a free or a slave state

Summary continues on next page

Kansas Bleeds Under Western Expansion

Both slaveowners and antislavery groups settled in Kansas. Most settlers were Northerners. Kansas had its first territorial election in 1854. But before the elections, 1,700 proslavery men came to Kansas. They were not citizens, and they voted illegally in the election. As a result, proslavery forces took over and wrote slavery into the constitution.

The antislavery people would not accept the results of the election and set up their own government. The situation became violent. In 1856, proslavery men attacked Lawrence, Kansas, and burned a hotel and looted stores. Then abolitionist John Brown attacked proslavery settlers. This began four months of **guerrilla** warfare. "Bleeding Kansas" became a slogan for antislavery fighters across the country.

guerrilla
(gə-rĭl′ə)
irregular warfare by independent forces

[?] More than two hundred fighters died during the skirmishes in "Bleeding Kansas." Why was this territory fought over so violently?

Buchanan Gains a Narrow Victory

In 1856, the presidential election became a three-way contest over slavery. The Republicans were against slavery in the West. The Democrats hoped to win votes from both the North and the South by pushing popular sovereignty. A third party, the Know-Nothing Party, was against slavery and immigration. The Democrats won the election. The Republicans received many votes, however. Antislavery forces took this as a sign to fight even harder.

[?] The Republicans lost the presidential election of 1856. Yet in many ways the campaign was a success for them. How can a losing election campaign still benefit a candidate or party?

Name: _____   Date: _____

CHAPTER 11
Lesson 4 Preview
The House Divided

(*A More Perfect Union* pp. 330–335)

Causes and Effects of the Election of 1860

Cause
- Harpers Ferry
- Dred Scott decision
- Lecompton Constitution
- Underground Railroad

→ **Election of 1860** →

Effects
- secession by Southern states
- rebels fire on Fort Sumter

1. **Look at the graphic organizer above. Then read the following sentences and fill in the blanks.**

   The election of _____ had many causes, including the _____ decision and the _____ Railroad. One of the effects of the election was the _____ of the Southern states.

2. **Look at the map on page 332 in your text. Then answer the following questions:**

   a. Which two states seem to have the highest percent of slaves in their population?
   _____
   _____

   b. Which state had a higher percent of slaves in its population, Virginia or Tennessee?
   _____
   _____

160 Chapter 11, Lesson 4 • Lesson Preview   Reading Support Resources

Name: _____ Date: _____

CHAPTER 11
Lesson 4 Reading Strategy
The House Divided

(*A More Perfect Union* pp. 330–335)

Predict/Infer This reading strategy helps you understand what you have read and what you will read next. Before you read a section, think about the titles, pictures, and captions. Then think about what will happen in the selection.

1. Read the section "Slavery Battled on All Fronts" on page 331 up to the heading "The Supreme Court Decision". What do you predict will happen next? Circle the letter next to the best answer.
   a. The Supreme Court will grant Scott his freedom.
   b. The Supreme Court will say that Scott must remain a slave.
   c. Scott will lead an uprising, just as John Brown did.

2. Name one clue from your reading that helped you make your prediction.
   _____
   _____

3. Read the headings "Antislavery Movement Forges Ahead" and "Slaves Ride the Underground Railroad" and look at the images on pages 332–334. What do you think these sections will be about?
   _____
   _____
   _____

4. Read the red and blue headings on pages 334 and 335. What can you infer about Southerners' reactions to Lincoln's election as President?
   _____
   _____
   _____
   _____

CHAPTER 11

Lesson 4 Summary
The House Divided

(*A More Perfect Union* pp. 330–335)

Thinking Focus: What events during the 1850s revealed that the conflict between the North and the South would never be resolved peacefully?

Slavery Battled on All Fronts

In 1857, the Supreme Court made an important decision in the *Dred Scott* v. *Sandford* case. Dred Scott was a slave who was owned by John Emerson in Missouri. For a short time, they lived in an area that had been a free state under the Missouri Compromise. Later, they returned to Missouri. After Emerson died, Scott sued for his freedom.

A Missouri court agreed with Scott, but the state Supreme Court did not. The Dred Scott case eventually reached the United States Supreme Court. Chief Justice Roger B. Taney said that African Americans were not citizens and as such, they had no right to sue in federal courts. Taney also said that the Missouri Compromise was unconstitutional, and that all territories should be open to slavery. Northern Republicans thought the decision was wrong. Antislavery settlers in Kansas would not vote for the new proslavery state constitution.

? Why didn't Chief Justice Taney's rulings dissolve the antislavery movement?

Antislavery Movement Forges Ahead

Northerners and other antislavery forces thought that the Fugitive Slave Act was very unfair. A person who was captured and charged with being an escaped slave was not even allowed to speak for himself or herself. Escaped slaves who were caught were not allowed to have lawyers. Often the word of the slaveholder alone decided the case.

? Why did Northerners think the Fugitive Slave Act was unfair?

Summary continues on next page

The House Divided (Lesson 4 Summary continued)

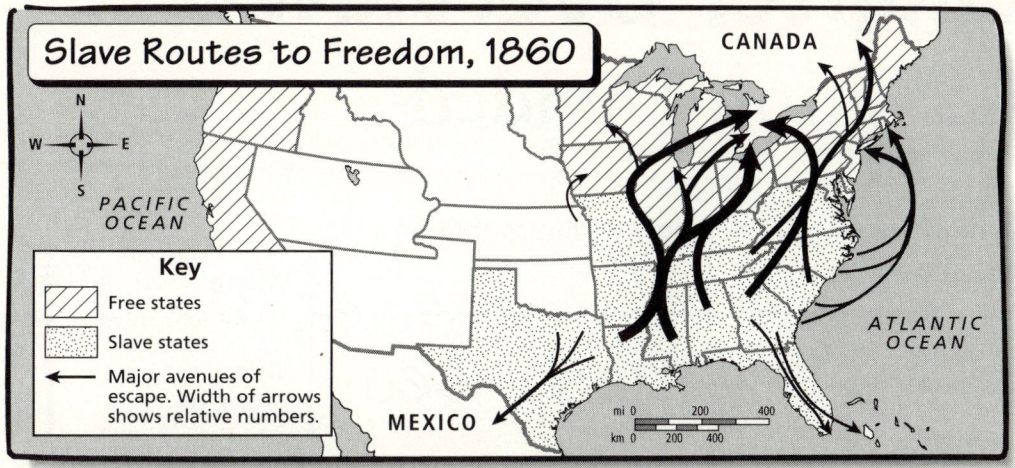

Slaves Ride the Underground Railroad

The antislavery forces set up a network of people known as the **Underground Railroad**. They moved slaves secretly from one safe hiding place to another until they reached a free state. It was very dangerous for both the slaves and the people helping them. People in the South knew about the Underground Railroad. It only made them angrier with the North.

[?] How did some abolitionists break the law to help the slaves?

Lincoln Inspires the Republicans

In 1858, Abraham Lincoln ran for the U.S. Senate in Illinois. He demanded that Stephen Douglas, the person running against him, take part in public debates on slavery. This was a new idea. Lincoln lost the election. But he was a winner in other ways. The public liked his ability to speak well, and Lincoln became the leader of the Republican Party. Two years later, the Republicans nominated him for President. Lincoln won. Now a man who was against slavery had been elected President.

Proslavery Southerners did not want to be part of a country that would elect an enemy of slavery. The Southern states decided to **secede** and set up the Confederate government. The North and South were ready to fight for their beliefs. The Civil War had begun.

[?] Abraham Lincoln lost the senatorial race of 1858 in Illinois but won the presidential election in 1860. Who elected him president?

Underground Railroad
(ŭn′dər-ground′ rāl′rōd′)
a network of people who helped escaped slaves travel north

secede
(sĭ-sēd′)
to leave or separate from a group or organization

Use with *A More Perfect Union* Pages 340–373

Chapter Overview
A Nation Divided

Fill in the blank spaces below with information from the chapter.

Where: The United States
Who: Americans

The Timeline of War, 1860–1865

1860

November 1860 Abraham Lincoln elected President

1861

April 12, 1861 _____

July 21, 1861 First battle of Bull Run

1862

September 17, 1862 Battle of Antietam

September 22, 1862 First Emancipation Proclamation

1863

January 1, 1863 Second Emancipation Proclamation

July 1-4, 1863 _____

May 22-July 4, 1863 Battle of Vicksburg

November 19, 1863 Gettysburg Address

1864

March 1864 General Grant appointed head of Union troops

Summer 1864 _____

1865

April 1865 _____

1866

Name: Date:

CHAPTER 12
Lesson 1 Preview
North Versus South

(*A More Perfect Union* pp. 342–346)

Strengths and Weaknesses of the North and South

	North	South
Soldiers	trained army	inexperienced recruits
Officers		highly trained and skilled
Supplies	well-supplied	lack of supplies
Motivation	fighting away from home	defending home, family

1. Look at the graphic organizer above. Then decide whether each statement that follows is true or false. Write *T* or *F* on the line. If a statement is false, rewrite the statement to make it true.

   a. The South had a trained army while the North had only inexperienced recruits.

   _____

   b. Both the North and South were well-supplied.

   _____

   c. Northern soldiers were probably very motivated to fight because they were defending their homes.

   _____

2. Look at the map on page 343 of your text. It shows which Confederate states seceded, or withdrew, from the Union. Then answer the following questions:

   a. Which six states were the first to secede?

   _____

   b. Which Union state was the farthest west?

   _____

   c. Which states seceded in May 1861?

   _____

Reading Support Resources · Lesson Preview · Chapter 12, Lesson 1

Name: _____ Date: _____

CHAPTER 12
Lesson 1 Reading Strategy
North Versus South

(*A More Perfect Union* pp. 342–346)

Cause and Effect This reading strategy helps you understand events and why they occur. As you read, think about the factors that caused an event. Then think about what the effects of that event may be.

1. Read the lesson introduction on page 342. What event caused Col. Robert E. Lee to make a painful decision? Circle the letter next to the best answer.

    a. his participation in the Mexican-American War

    b. the Confederate attack on Fort Sumter

    c. his taking command of southern military forces

2. Read the section "Build-Up of Southern Forces." What was the effect of President Lincoln's election?

    _____

    _____

3. Read the section "The Powerful North." Then fill in the chart below.

Cause	Effect
The North's navy blocked Southern ports.	
	Shortages of goods occurred in the South.
	It took five Confederate dollars to buy a cup of coffee.
Great Britain did not want to become involved in the war.	

CHAPTER 12
Lesson 1 Summary
North Versus South

(*A More Perfect Union* pp. 342–346)

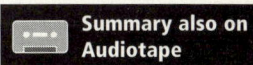

Thinking Focus: What advantages and disadvantages did each side have as it prepared to fight the Civil War?

Build-Up of Southern Forces

When the Civil War began, Colonel Robert E. Lee became the military leader of the **Confederacy**. His job was hard because the South did not have an organized army. Lee had to find and train men to fight. The Confederacy did not have much money to buy weapons. Many men had to bring their own guns, horses, and uniforms to battle.

The seven cotton-growing states in the South **seceded** from the United States right after Abraham Lincoln was elected President. They formed the Confederacy. Jefferson Davis became its president. One by one, four other states joined the Confederacy. Davis had to find a way to have these states work together and create a new government. Even though the South was not as rich, and did not have as many people as the North, it had some strengths. The Confederates were fighting on their own ground—land that they knew. This put them close to their supplies and supporters. The army had very good officers. Most people were confident and were willing to fight to keep their way of life.

? What challenges did the South face in preparing for war?

Confederacy
(kən-fĕd′ər-ə-sē)
the 11 southern states that separated from the United States

secede
(sĭ-sēd′)
to withdraw formally from membership in an organization, association, or alliance

The Powerful North

The North had many advantages over the South. Those in the Union believed they would quickly and easily defeat the Confederacy because of the following things:

- The Union forces included more than two million men. The Confederate troops included about one-half as many, just 800,000 men. The Union had more ships. With a stronger navy, the North blocked Southern ports. This hurt the South's trade with Europe, which it needed for money and supplies.

Summary continues on next page

North Versus South *(Lesson 1 Summary continued)*

- Industry was controlled by the North. Before the war, the South sold its farm goods to the North. The South also had bought most of its manufactured goods from the North. Now, these markets were cut off. The North also controlled most of the country's railroads, which could move men and supplies where they were needed.
- Money printed in the South was worth less than Union money. Prices for everything became very high during the war. Many Southerners did not have enough money to feed their families.

[?] Why was a strong navy so important to the North's military success?

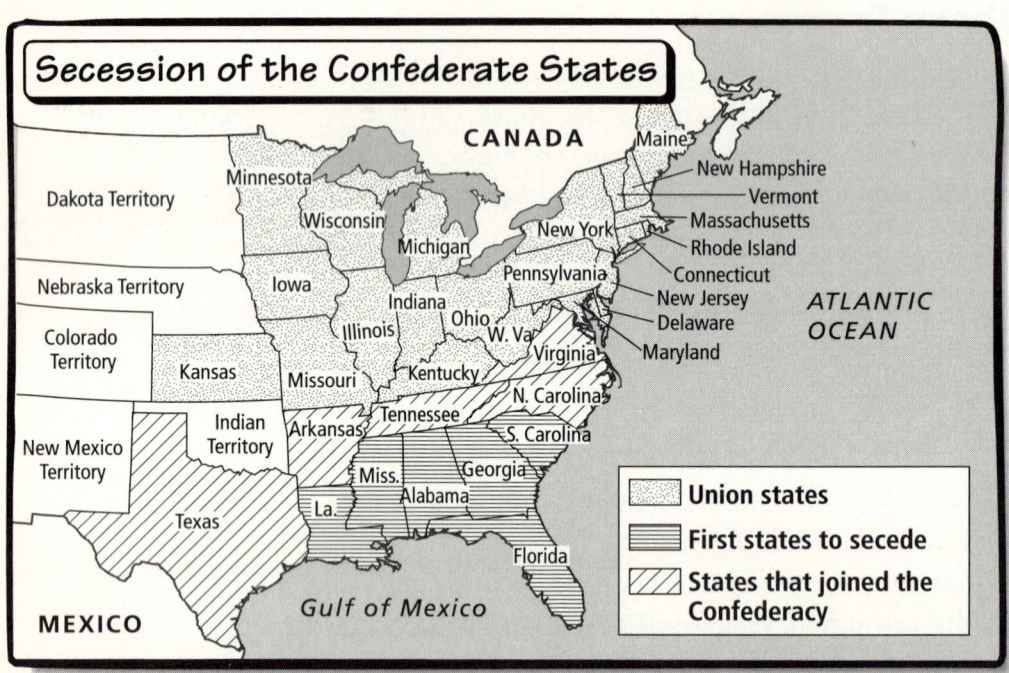

Name: _____   Date: _____

CHAPTER 12
Lesson 2 Preview
The Nation at War

(*A More Perfect Union* pp. 347–354)

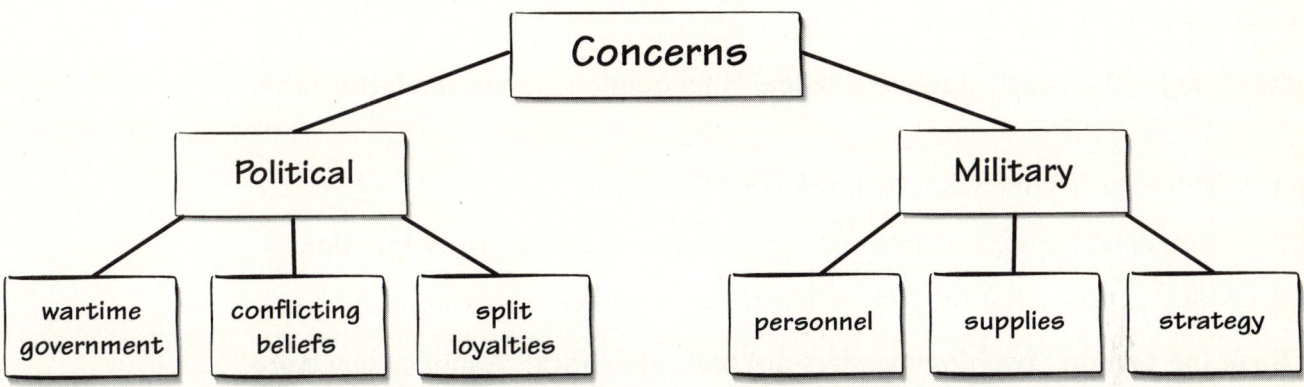

1. Look at the graphic organizer above. Then read the following sentences and fill in the blanks.

   The Union's and Confederacy's concerns were divided between _____ and _____ issues. Running a wartime _____ and dealing with _____ beliefs within one government were two of the main political concerns. Military concerns were not any easier. There never seemed to be enough _____ and _____ to carry out their strategies.

2. Look at the map and chart on page 350 in your text. Then answer the following questions.

   a. What main topic do both the map and chart show?
   _____

   b. What are the dates of the first significant battle?
   _____

   c. What battle was fought directly east of Fort Henry?
   _____

Reading Support Resources

Name: _____ Date: _____

CHAPTER 12
Lesson 2 Reading Strategy
The Nation at War

(*A More Perfect Union* pp. 347–354)

Evaluate This reading strategy helps you recognize the difference between facts and opinions. A fact is something that can be proven to be true. An opinion is a belief based on what a person thinks or feels.

1. Read page 347. Which statement below is an opinion? Circle the letter next to the best answer.

   a. The Union troops will crush the rebel forces.

   b. Confederate troops waited for the Yankees near Manassas Junction.

   c. Many people from the city of Washington gathered to watch the battle.

2. Read the section "Two Commanders-in-Chief Take Stock." Suppose you were living during the Civil War. Write a sentence in which you give an opinion of either Confederate President Davis or President Lincoln.

   _____

   _____

3. Read page 351. Which statement below is an opinion? Circle the letter next to the best answer.

   a. By fall 1862, the Civil War had been going on for more than a year.

   b. The battle at Antietam Creek was a great victory for the North.

   c. Santos Benavides was a member of the 33rd Texas Cavalry.

4. Read the section "The Hinge of Fate." Then write your own opinion of Grant's attack on Vicksburg and explain whether you think his strategy was too harsh.

   _____

   _____

   _____

   _____

CHAPTER 12

Lesson 2 Summary
The Nation at War

(*A More Perfect Union* pp. 347–354)

Summary also on Audiotape

Thinking Focus: How did ideas about the nature of war change from the First Battle of Bull Run in 1861 to the Battle of Gettysburg in 1863?

Two Commanders-in-Chief Take Stock

Union President Lincoln and Confederate President Davis had very different backgrounds. Davis grew up on a large plantation and had been trained as a soldier. Lincoln came from a poor frontier family and was a lawyer. But both men were political **moderates**. Davis supported states' rights, although he had to organize a strong government to be able to fight the war. This made some Southerners angry. They thought Davis was forgetting the ideas for which the South was fighting.

At the start of the war, Lincoln spent a lot of time running the war because he could not find a good leader for the army. In 1864, he chose Ulysses S. Grant, who was an excellent soldier. Lincoln also had to find a way to unite the Union states to support a single cause in the war. At first, Lincoln said the Union was fighting to save the nation and not to end slavery. This made many who were against slavery angry. Later, Lincoln gained support by saying that slavery was wrong.

moderate
(mŏd´ər-ĭt)
an individual opposed to extreme views or measures in politics or religion

[?] What were the similarities and differences between President Lincoln and President Davis?

War Rages On

The war had been going on for more than a year, with no end in sight. On September 17, 1862, one of the war's bloodiest battles took place at Antietam Creek in Maryland. In one day of fighting, more than 20,000 men died—more men than in the War of 1812, the Mexican War, and the Spanish-American War combined. Lincoln declared Antietam a victory for the North. But neither side was really a winner. Both sides lost many men and much property. And still there were no signs of peace. As the war continued, family loyalties were divided.

Summary continues on next page

Members of the same family sometimes fought on different sides. Women also had to sometimes choose between supporting their country or their family.

? Evaluate how the battle at Antietam helped to convince citizens that the nature of the Civil War would be neither glorious nor short-lived.

The President Proclaims an End to Slavery

In 1862, Lincoln issued his first **Emancipation** Proclamation. This made it clear that the Union believed in freedom. It also helped to create support for the war in the North. The Proclamation said that all slaves in the Confederacy would be free. This would mean that the South could lose most of its workers. Freed slaves could now move to the North and join the Union forces. The North would accept and pay free black soldiers to fight. The Confederacy refused to accept the Proclamation. On January 1, 1863, President Lincoln signed a second Proclamation. Many African Americans took advantage of it and joined in the fight against the South. Almost 200,000 African Americans served in the army and in the navy during the Civil War.

emancipation
(ĭ-măn´sə-pā´shən)
the state of being freed from oppression, bondage, or restraint

? With the enactment of the Emancipation Proclamation, blacks could enlist in the military. How did this new policy influence the North's military strength?

The Hinge of Fate

For two years, both the North and the South won and lost important battles. The North wanted to capture the Confederacy's capital of Richmond, Virginia. But they could not. Many battles were also fought along the Mississippi River. General Grant's troops attacked Vicksburg, Mississippi, from the land and the river for six weeks. Vicksburg finally surrendered. The North won a major victory. From Vicksburg, the North could block Southern trade along the Mississippi River.

The North also won a major battle at Gettysburg, Pennsylvania. In July, 1863, General Lee crossed the Potomac River and invaded the North near Gettysburg. After three days of fighting, Union troops forced Lee's men back across the river. Thousands of men from both sides were killed. These two battles were important victories for the North.

? Why were the battles at Vicksburg and Gettysburg referred to as "the Hinge of Fate"?

Name: _____ Date: _____

CHAPTER 12
Lesson 3 Preview
War on the Homefront

(*A More Perfect Union* pp. 355–359)

1. **Look at the graphic organizer above. From the information in the organizer, decide whether each statement that follows is true or false. Write *T* or *F* on the line.**

   a. New taxes were brought on by the lengthy war. ____

   b. Desertion by soldiers led to the draft. ____

   c. Civil rights were restricted because of food shortages and the draft. ____

   d. Food shortages, the draft, and other hardships led to riots and the formation of guerilla bands. ____

2. **Look at the illustration on page 359 in your text and read the caption. Why do you think women were working in factories instead of men?**

   _____

   _____

   _____

Name: _____ Date: _____

CHAPTER 12
Lesson 3 Reading Strategy
War on the Homefront

(*A More Perfect Union* pp. 355–359)

Predict/Infer This reading strategy helps you understand what you have read about and what you will read next. Before you read a section, think about the titles, pictures, and captions. Then think about what will happen in the selection.

1. **Read the lesson title. From your reading so far, what do you predict was the effect of the war on daily life? Circle the letter next to the best answer.**

    a. The war probably had little effect on daily life.

    b. People suffered from lack of money, food, and housing.

    c. Most people prospered during the war.

2. **Look at the pictures on pages 356 and 357 and read the captions. Name two issues that you predict will be discussed in these pages.**

    _____

    _____

3. **Look at the pictures on page 358. How do you think the war affected boys under the age of 18?**

    _____

4. **Read the red heading on page 359. Then look at the picture and read the caption. Fill in the chart below to help you predict how the war affected women.**

What I Know	What I Predict

CHAPTER 12
Lesson 3 Summary
War on the Homefront

(*A More Perfect Union* pp. 355–359)

 Summary also on Audiotape

Thinking Focus: What major changes took place in American society as a result of the Civil War?

Crisis of Wartime Leadership

President Lincoln delivered his famous Gettysburg Address after the Battle of Gettysburg. He honored the soldiers who died there, and called for "a new birth of freedom." This was hard to do. Although some slaves had been freed, they did not have many rights. The **civil rights** of Union citizens had also been limited by Congress as they tried to win the war.

The North and the South faced many social and economic problems during the war. Both governments needed to pay the high cost of the war. People paid heavy taxes on things that they bought and on the money that they made. Many people's civil rights were limited. For example, soldiers arrested and held people without a trial. People who were against the **draft** could be sent to jail without a trial. The draft caused many problems too. In the Union, any man between the ages of 20 and 45 could be drafted. But those who could afford to pay $300 did not have to serve. This made the poor very angry. There were riots across the country because of the draft. Thousands of people were hurt or killed before the government changed the Draft Law. In the South, slaveowners with more than 20 slaves did not have to serve. Food shortages in the South also caused riots. Many Confederate soldiers deserted the army to help their families save their lands.

civil rights
(sĭv′əl rīts)
rights and freedoms belonging to all citizens or members of society

draft
(drăft)
a call to military service

[?] Why did both Northern and Southern citizens resent the terms of the draft? What caused citizens to riot?

Draft Sends Youth to War

More than one half of the soldiers and sailors in the Civil War were 25 years old or younger. Boys between the ages of 10 and 12 were drummer boys who marched with the army. Boys in both navies carried gunpowder to the men shooting the cannons. 13- and 14-year-old boys marched and fought alongside older men. Once a boy was in

Summary continues on next page

the military, he did not get special treatment. Teenagers even became officers and received medals for their bravery. A young soldier could even be put on trial and hanged as a spy.

[?] What kinds of jobs were held by the young in the Civil War?

War Creates New Roles for Women

Women took on new roles during wartime. They supported and protected their homes. Women worked in factories making weapons for war. Many women took jobs that had been open only to men, such as printers, blacksmiths and farmers. Hundreds of women worked for the government, some in very important jobs. One woman, Sally Tomkins, was a captain in the Confederate army. Thousands were cooks and nurses in the army and navy. Women also worked as spies. Many dressed like men and joined the army so they could fight next to their husbands.

[?] How did many women, who were not allowed to fight in the Civil War, find a way to help the war effort?

| The Civil War Forces Changes ||
Women's Roles	In Society
• take responsibility for homes and farms • work in factories • fight as soldiers	• Citizens are heavily taxed. • Civil rights can be denied. • Unfair draft laws cause riots.

CHAPTER 12
Lesson 4 Preview
The Long March to Surrender
(*A More Perfect Union* pp. 362–367)

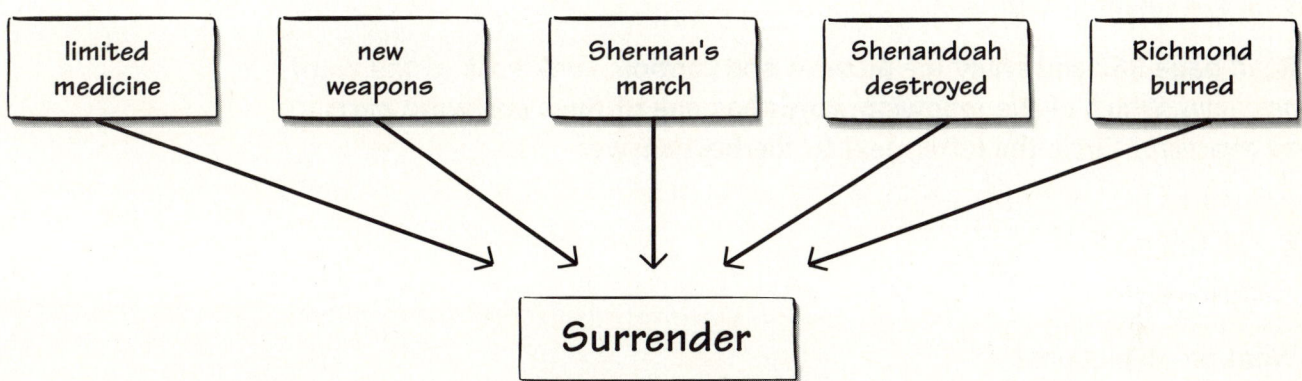

1. **Look at the graphic organizer above. Then read the following sentences and fill in the blanks.**

   Many factors led to the South's surrender to the North. Limited _____ coupled with the destruction caused by new _____ severely weakened the Southern forces and resulted in many deaths. The Southern morale was severely shaken during _____ march and after the city of _____ was burned.

2. **Look at the photograph of Clara Barton on page 363 in your text and read the caption. What did this nurse do that history still remembers her for today?**

   _____
   _____
   _____

Name: _____ Date: _____

CHAPTER 12
Lesson 4 Reading Strategy
The Long March to Surrender

(*A More Perfect Union* pp. 362–367)

Think About Words This reading strategy helps you figure out the meaning of new words. When you come to an unfamiliar word, look for word parts you already know and use clues such as context and pictures.

1. Read page 362 and study the pictures and caption. Look back at the word *depictions*. Which of the following words has one of the same word parts as *depictions*? Circle the letter next to the best answer.

    a. deaths
    b. pictures
    c. designs

2. What are depictions?

   _____

3. Read the first two paragraphs of page 363. Then look at the word *tactics* near the end of that selection. Based on the context of the paragraph, what do you think *tactics* means?

   _____

4. Read the rest of the lesson. Choose a word from the lesson that is new to you. Then fill in as much of the chart below as you can to help you figure out what the word means.

   WORD: _____

   clues from the reading:

   clues from the pictures:

   similar words I already know:

   parts of words I already know:

   the word means

CHAPTER 12

Lesson 4 Summary
The Long March to Surrender

(*A More Perfect Union* pp. 362–367)

Thinking Focus: What events led to General Lee's surrender at Appomattox?

The Final Tally

The North wanted the war to end. It wanted to make the South give up fighting by trying to destroy the spirit of the people in the South. To do this, they decided to bring "total" war to the Confederacy. Union forces burned houses and fields. People starved to death.

New weapons such as cannons, the repeater rifle, gas shells, machine guns, and flame throwers caused horrible injuries and caused many more to die. Medical practices during the war were very simple. Doctors often did not have much training. As a result, many soldiers died of their wounds. Clara Barton was the first person to set up emergency care in the battlefield. This helped, but still, one out of every fifty Americans died in the Civil War.

Fighting the "total war" destroyed entire cities and areas. After General William Sherman's Union soldiers captured the city of Atlanta, they took anything the Confederates might use. Sherman forced everyone to leave, and then the troops burned the city to the ground. The soldiers continued toward the Atlantic coast, taking what they needed and burning as they went. Another Union General, Philip Sheridan, and his troops destroyed entire farms in the Shenandoah Valley in Virginia. These farms produced most of the food for Lee's army. Sheridan's attack destroyed the Confederate army's food supply.

❓ Why did Grant and his generals believe that "total war" was necessary?

Summary continues on next page

New Tools for Warfare

Hot air balloons used for troop observation and message drops

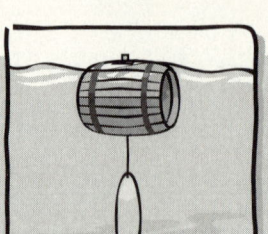
Torpedoes used as underwater mines to sink boats

.44 Colt Revolver could shoot many bullets at close range

Cannons used by the North; largest ever made

Surrender at Appomattox

By 1865, General Lee's 35,000 troops could no longer fight. They were starving. There was little left of the soldier's boots or uniforms. The troops were running out of ammunition. To make things worse, 80,000 Union soldiers under General Meade were moving closer to Lee's men. Lee had no choice. He had to meet with General Grant to end the war. That meeting took place at Appomattox Court House, Virginia. General Lee surrendered to Grant. Grant's terms were simple. He set Lee's troops free. He gave them food. He allowed them to take their horses and mules home. The war was over.

? What terms did Grant set for Lee's surrender?

Use with *A More Perfect Union* Pages 374–405

Chapter Overview
Reconstruction

Fill in the blank spaces below with information from the chapter.

When: 1865–1877

Where: The South

Who: Northerners, Southerners

Reconstruction

The Southern Way of Life Changed
- slaves freed
- _____
- farms destroyed

Plans for Reconstruction
- Lincoln Plan (13th Amendment)
- Johnson Plan
- _____

_____
- Radicals dominate Congress
- African Americans enter politics
- carpetbaggers and scalawags
- 14th and 15th Amendments

After Reconstruction
- Black codes
- _____
- secret societies
- African American migration

Reading Support Resources • Chapter Overview • Chapter 13 • **181**

CHAPTER 13
Lesson 1 Preview
A Time for Reconciliation

(*A More Perfect Union* pp. 376–384)

Steps Leading to Reconstruction and the 14th Amendment

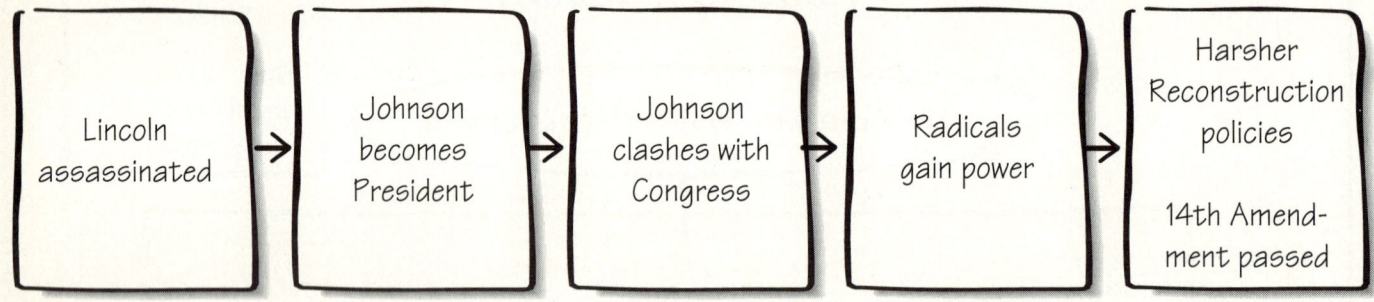

1. Look at the graphic organizer above. Then put the following items in the correct order. Number the items from one to five.

   ___ Radicals gain power.

   ___ Johnson becomes president.

   ___ Lincoln assassinated.

   ___ harsher Reconstruction policies/Fourteenth Amendment passed

   ___ Johnson clashes with Congress.

2. Look at the chart titled *Reconstruction Amendments* on page 384 of your text. Then answer the following questions:

   a. Which amendment defined national citizenship?
   _____

   b. What was the purpose of the Fifteenth Amendment?
   _____
   _____
   _____

Name: _____ Date: _____

CHAPTER 13
Lesson 1 Reading Strategy
A Time for Reconciliation

(*A More Perfect Union* pp. 376–384)

Compare and Contrast This reading strategy helps you understand how events are similar and different. As you read about historical events, think about how they compare and contrast with events you already know.

1. Read the section "Lincoln Plans for Reconstruction." Circle the letter next to the best ending for the following sentence: Moderate Republicans wanted easy terms for the South to reenter the Union, but Radical Republicans

    a. required more difficult terms.
    b. proposed the Thirteenth Amendment.
    c. wanted amnesty for all southerners.

2. Read the section "Lincoln Assassinated." Write a sentence about Lincoln's abilities to negotiate and compromise. Then write a sentence about Johnson's negotiating skills.

    Lincoln: _____
    _____

    Johnson: _____
    _____

3. Were Lincoln's and Johnson's negotiating skills similar or different?
    _____

4. Read the section "Freed People Struggle for Rights." Then fill in the chart below comparing life for black Americans before and after Emancipation.

	Before	After
family ties		
education		
citizenship		

Reading Support Resources   Reading Strategy • Chapter 13, Lesson 1 **183**

CHAPTER 13

Lesson 1 Summary
A Time for Reconciliation

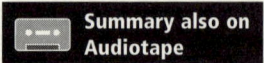 Summary also on Audiotape

(*A More Perfect Union* pp. 376–384)

Thinking Focus: What social, political, and economic challenges faced the South following the Civil War?

The Southern Way of Life Is Destroyed

The Civil War almost destroyed the South. In 1865, most of the farms were in ruins. Crop fields were now nothing but weeds. Roads, bridges, buildings, and machinery were destroyed. It would take a lot of money and work to rebuild. But Confederate money was worthless. Farmers could not get credit to buy seeds to plant new crops. Over one-fifth of the men had been killed in the war. Thousands of slaves had died fighting for the Union. Others wanted to leave the South for a better life. All of this made it hard to get workers. Many plantation owners offered freed blacks land to farm as **sharecroppers**. This helped them to start growing crops again.

[?] How did the widespread destruction of the South affect agriculture?

Lincoln Plans for Reconstruction

Even before the Civil War ended, Lincoln had thought about how the South could peacefully rejoin the Union. His plan was called **Reconstruction**. Lincoln organized new governments in the Southern states where there were Union troops. He tried to treat people fairly. He presented a plan for **amnesty** and Reconstruction to Congress. A group of congressmen called Radical Republicans proposed another plan, the Wade-Davis Bill. It protected black Americans' civil rights more than Lincoln's plan. It also demanded greater loyalty from the Southern states. The Wade-Davis Bill was passed, but the President refused to sign it. The bill was defeated. Many congressmen were angry. Lincoln settled their differences with the Thirteenth Amendment, which would outlaw slavery. States that were in the Confederacy had to approve this amendment before they would be allowed to rejoin the Union.

[?] What compromise did Lincoln offer between his own plan and the Wade-Davis bill?

sharecropping
(shâr′krŏp′ĭng)
the practice of a tenant farmer giving a share of his or her crop to the land owner instead of paying rent

Reconstruction
(rē′kən-strŭk′shən)
the period (1865–1877) following the Civil War, when the federal government took charge of the former Confederate states

amnesty
(ăm′nĭ-stē)
a general pardon for offenders by a government, especially for political offenses

Summary continues on next page

A Time for Reconciliation (Lesson 1 Summary continued)

Lincoln Assassinated

Six days after the Civil War ended, President Lincoln was shot by a pro-South actor while at the theater with his wife. Lincoln died the next day. Vice President Andrew Johnson was quickly sworn in as President. Even though Johnson was from the South, he was loyal to the Union. His Reconstruction plans, like Lincoln's, outlawed slavery, but did not demand civil rights for black Americans. Johnson's plan made it easy for Southern states to rejoin the Union. Southern states used new laws, known as Black Codes, to keep former slaves from being truly free. In Mississippi, freed blacks could be forced to work for their former owners. In South Carolina, the only job blacks could hold was either servant or farmer. Plantation workers could not leave without the permission of their former owners.

? How did the Black Codes keep freed blacks in virtual slavery?

Freed People Struggle for Rights

In spite of the Black Codes, former slaves enjoyed new freedoms. They could join churches, schools, and social groups. Before the war, laws would not let black Americans learn to read and write. After 1868, Southern states set up their first public school systems. They were **segregated**, but all children were finally able to get an education. In 1866, Congress passed a bill that guaranteed citizenship to blacks. President Johnson vetoed it, but Congress outvoted his veto. The Republicans thought the Supreme Court might overturn the law, so they passed the Fourteenth Amendment. It defined citizenship as anyone born or naturalized in the United States. It also said that states could not take away anyone's civil liberties.

segregated
(sĕg'rĭ-gāt'əd)
having separate facilities, such as public schools or drinking fountains, for people of different races

? What led to the passing of an amendment to the Constitution, rather than a bill, to guarantee federal citizenship to black Americans?

Name: _____   Date: _____

CHAPTER 13
Lesson 2 Preview
Radical Reconstruction

(*A More Perfect Union* pp. 385–390)

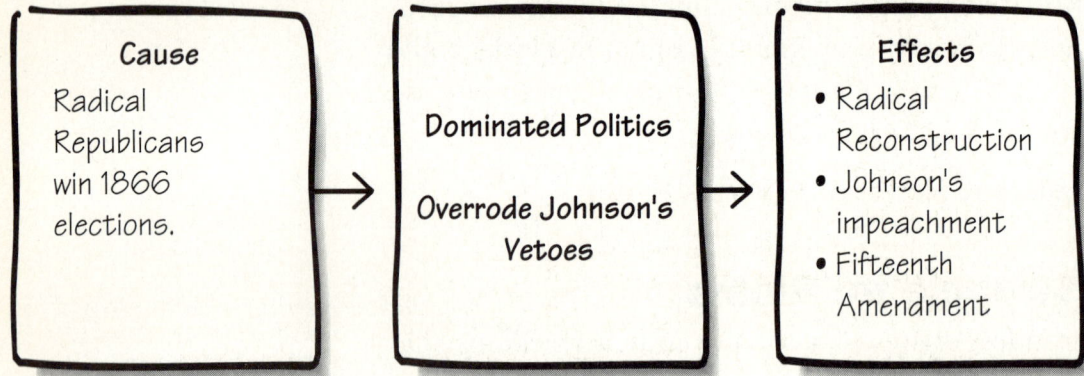

1. Look at the graphic organizer above. Then read and answer the following questions:

   a. Which group won the 1866 election?
   _____

   b. What did Radical Republicans do to President Johnson's vetoes?
   _____

   c. What were the three effects of politics dominated by Radical Republicans?
   _____
   _____
   _____

2. Look at the map in your textbook on page 386. What states were readmitted to the Union in 1868?
   _____
   _____
   _____

186 Chapter 13, Lesson 2 • Lesson Preview   Reading Support Resources

Name: _____ Date: _____

CHAPTER 13
Lesson 2 Reading Strategy
Radical Reconstruction

(*A More Perfect Union* pp. 385–390)

Cause and Effect This reading strategy helps you understand events and why they occur. As you read, think about the factors that caused an event. Then think about what the effects of that event may be.

1. Read the section "Congress Challenges Johnson." Which of the following was an effect of the Military Reconstruction acts? Circle the letter next to the best answer.

   a. The South was divided into five military districts.
   b. Race riots occurred in New Orleans and Memphis.
   c. The Radicals gained enough seats in Congress to control Reconstruction policy.

2. Read the section "Johnson Stands Trial." Which of the following was a cause of Congress's impeachment of President Johnson? Circle the letter next to the best answer.

   a. Senator Edmund G. Ross refused to announce his verdict until the last minute.
   b. Many white southerners refused to vote for their state's constitution.
   c. Johnson challenged the authority of Congress to decide Reconstruction policy.

3. Read the section "African Americans Enter Politics." What was one effect of Reconstruction on African Americans in politics?

   _____

4. Read to the end of the lesson. Then complete the chart below.

Cause	Effect
Carpetbaggers arrive in the South.	
Scalawags support Reconstruction.	
	passage of 15th Amendment
15th Amendment	

Reading Support Resources

CHAPTER 13
Lesson 2 Summary
Radical Reconstruction

(*A More Perfect Union* pp. 385–390)

Thinking Focus: What were the effects of Radical Reconstruction on the South, and how did Southerners respond to the changes?

Congress Challenges Johnson

President Johnson was against Congress having a part in the Reconstruction. He wanted to give some rights back to former Confederates, and he did not want Southern states to accept the Fourteenth Amendment. Radical Republicans, however, wanted to punish white Southerners and protect black Americans' rights to vote. In 1866, the Radical candidates won many seats in Congress. Now, with more power, they threw out Johnson's plan and created their own. This plan was called Radical Reconstruction. They removed all of the Confederate governments except one. The rest of the South was divided into five districts and put under **martial law**. The states under martial law had to allow black Americans to vote.

❓ How did Congress respond to Johnson's attempts to take control of Reconstruction policy?

martial law
(mär′shəl lô)
rule or law of a civilian population carried out by the military

impeachment
(ĭm-pēch′mənt)
procedure of accusing a person holding public office of misconduct

Johnson Stands Trial

President Johnson worked against the Radical Republicans' plan. He limited the power of the military governors who had control of the five Southern districts. He also supported leaders who let former Confederates vote. Under the Radicals' plan, former Confederate officials and army officers could not vote. By letting them vote, Johnson gave more power to people who did not want black Americans to have more rights. This made Congress very angry. The House passed a charge of **impeachment**. The Senate acted as jury in Johnson's trial. One senator's vote of "not guilty" saved him and allowed him to stay in office.

❓ How did President Johnson's resistance to Congressional authority lead to his impeachment?

Summary continues on next page

Radical Reconstruction (Lesson 2 Summary continued)

African Americans Enter Politics

Most black Americans voted. They elected many of their own candidates, especially in South Carolina and Louisiana. Many black Americans also became members of Congress. But white leaders still controlled the Republican Party in the South and no black American governors were elected.

[?] How do you think white Southerners regarded black officeholders?

Reshaping the South

After the Civil War, many people from the North went to the South. Some wanted to make money, while others wanted to help the South rebuild. Many went to help blacks get their full rights. Southerners called these people **carpetbaggers**. Some Southerners had sided with the Republicans during the war and supported Reconstruction. Southern white conservatives called them **scalawags** and thought they were traitors.

[?] Why were some Southerners angry at carpetbaggers and scalawags?

carpetbaggers
(kär′pĭt-băg′ər)
a person from the North who went to the South after the Civil War to gain financially or politically

scalawag
(skăl′ə-wăg′)
a white Southerner who supported Reconstruction

Rebuilding the South

There was much illegal behavior during Reconstruction. White Southerners blamed it on the carpetbaggers and the black voters. The "get rich quick" spirit was almost everywhere.

In order to make sure that blacks could vote, Congress passed the Fifteenth Amendment. It guaranteed that the right of a citizen to vote could not be taken away "on account of race, color, or previous condition of servitude." Some Democrats thought this gave blacks special favors. Some Radicals thought the amendment was too weak because it did not set up standard voting requirements for all states.

[?] Review the arguments for and against the Fifteenth Amendment. Why did Republicans think an amendment was necessary?

Name: Date:

CHAPTER 13

Lesson 3 Preview

Southern Life Under Reconstruction

(*A More Perfect Union* pp. 391–397)

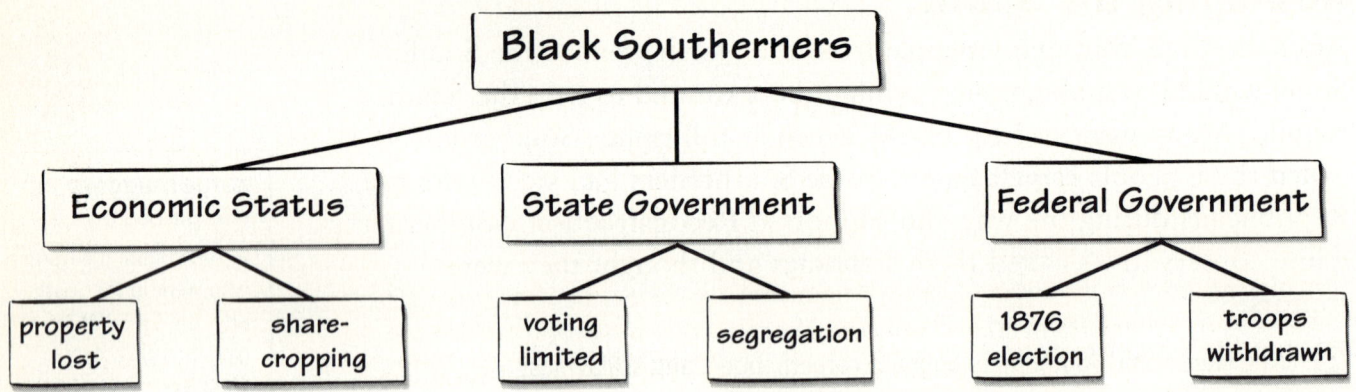

1. Look at the graphic organizer above. Then read and answer the following questions:

    a. What was the economic status of black Southerners?

    _____

    _____

    b. What actions did state governments take that affected black Southerners?

    _____

    _____

2. Look at the timeline in your textbook on page 395. Then read and answer the following questions:

    a. In what year was President Lincoln assassinated?

    _____

    b. In what year was the first black U.S. Senator elected?

    _____

    c. What happened in 1875?

    _____

Name: _____ Date: _____

CHAPTER 13
Lesson 3 Reading Strategy
Southern Life Under Reconstruction

(*A More Perfect Union* pp. 391–397)

Self-Question This reading strategy helps you stay focused on what you read. Ask yourself questions before you read a section. Then read to see if you can find the answer to your questions.

1. The chart below shows what kinds of questions you might ask before you read the section "Forty Acres and a Mule." As you read the section, look for the answers to these questions and fill in the chart.

Question	Answer
a. Who received forty acres of land?	
b. From whom did these people receive the land?	
c. What did they do with the land?	
d. What eventually happened to the land?	

2. Read the red and blue headings on page 394. Which question do you expect you will be able to answer when you read the section? Circle the letter next to the best answer.

    a. What was sharecropping?

    b. What was the purpose of secret societies?

    c. What farming methods were used during Reconstruction?

3. Read the heading "Legacies of Reconstruction." Write a question you expect you will be able to answer when you read the section.

    _____

4. Now read the section "Legacies of Reconstruction" and write the answer to your question, or something else you learned, in the space below.

    _____
    _____

Reading Support Resources

CHAPTER 13

Lesson 3 Summary
Southern Life Under Reconstruction

(*A More Perfect Union* pp. 391–397)

Summary also on Audiotape

Thinking Focus: How did Reconstruction policies end in mixed results?

Forty Acres and a Mule

After the war, freed blacks in the South started farming their own land. General Sherman gave them large areas of land under his control. Later, Congress let black American rent some of its "abandoned" land. Some bought this land later. But the land was hard to farm. In some areas, Congress did not actually own the "abandoned" land. So it could not legally rent or sell it. When President Johnson gave rights back to white Southerners, they went back to their own land. The plantation owners did not want to accept the freedom of former slaves. They still wanted slavery. Many black Americans who could not buy their own farms or survive on them became sharecroppers. They worked on the white landowners' land. In return, sharecroppers had to give the white owners a part of their crops. The sharecroppers felt this gave them independence. But most sharecroppers could not earn enough to pay the white owners.

? Why did many blacks become sharecroppers?

The Reaction of White Southerners

Many white Southerners refused to accept that their style of life had to change. They elected Democratic representatives. Some Democrats promised to **redeem** the South and to restore "Home Rule." That meant the Southern states would be able to rule themselves and ignore federal laws. These Democratic Redeemers did not want black Americans to be able to vote against them. They set up systems that did not let them vote. This was against the Fifteenth Amendment. For example, some states set up a poll tax, which had to be paid in order to vote. Most black Americans could not afford to pay the tax. Some white Southerners turned to violence to protect their interests. They organized secret groups such as the Ku Klux Klan to frighten black

redeem
(rĭ-dēm´)
to recover or reclaim

Summary continues on next page

Southern Life Under Reconstruction (Lesson 3 Summary continued)

Americans. These societies became more powerful as feelings against Reconstruction grew. Many of the societies became **vigilante** groups.

[?] How did Southern whites seek to counter the effects of the Fifteenth Amendment?

vigilante
(vĭj´ə-lăn´tē)
citizen who is part of a group that takes the law into its own hands, punishing those it feels are criminals without any legal authority to do so

The End of Reconstruction

The South continued to refuse to accept Reconstruction. Eventually the North lost patience. Many Northerners began to feel that the South should be left alone to solve its own problems. In a very close election in 1876, Republican Rutherford B. Hayes was elected President through a bargain with the Democrats. The Republicans agreed to remove all federal troops from the South in return for votes for Hayes. This was called the Compromise of 1877. It left black Americans in the South with no federal protection. Reconstruction was over.

[?] How and why did Reconstruction end?

Legacies of Reconstruction

Reconstruction brought many changes. Slavery had ended forever. The federal government had established its authority over states. Many civil rights had been set up by the Fourteenth and Fifteenth Amendments. But black Americans still had less than complete freedom. In place of slavery, the South had set up segregation of the races. Black Americans still did not have opportunity there. Many moved away. Some joined the westward movement. Many moved to cities in the North. The ideas behind Radical Reconstruction did not die, however. The civil rights movement of the 1950s and 1960s continued the same ideals.

[?] Would you say that Reconstruction was a failure or a success? Explain your answer.

Reconstruction: 1865—1877

- 1865 — 13th Amendment
- 1866 — Ku Klux Klan established
- 1867 — Reconstruction Acts
- 1868 — 14th Amendment
- 1869 — First black U.S. Senator elected
- 1870 — 15th Amendment
- 1875 — Civil Rights Acts
- 1877 — Federal troops withdraw from South

Use with *A More Perfect Union* Pages 408–439

Chapter Overview
Reshaping the Great Plains

Fill in the blank spaces below with information from the chapter.

When: 1850–1900

Who: Plains Indians, White settlers

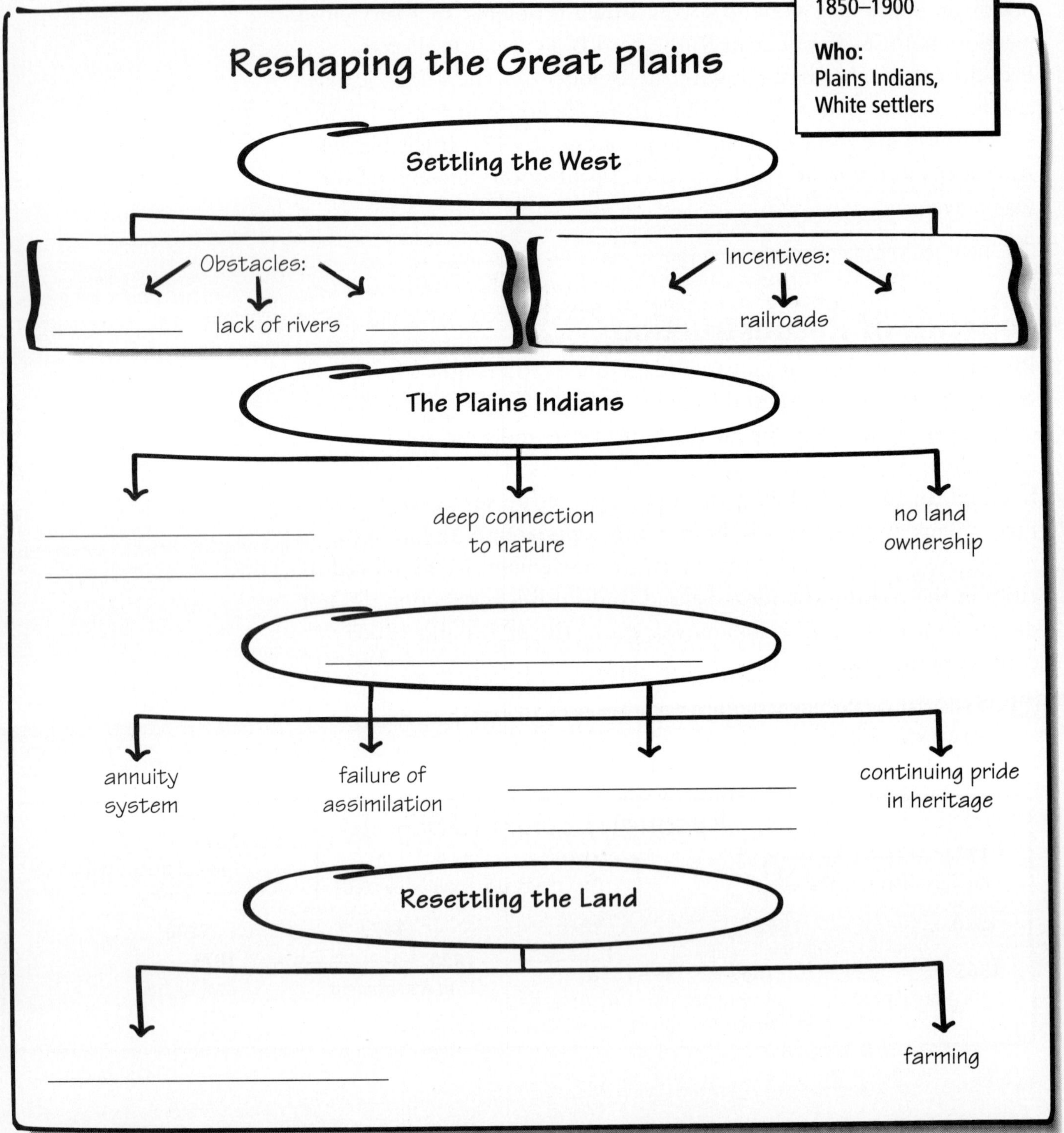

Reshaping the Great Plains

- Settling the West
  - Obstacles: _____, lack of rivers, _____
  - Incentives: _____, railroads, _____
- The Plains Indians
  - _____
  - deep connection to nature
  - no land ownership
- _____
  - annuity system
  - failure of assimilation
  - _____
  - continuing pride in heritage
- Resettling the Land
  - _____
  - farming

Name: Date:

CHAPTER 14
Lesson 1 Preview
A Time of Change
(*A More Perfect Union* pp. 410–414)

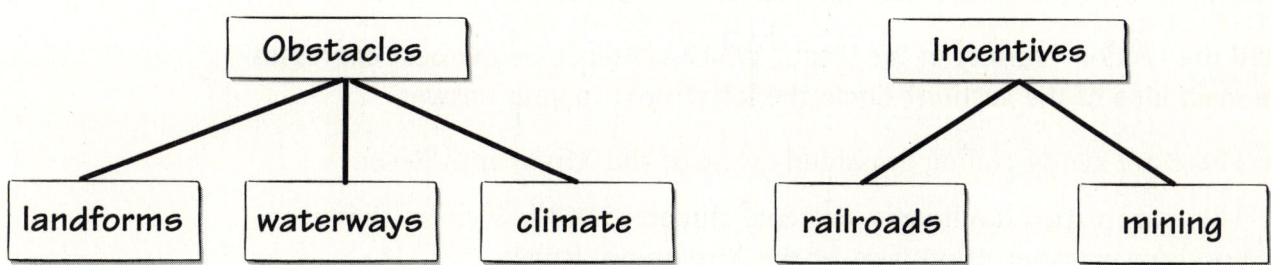

1. Look at the graphic organizer above. Then read the following sentences and fill in the blanks.

   Railroads and _____ were two reasons for settling in the West. But settlement was not always easy. There were many _____ to living there. For example, the _____ were beautiful but were difficult to get around. The waterways were challenging and the _____ could be very cold or very hot, with droughts, blizzards, and thunderstorms.

2. Look at the picture of the Rocky Mountains and read the caption on page 410 of your text. Write two sentences that describe what you see in the picture.

   _____
   _____
   _____
   _____

Name: _____ Date: _____

CHAPTER 14

Lesson 1 Reading Strategy
A Time of Change

(*A More Perfect Union* pp. 410–414)

Finding the Main Idea This reading strategy helps you organize and remember what you read. When you finish a selection, jot down the main idea and its supporting details.

1. Read the section "Variety of the West." Which sentence below best expresses the main idea of the section? Circle the letter next to your answer.

   a. There are gently rolling grasslands west of the Mississippi River.

   b. There are varied landforms, extreme climates, and few rivers that are good for transportation west of the Mississippi River.

   c. Climates can vary greatly west of the Mississippi River.

2. Read the section "Railroads Arrive." What is the main idea of this section?

   _____

3. List three supporting details in the section "Railroads Arrive."

   _____
   _____
   _____

4. Read the section "Mining Develops." Then fill in the chart below with the main idea of the section and at least two supporting details.

Main Idea	Supporting Details

CHAPTER 14

Lesson 1 Summary
A Time of Change

(*A More Perfect Union* pp. 410–414)

Thinking Focus: How did people's view of the Great Plains change after 1860?

Variety of the West

The area known as the Great Plains lies between the Mississippi River and the Rocky Mountains. It is a flat grassy region with few trees, that slowly rises up to the foothills of the Rocky Mountains. The climate in the Plains can range from very hot to very cold with long periods of dryness. There are also times of the year when the Plains has heavy thunderstorms and snowstorms.

The Rocky Mountains lie west of the Great Plains. An area called the intermountain zone sits between the Rocky Mountains to the east and the Cascade Mountains and the Sierra Nevada range to the west. This region has a mixture of deserts, basins, deep canyons, and plateaus. Fertile farming land lies in the valleys between these ranges and the mountains along the north Pacific coast.

The Missouri, Platte, Arkansas, and Red rivers of the Great Plains provided Indians, explorers, and settlers with water for drinking. But fast-moving rapids made few rivers usable for transportation. Most people traveled over land by horseback, wagon train, or stagecoach.

? Explain why the West is said to have a variety of environments.

Railroads Arrive

In 1869, the **transcontinental** railroad linked the Central Pacific to the Union Pacific Railroads. Teams of men from each railroad raced the other to see who could lay the most track. Chinese workers for the Central Pacific began laying track in California and continued east over the Sierra Nevada Mountains and across the Great Basin. The climate in these regions made the work even more difficult. Avalanches and blizzards fell as the men dug tunnels and cut passes through the mountains. They suffered in dust storms in the summer. Often the workers did not have enough food or a place to sleep.

transcontinental
(trăns′ kŏn-tə-nĕn′ tl)
crossing a continent

Summary continues on next page

A Time of Change (Lesson 1 Summary continued)

The workers for the Union Pacific were mostly from Ireland and other European countries. This crew worked across the Great Plains and over the Rocky Mountains. They also faced problems caused by the climate and attacks from American Indians. They met the Central Pacific crew in Utah.

[?] Describe some of the problems faced by the men who built the transcontinental railroad.

Mining Develops

The railroads made it easier to bring silver and other ores from the West to the industrial centers in the East. In 1859, prospectors discovered a rich vein of silver in Nevada. This became known as the Comstock Lode. It was difficult to mine this silver. The miners needed heavy machinery to cut deep tunnels into the hard rock around the vein. Other machines were needed to carry the silver up to the surface and then crush the stone and separate the silver from it. Individual prospectors could not afford to buy all of this expensive equipment. But large companies could, and soon they took over mining.

The **bonanza** lay 1,000 feet below the ground. Many people became wealthy from this silver-rich rock. Miners rushed to Nevada. Everybody wanted to get rich. **Boom towns** were quickly built around the mines. When the demand for silver dropped and the price fell, mining became less profitable. So miners left the boom towns. They became ghost towns just as quickly as they had appeared.

[?] Why was mining after 1850 often undertaken by large companies rather than by individual prospectors?

---

bonanza
(bə-năn´ zə)
rich, valuable (ore-bearing) rock

boom town
(bo͞om toŭn)
a town that is built very quickly

Name: _____ Date: _____

CHAPTER 14
Lesson 2 Preview
Culture of the Plains Indians

(*A More Perfect Union* pp. 415–419)

Plains Indians

	Before Europeans	After Europeans
Homes	lodges	tepees
Economy	farming	hunting
Travel	foot, dog sledge	horse
Weapons	bow and arrows	guns

1. Look at the graphic organizer above. It describes the Plains Indians before and after the arrival of Europeans. From the information in the graphic organizer, decide whether each statement that follows is true or false. Write *T* or *F* on the line.

    a. The Indians farmed before Europeans arrived. ___

    b. Indians did not begin to use guns until after the Europeans arrived. ___

    c. Indians lived in tepees before they lived in lodges. ___

    d. The dog sledge was more efficient than traveling on a horse. ___

2. Look at the map on page 419 of your text. Then answer the following questions:

    a. What does this map show?
    _____
    _____

    b. What river runs through Cherokee and Creek territory?
    _____

Reading Support Resources   Lesson Preview • Chapter 14, Lesson 2

CHAPTER 14
Lesson 2 Reading Strategy
Culture of the Plains Indians

(*A More Perfect Union* pp. 415–419)

Summarize is a strategy that helps you remember key points about what you have read. When you get to a good break in your reading, stop and write down the main ideas of what you have read.

1. Read page 415 and the first column of page 416. What is the best summary of the Plains Indians' way of life before the arrival of Europeans? Circle the letter next to your choice.

    a. Indians used horses and guns to help them hunt buffalo.

    b. Many Indians were settled farmers.

    c. Most Indians lived in tipis.

2. Read the section "A Nomadic Way of Life." What is the best summary of the Plains Indians' way of life after the arrival of Europeans? Circle the letter next to your choice.

    a. Many Indians became nomads who followed the buffalo herds.

    b. Many Indians stopped hunting and became farmers.

    c. Many Indians moved to the northwestern United States.

3. Read the section "Tribal Status." Write a few sentences in the chart below summarizing what you have learned about how Indians viewed the land.

How Indians Viewed the Land

CHAPTER 14

Lesson 2 Summary
Culture of the Plains Indians

(*A More Perfect Union* pp. 415–419)

Summary also on Audiotape

Thinking Focus: What are four characteristics of the Plains Indians' lives?

Hunters of the Buffalo

Before Europeans arrived, the Plains Indians were farmers who lived mostly in one place. They built homes from earth and wood poles. They grew crops in the fertile soil around rivers. Small groups of men would go out on foot and hunt buffalo. They traded with nearby tribes.

The Plains Indians' way of life changed at the end of the 1600s. The Chippewa Indians received guns from European fur traders in Canada. They used them in fights against the Sioux, also called the Lakota. At the same time, Indians in New Mexico revolted against Spanish settlers. As the Spanish left, they did not take many of their horses. The Indians adopted these horses. Now they could travel farther and faster on horseback than on foot. Hunting became much easier. The Indians began to follow buffalo herds as they moved across the Plains. Tribal life was no longer settled. Instead, life became nomadic—Indians moved from one place to another, rather than living in one place.

? How did the horse and gun transform the life of the Plains Indians?

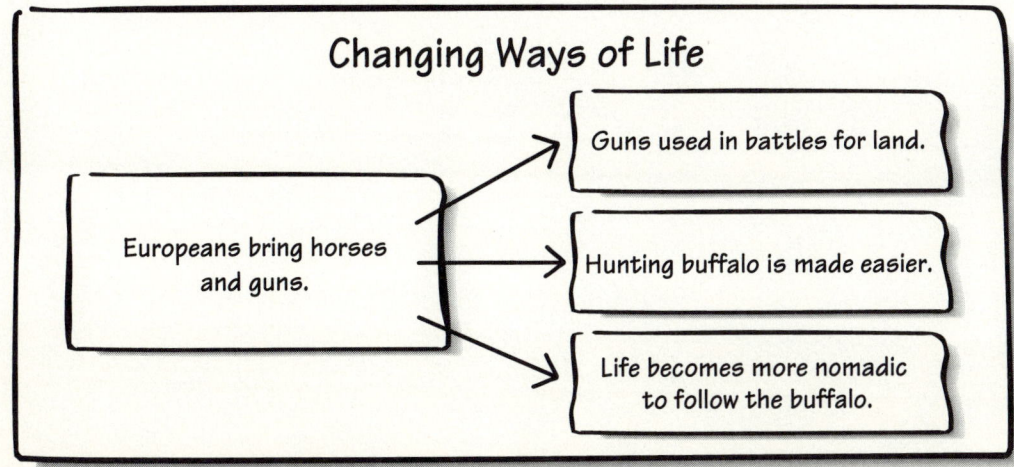

Summary continues on next page

Culture of the Plains Indians *(Lesson 2 Summary continued)*

Tribal Status

In order to get the horses they needed, Plains Indians stole horses from other tribes or pioneer settlements. Success in warfare and in raids made a man important in his tribe. A young boy was able to get status by joining men on a hunt. As he grew older, his status could grow by stealing horses, fighting as a warrior, or leading a hunt or a war party. A man's status was important because it showed his bravery.

The tribes also tested a man's ability by "counting coup." A coup was a daring act that must be done under difficult conditions. The greater the danger, the greater the coup. A chief was a great fighter or experienced leader. Tribes could have more than one chief depending on what the tribe needed. A council of elders was also in charge of the tribes. They made decisions about tribal problems.

Even though each tribe was different, they all shared certain beliefs. The Plains Indians believed that people were connected to the land and to the natural world. They thought that a tribe could use the land, but individuals should not own it. Certain areas were considered sacred. The Indians did not want to give up or sell their tribal lands to the U.S. government.

? How did a man on the Plains acquire status in his tribe?

Name: _____ Date: _____

CHAPTER 14
Lesson 3 Preview
Indian Lands Lost

(*A More Perfect Union* pp. 422–426)

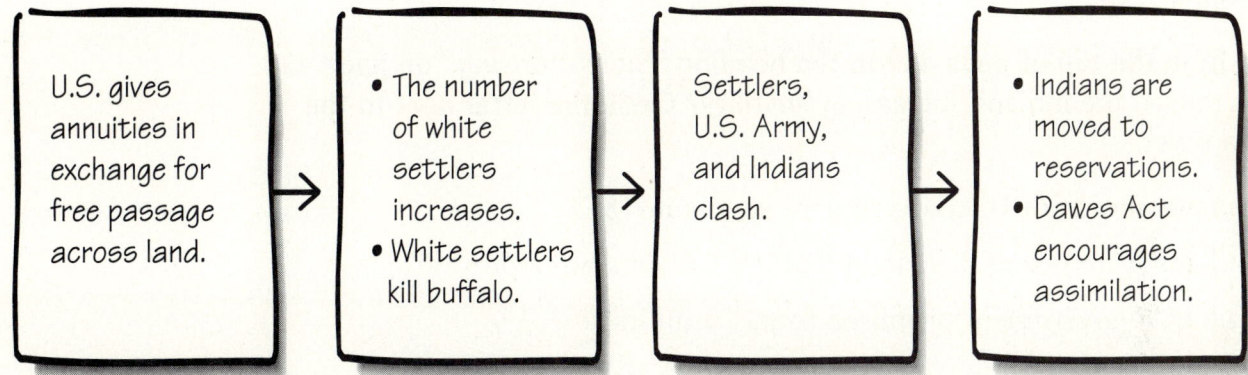

1. **Look at the graphic organizer above. Read the following sentences and put them in the correct order.**

    ___ A growing number of white settlers move to the Plains.

    ___ Indians move to reservations and are encouraged to assimilate.

    ___ Americans and Indians clash.

    ___ Indians receive annuities for allowing pioneers to pass through their lands.

2. **Look at the map on page 425 in your text. The largest grouping of Indian reservations in 1890 was in Oklahoma. Name the tribes who lived there.**

    _____

    _____

    _____

    _____

Reading Support Resources   Lesson Preview • Chapter 14, Lesson 3 **203**

Name: _____   Date: _____

CHAPTER 14
Lesson 3 Reading Strategy
Indian Lands Lost

(*A More Perfect Union* pp. 422–426)

Cause and Effect This reading strategy helps you understand events and why they occur. As you read, think about factors that caused an event. Then think about what the effects of that event may be.

1. Read from the top of page 422 to the heading "Sioux Uprising" on page 423. What caused the Indians' increasing hostility? Circle the letter next to the best answer.

    a. Indians met with U.S. government agents in 1851.

    b. Indians were losing their land and their main source of food.

    c. The U.S. government promised to pay annuities.

2. Read sections "Sioux Uprising" and "Sand Creek Massacre." What caused the Sand Creek Massacre?

    _____

3. What was the effect of the massacre?

    _____

4. Read the section "Policies that Changed Indian Life." Then fill in the chart below.

Cause	Effect
	Indians move to reservations.
Dawes Act gives each tribal family 160 acres.	
Indian children are sent to special schools to learn about white culture.	

204 Chapter 14, Lesson 3 • Reading Strategy   Reading Support Resources

CHAPTER 14

Lesson 3 Summary
Indian Lands Lost

(*A More Perfect Union* pp. 422–426)

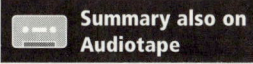

Thinking Focus: What factors combined to end the Plains Indians' nomadic way of life?

Indians and White Settlers Clash

During the gold rush of 1849, the Indians agreed to let pioneers cross their lands. But the pioneers and their animals threatened the buffalo. The animals ate the grass that the buffalo needed. Many pioneers killed the buffalo for food. The Indians were upset by this because the buffalo were very important to their way of life. They began to attack groups of pioneers.

The U.S. government wanted to have peace treaties with the Indians. It promised to supply the tribes with an **annuity** if the Indians would let pioneers pass across their land. But the government agents who supplied the annuities were often corrupt. Many times the Indians did not receive their annuity. If they did, the food was spoiled, the clothing was of poor quality, or the guns were broken.

When the transcontinental railroad was finished in the late 1860s, many more white people came to the Plains and to Indian lands. White hunters killed the buffalo for no good reason. After the white settlers arrived, only a few of the millions of buffalo that had existed were left. The Indians were in danger of starving without the buffalo. Again, the Indians responded by attacking and killing hundreds of pioneers. These years of uprisings were some of the bloodiest in the history of the West.

annuity
(ə-no͞oʹĭ-tē)
a yearly provision to American Indians of food, clothing, and other necessary items (as part of an agreement with the U.S. Government)

[?] Why did the U.S. government want to settle the Plains Indians on reservations?

Summary continues on next page

Indian Lands Lost *(Lesson 3 Summary continued)*

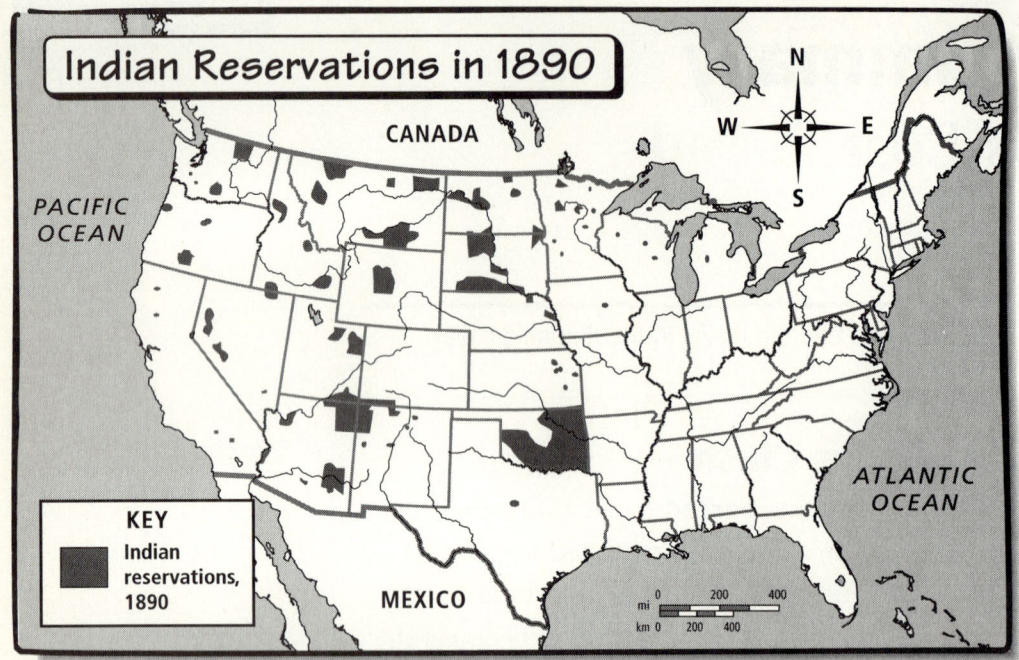

Policies That Changed Indian Life

The government wanted to make the Indians give up their nomadic life by moving them onto **reservations**. They believed that once there, the Indians would **assimilate** into the white culture.

During the 1870s, some Indians tried to resist this change. They were attacked by the U.S. Army. Many tribes moved to reservations. In 1887, the Dawes Act gave each Indian family 160 acres of reservation land to farm, and let white settlers move onto the remaining reservation land. Instead of helping the Indians assimilate, this law only made their life harder. Many did not know how to farm. Some went into debt and lost their land. Others sold it to whites for very little money. In the end, the Indians lost more than 60 percent of their land.

To encourage assimilation, Indian children were sent to special schools and given new names and new clothes. They were forced to speak English and taught about Christianity and the customs of white society. Many children were unhappy and many tried to run away. In spite of all their losses, the Plains Indians never lost pride in their heritage.

? Explain how the Dawes Act and government education programs were used as part of the assimilation policy.

reservation
(rĕz´ər-vā´shən)
land set aside for American Indians that was off-limits to white settlers

assimilate
(ə-sĭm´ə-lāt´)
to adopt the mainstream culture and give up one's own beliefs and culture

Name: _____ Date: _____

CHAPTER 14
Lesson 4 Preview
Resettlement of the Land

(*A More Perfect Union* pp. 427–432)

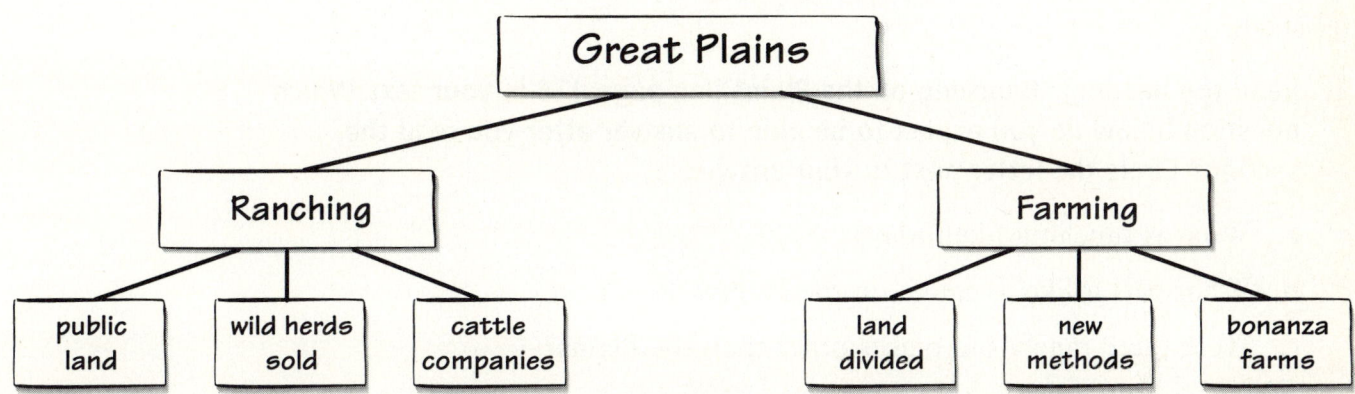

1. **Look at the graphic organizer above. Then read the following sentences and fill in the blanks.**

   New settlers to the Great Plains were either farmers or _____.

   Some ranching was done on _____ land. Large

   _____ were formed as the result of ranching. New

   _____ of farming helped create _____ farms,
   which were very profitable.

2. **Look at the picture of a branding iron and read the caption on page 428 in your text. Why was it necessary to mark cattle with the iron?**

   _____

   _____

   _____

Reading Support Resources   Lesson Preview • Chapter 14, Lesson 4 **207**

Name: _____ Date: _____

CHAPTER 14
Lesson 4 Reading Strategy
Resettlement of the Land

(*A More Perfect Union* pp. 427–432)

Self-Question This reading strategy helps you stay focused on what you read. Ask yourself questions before you read a section. Then read to see if you can find the answer to your questions.

1. Read the heading "Ranching on the Plains" on page 428 in your text. Which question below do you expect to be able to answer after you read the section? Circle the letter next to your answer.

   a. What is ranching like today?

   b. What was it like to ranch on the Plains?

   c. Were there ranches in places other than the Plains?

2. Read the section to see if the question you chose above was answered. If it was, write the answer to the question.

   _____

   _____

   _____

3. Read the red and blue headings and look at the photographs on pages 431 and 432. Then write two questions on the left side of the chart below. After you have read the section, fill in the right-hand column of the chart.

Questions	What I Learned
A.	
B.	

208 Chapter 14, Lesson 4 • Reading Strategy   Reading Support Resources

CHAPTER 14

Lesson 4 Summary
Resettlement of the Land

(*A More Perfect Union* pp. 427–432)

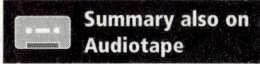

Thinking Focus: In what ways did ranching and farming transform the American West?

Ranching on the Plains

The **Homestead** Act of 1862 allowed settlers to claim 160 acres of land, build a house, and work the land for five years. If a homesteader did all of these things, he became the owner of the land. Some homesteaders farmed their land. Others chose cattle ranching.

Thousands of wild cattle roamed the Plains. Over time, ranchers brought in cattle from Britain that were better to eat. Each steer of this type needed 15 acres of grazing land. Ranchers did not own enough land, so they shared government-owned public land with other ranchers.

At roundup time, all the cattle were brought together and branded with the mark of each rancher. The cattle were then sold. New methods of packing and refrigeration helped ranchers send their beef to the East. The growing railroad network delivered the beef faster. Cattle ranching became a big business. Businessmen from the East, England, and Scotland soon organized their own cattle companies.

By the 1890s, ranching was no longer a good business. New barbed wire fences limited where the cows could graze. Ranchers had to rent or buy land that had once been free. Two hard winters killed many cows and the price of beef fell.

[?] How did barbed wire change ranching?

homestead
(hōm´stĕd´)
to file a claim for land, build a house, and work the land for five years

Summary continues on next page

Resettlement of the Land *(Lesson 4 Summary continued)*

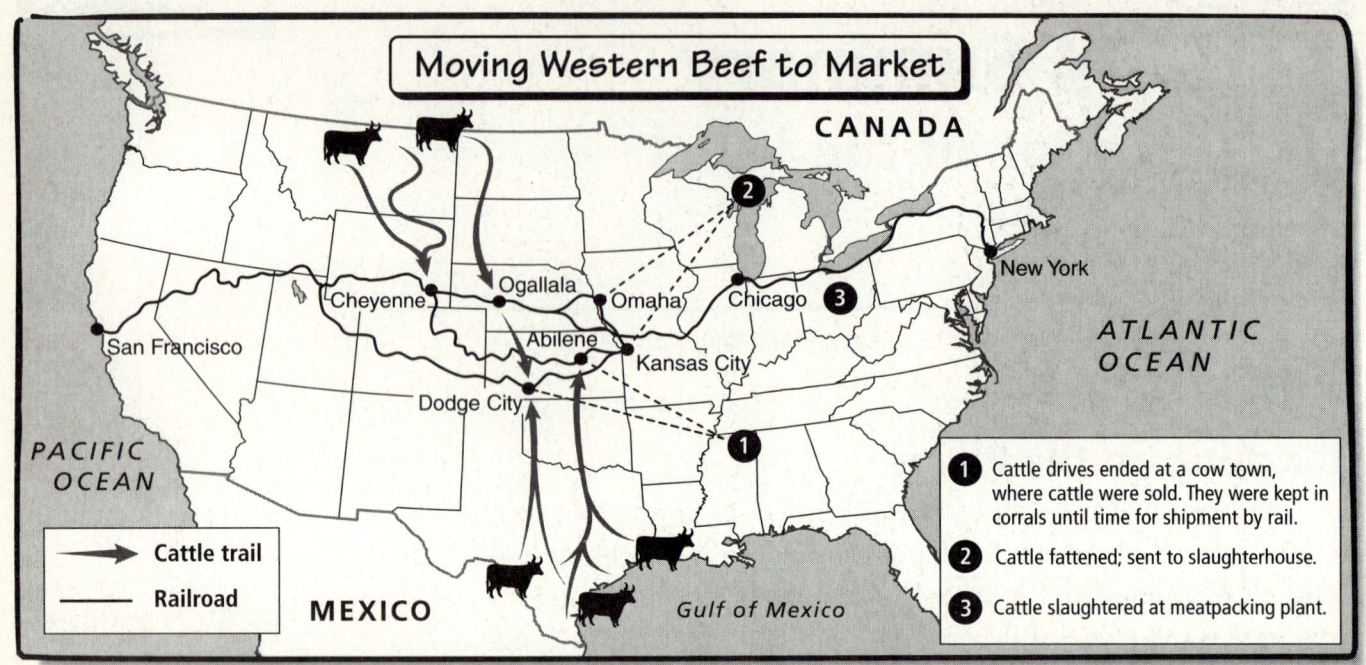

Farming on the Plains

Good railroads and the Homestead Act brought many people to the Plains. One group that came was recently freed African Americans from the South. By 1900, approximately 500,000 new families had arrived. They had to quickly build a shelter and find water.

The climate was very dry in the Plains. Homesteaders had to break up the soil so they could plant crops. They also had to use special techniques called dry farming. This meant planting only half of the fields each year to save the moisture in the other half. Fields were plowed very deeply. Farmers planted fewer seeds per acre. They planted crops like wheat, which grew well in the Plains climate. The homesteaders also built windmills to pump water up from deep under the ground. Farmers needed all these methods, and good luck, to succeed. Others became successful by starting farming projects with big companies that used new technology.

Not all homesteaders succeeded. Many did not have enough money to buy machinery, seed, and livestock. They had to borrow money and fell into debt. Property taxes increased and put homesteaders further into debt. Some had to sell their farms to pay the bills.

? What methods did farmers use to grow crops successfully on the Great Plains?

Use with *A More Perfect Union* Pages 440–469

Chapter Overview
Industry and Workers

Fill in the blank spaces below with information from the chapter.

Industrial America, 1850-1920

Growth of Industry
- new inventions
- capital
- _____

Growth of Cities
- industry
- steel
- _____
- jobs

America Changes

_____
- mass production
- low wages, long hours
- labor unions

Immigration
- hardships
- _____
- contributions

CHAPTER 15

Lesson 1 Preview
Building the American Dream

(*A More Perfect Union* pp. 442–446)

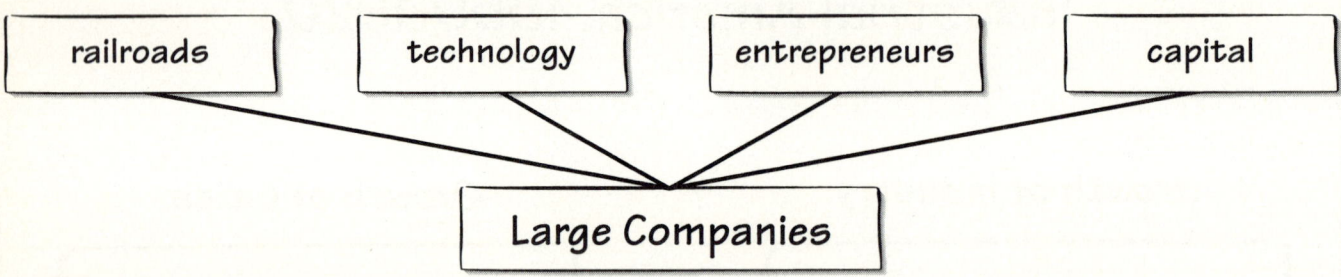

1. Look at the graphic organizer above. Use the information to fill in the blanks below.

   In the late 1800s, many new large companies formed as a result of the building of _____ and the development of technology. The dreams and commitment of people in business, or _____, and the investment of wealth, or capital, also contributed to the development of large companies.

2. Look at the photographs of Alexander Graham Bell's first telephones on page 443 and read the captions. Then answer the following questions:

   a. In what year was the first New York to Chicago telephone connection made? _____

   b. How might the invention of the telephone have made it easier to do business?

   _____
   _____
   _____
   _____

Name: _____ Date: _____

CHAPTER 15
Lesson 1 Reading Strategy
Building the American Dream

(*A More Perfect Union* pp. 442–446)

Finding the Main Idea This reading strategy helps you organize and remember what you read. When you finish a selection, jot down the main idea and its supporting details.

1. Read the section "Amazing Inventions" on pages 443–444. Which sentence below best expresses the main idea of the selection? Circle the letter next to the best answer.

    a. Thomas Alva Edison invented the first electric light.

    b. The linotype machine speeded up the production of newspapers and magazines.

    c. Many new inventions became part of daily life between the years 1870 and 1920.

2. Read the section "The Economy Transformed" on page 445. Then fill in the chart below with at least two details from the section.

Main Idea	Supporting Details
Entrepreneurs built factories and businesses that helped turn the United States into a major industrial nation.	

3. Read the section "Realizing the American Dream." Write the main idea in the space below.

    _____

4. Now write down three details that support the main idea of the section.

    _____
    _____
    _____

Reading Support Resources   Reading Strategy • Chapter 15, Lesson 1   **213**

CHAPTER 15
Lesson 1 Summary
Building the American Dream

(*A More Perfect Union* pp. 442–446)

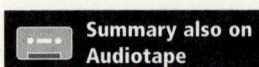

Thinking Focus: What caused the massive economic growth that occurred in the United States following the Civil War?

Amazing Inventions

Many new machines were invented in America between 1870 and 1920. One great inventor was Thomas Alva Edison. He made the first practical electric light. Electric lights replaced oil and gas lamps. Electric lights made factories, homes, and the streets safer places in which to live and work. Alexander Graham Bell was another inventor who lived during this time. He invented the telephone. Businesses wanted to have telephones because communication could be faster and easier. Other important inventions developed at this time include the typewriter, the sewing machine, and the linotype machine. The linotype set type for printing books, newspapers, and magazines.

[?] How did Edison's and Bell's inventions change American industry?

The Economy Transformed

I.M. Singer did not invent the sewing machine. But he made it better. He used good manufacturing and business ideas to make and sell his machines. This helped him to build a huge company. Singer was an **entrepreneur**. The period from 1870 to 1920 was a great time for entrepreneurs. Many borrowed **capital** to start companies. J. Pierpont Morgan became a wealthy banker. He loaned money to other entrepreneurs. They paid back the loans with interest. Morgan made high **profits** famous. Some entrepreneurs combined smaller companies into much larger companies that made a lot of money. John D. Rockefeller and Cornelius Vanderbilt were other famous entrepreneurs. Rockefeller made a fortune in the oil industry. Vanderbilt became rich in the railroad industry.

[?] Explain how early entrepreneurs operated in the business world.

entrepreneur
(ŏn'trə-prə-nûr')
a person who organizes a new business and takes the financial risk

capital
(kăp'ĭ-tl)
money or property invested to produce more money

profit
(prŏf'ĭt)
the money earned from a business after expenses have been paid

Summary continues on next page

Building the American Dream *(Lesson 1 Summary continued)*

Realizing the American Dream

Many of the successful entrepreneurs were examples of "the American Dream." This was an idea that poor people could become rich through hard work, good behavior, and a bit of luck. Author Horatio Alger wrote many books with this theme. One example of the American Dream was Andrew Carnegie. He came from Scotland and began to work in America at the age of 12. Carnegie was ambitious and smart. He became wealthy when he was a young man. Carnegie began to use a new furnace to make steel. This new way of making steel lowered prices and made steel more available. Steel became very important for railroads, buildings, bridges, and so on. Carnegie became one of the world's richest men. He also became a **philanthropist**. He helped to build libraries and support education.

> **philanthropist**
> (fĭ-lăn'thrō-pĭst)
> a person who gives money to public institutions

[?] What does the term "rags to riches" mean? Give an example of someone who "realized" the American Dream.

America Becomes an Industrial Nation

Thomas Edison	develops first practical electric light
Alexander Graham Bell	invents the telephone
I.M. Singer	improves the sewing machine; his company becomes the world's largest maker of a single product
Andrew Carnegie	develops the steel industry
John D. Rockefeller	develops the oil industry
Cornelius Vanderbilt	builds a railroad empire
J. Pierpont Morgan	becomes investment banker and financier

CHAPTER 15

Lesson 2 Preview
Moving into Industrial Cities

(*A More Perfect Union* pp. 447–453)

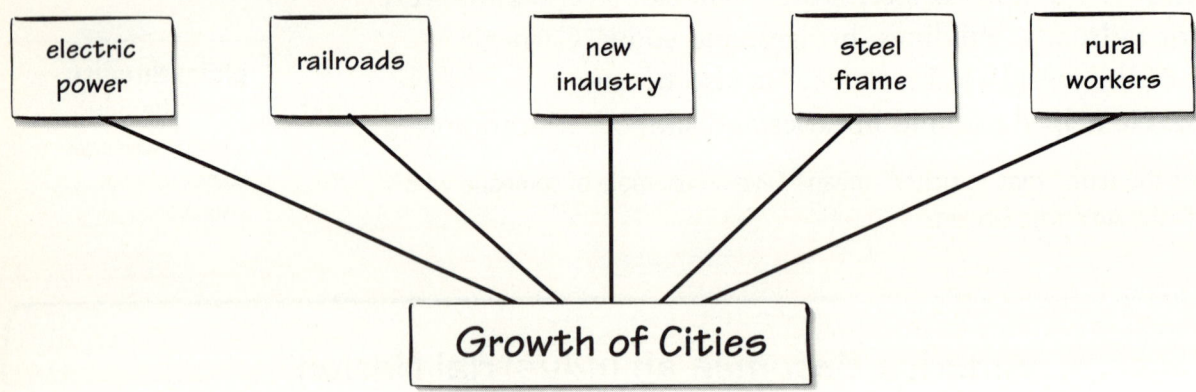

Factors that Led to the Growth of Cities

electric power • railroads • new industry • steel frame • rural workers → Growth of Cities

1. Look at the graphic organizer above. Then read the following sentences and fill in the blanks.

   Many factors contributed to the _____ of cities. With the development of _____, transportation of people and goods became faster and more efficient. New industries quickly developed when _____ power was used in factories. _____ moved to cities as they lost their farming jobs. Buildings and bridges became larger and stronger with the use of _____ construction.

2. Look at the graph on page 453 in your text. It shows the number of African Americans in Chicago between 1880 and 1920. Between what ten-year period did the black population increase the most?

   _____

Name: _____ Date: _____

CHAPTER 15
Lesson 2 Reading Strategy
Moving into Industrial Cities

(*A More Perfect Union* pp. 447–453)

Cause and Effect This reading strategy helps you understand events and why they occur. As you read, think about the factors that caused an event. Then think about what the effects of that event may be.

1. Read page 447. What was the effect of the Chicago fire? Circle the letter next to the best answer.

    a. The fire started in the O'Leary barn.

    b. Legend says that a cow may have kicked over a lantern.

    c. The rebuilding of Chicago revolutionized city architecture.

2. Read the section "Industrial Cities Develop." Write one effect of the growth of industry in cities in the space below.

   _____

3. Read the section "Rural People Migrate to Cities." Then decide if each statement below is a cause or an effect of the migration of rural people to cities. Write a *C* next to causes and an *E* next to effects.

    ___ Railroads reduced travel time.

    ___ People lost their farm jobs because of new farming inventions.

    ___ By 1910, a third of the people living in cities had come from the countryside.

4. Read the section "Southern Blacks Move North." Then fill in the chart below.

Cause	Effect
	Black Americans learned trade-related skills and took courses in teaching.
There were many crop failures in the South in 1919–1920.	
A growing need for factory workers developed in industrial cities.	

Reading Support Resources   Reading Strategy • Chapter 15, Lesson 2   **217**

CHAPTER 15
Lesson 2 Summary
Moving into Industrial Cities

(*A More Perfect Union* pp. 447–453)

Summary also on Audiotape

Thinking Focus: How did industrial development and the growth of cities change American life during the late 1800s and early 1900s?

Industrial Cities Develop

Between 1850 and 1900, America was changing to an **urban society**. New sources of power such as oil and electricity helped cities grow. So did the railroad system.

Cleveland, Ohio, became an industrial center because trains could bring raw materials to the factories and take away finished products to sell. Some cities specialized in one product. Cleveland built locomotives, Pittsburgh made steel, Minneapolis processed flour, and Memphis made cottonseed oil. Chicago became the center of railroad traffic because of its location in the center of the country.

As cities grew crowded, space became more valuable. Builders began to use steel frames to make stronger and taller buildings. The first skyscraper with a metal frame was built in 1884 in Chicago. Steel frames also made longer, stronger bridges possible. These new bridges could hold trains and other traffic.

? How did the new uses of steel change ways of constructing buildings? How did such changes aid transportation?

urban society
(ûr´ bən sə-sī´ ĭtē)
a way of life based on living in cities

Rural People Migrate to Cities

Cities grew as people from rural areas moved to urban areas looking for jobs. New machinery had taken over many farming jobs, and fewer workers were needed. Large businesses had also often driven small rural companies out of business. Railroads had made travel fast and cheap. So it was easy for people to take the train to the cities where they could look for work.

? What led people living on farms and in small towns to move to cities?

Summary continues on next page

Moving into Industrial Cities *(Lesson 2 Summary continued)*

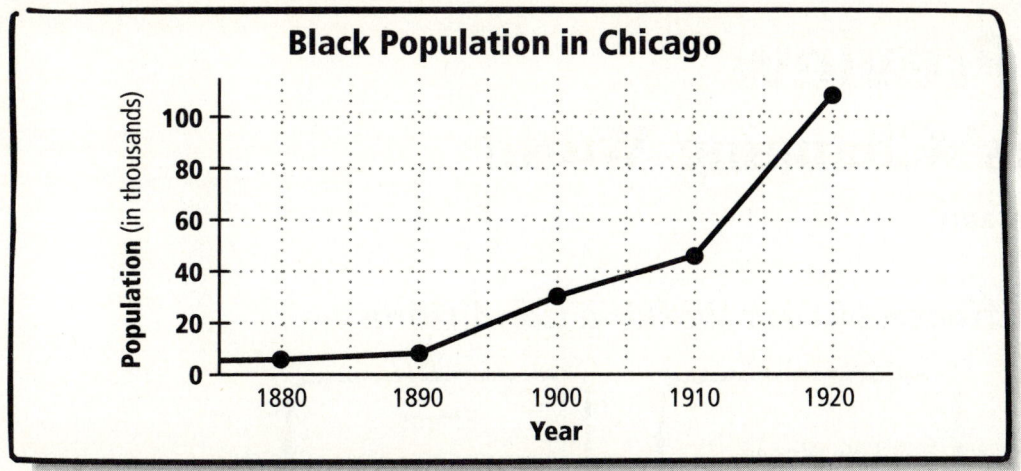

Southern Blacks Move North

Many black Americans from the South moved to northern cities looking for work. They also left to get away from bad treatment by whites. But most blacks still lived in the South.

In 1881, Booker T. Washington started the Tuskegee Institute. This was a school where African Americans could learn trade skills or how to become a teacher. Washington believed that blacks needed good jobs to make their lives better.

Another large wave of black Americans moved to northern cities during World War I. Although many found a better life in the North, some Southern blacks found the change in lifestyle difficult. Organizations such as churches and the National Urban League helped them fit in more easily. They helped those new to the city find housing, and they provided information about jobs and training.

? How did black communities help people adjust to city life?

Name: _____   Date: _____

CHAPTER 15

Lesson 3 Preview
The Workers' Changing World

(*A More Perfect Union* pp. 455–461)

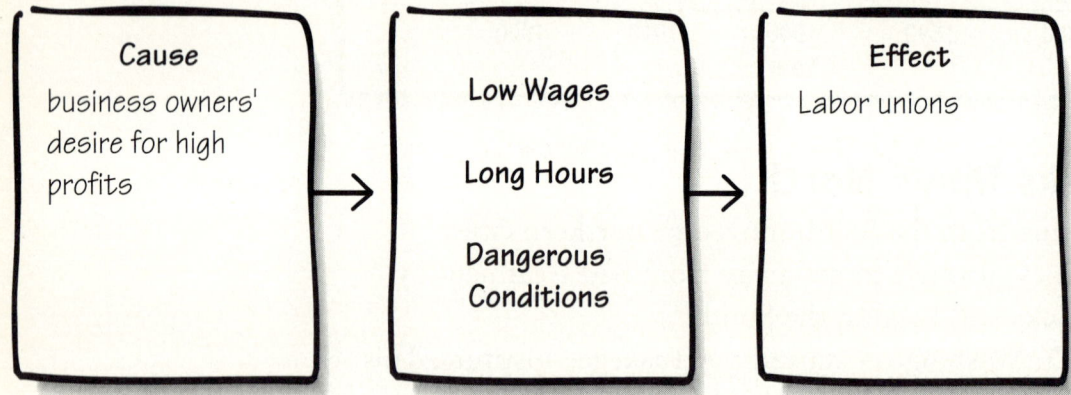

Causes and Effects of Poor Working Conditions

Cause: business owners' desire for high profits → Low Wages, Long Hours, Dangerous Conditions → Effect: Labor unions

1. Look at the graphic organizer above. Then read the following sentences and fill in the blanks.

   a. Low wages, long hours, and dangerous conditions were the result of business _____.

   b. In order to overcome unacceptable working conditions, workers formed _____.

2. Look at the picture on page 457 in your text and read its caption. Do you think young children should work in factories? Explain your answer.

   _____
   _____
   _____
   _____
   _____

Name: _____   Date: _____

CHAPTER 15
Lesson 3 Reading Strategy
The Workers' Changing World

(*A More Perfect Union* pp. 455–461)

Using the Visuals This reading strategy helps you use photographs, maps, charts, and illustrations to help you understand what you read. As you read, be sure to study the visuals and carefully read the captions.

1. Look at the picture on page 455 and read the caption. What can you learn from the picture and caption? Circle the letter next to the best answer.

    a. The factory was in Germany.

    b. Factory workers wore uniforms.

    c. Factory work was not just for men.

2. Look at the picture on page 457 and read the caption. What does the picture tell you about working conditions in the factory? Circle the letter next to the best answer.

    a. There were rules against child labor.

    b. Children worked in factories under dangerous conditions.

    c. Protective clothing was required.

3. Look at the statements below. Then look for a picture in the lesson that supports each of the statements. Write the page number of the picture in the blank space.

    ___ Some factory workers lived in special towns that surrounded the factory in which they worked.

    ___ Both men and women participated in strikes.

    ___ Strikes sometimes were very difficult to settle.

4. Choose one of the pictures in the lesson. Write a sentence explaining what that picture tells you about factory workers in the early 1900s.

    _____

    _____

Reading Support Resources   Reading Strategy • Chapter 15, Lesson 3 **221**

CHAPTER 15
Lesson 3 Summary
The Workers' Changing World

(*A More Perfect Union* pp. 455–461)

Thinking Focus: How did changes in production affect the way in which Americans lived and worked during the late 1800s and early 1900s?

Production Speeds Up

In 1913–1914, Henry Ford began to use the first **assembly line** to make cars. This system was later used in other industries. In it, each worker did the same task over and over. Work was often boring and low paying, so workers changed jobs often. Setting up tasks in this logical order helped to make products faster and cheaper. This led to mass production, or making many of the same item. Mass production also made it possible for factory owners to order large amounts of raw materials at a lower price. Machinery could also be used over and over. All of this helped owners make a bigger profit.

assembly line
(ə-sĕm´ blē līn)
manufacturing method that carries parts past workers on a moving belt so that each piece of work can be carried out by the same worker over and over

[?] Explain how the assembly line changed production.

The Workers Struggle

Factories often paid low wages. Workers were on the job 10 to 12 hours a day, six days a week. The high cost of rent left little money for food, clothing, or emergencies. Workers were afraid of losing their jobs, and managers and owners took advantage of them. Workers sometimes used dangerous machinery and poisonous materials without any protection. There was no help for the unemployed, the sick, or those hurt on the job. A few businesses set up towns where workers lived in houses and shopped in stores owned by the company.

[?] What factors contributed to the poor working conditions in most industries?

Summary continues on next page

The Workers' Changing World *(Lesson 3 Summary continued)*

Unions Develop

Workers began to complain about their poor working conditions. But companies ignored them. Workers then joined together in **labor unions**. As a group, they could go on **strike** until the company met their demands.

The first really successful union was the American Federation of Labor (AFL). It was set up in 1886 by Samuel Gompers. He believed in using strikes and boycotts. A boycott meant that union members would not buy or use a company's products until the union's demands were met.

[?] How did workers use strikes and boycotts to change their working conditions?

Unions Meet Opposition

Companies did not like organized labor and the power it had to strike. In 1886, strikers at Chicago's McCormick Harvester Company fought with strike breakers, who were workers hired to take their place. The company called in the police. In the end, several policemen and workers were killed, and many were injured. The unions were blamed for the violence.

Eight years later, AFL workers at a Pennsylvania steel factory asked for a raise. The company locked them out of the factory. The National Guard was called in to protect the strikebreakers. Finally the union had to give up.

In 1894, another famous strike took place in the company town of Pullman, Illinois, where workers made railway cars. When business slowed down, the company cut workers' wages. But they didn't lower their rent or prices at the company store. Workers went on strike. Pullman shut down the plant. Railroad workers who agreed with the strikers would not handle Pullman railroad cars. Finally, federal courts ordered the strike to end because it was upsetting trade and the U.S. mails.

[?] What methods were used in the Pullman and Homestead strikes to stop unions from influencing workers?

---

labor union
(lā´ bər yōōn´yən)
an organization of workers formed to help them get the wages and working conditions that they want

strike
(strīk)
a period of time during which workers stop working until their demands are met by their employers

Name: _____ Date: _____

CHAPTER 15

Lesson 4 Preview
Destination: America

(*A More Perfect Union* pp. 462–467)

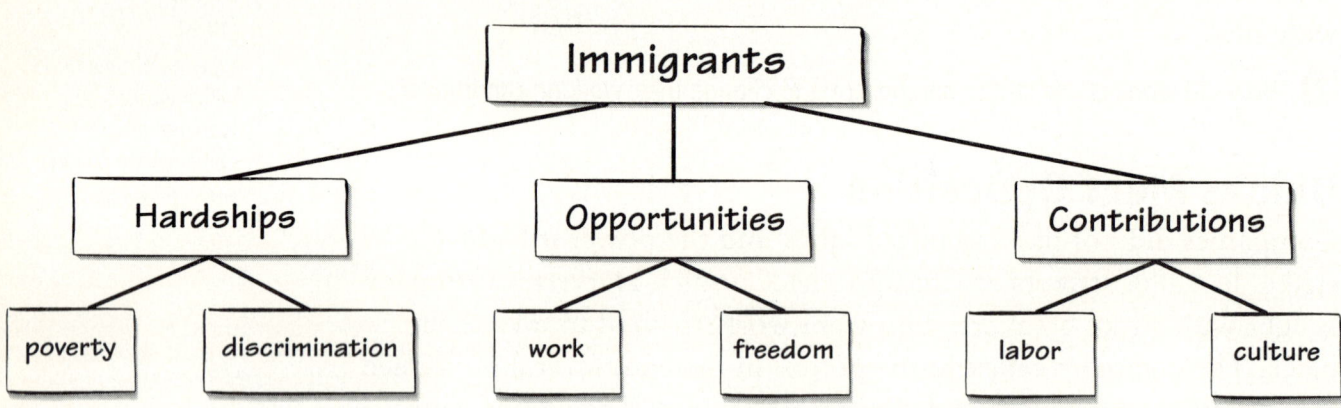

1. **Look at the graphic organizer above. Then read and answer the following questions.**

   a. What hardships did immigrants face when they arrived in America?
   _____
   _____

   b. What opportunities were immigrants looking for when they came to America?
   _____
   _____

   c. What contributions did immigrants make to America?
   _____
   _____

2. **Look at the graph on page 467 in your text. Which city had about 750 thousand (.75 million) immigrants? Which city had about 250 thousand (.25 million) immigrants?**
   _____
   _____

Name: _____ Date: _____

CHAPTER 15
Lesson 4 Reading Strategy
Destination: America

(*A More Perfect Union* pp. 462–467)

Self-Question This reading strategy helps you stay focused on what you read. Ask yourself questions before you read a section. Then read to see if you can find the answer to your questions.

1. Read the red and blue headings on pages 462 and 463 and study the map on page 463. Which question below do you think you will be able to answer after you read the section?

    a. What countries did new immigrants come from in the late 1800s and early 1900s?

    b. How many immigrants came to the United States in the 1970s?

    c. How many people leave the United States to live in other countries each year?

2. Write an additional question that you expect to be able to answer after you read the section "Promise of America."

   _____

3. Read the red and blue headings on pages 466 and 467. Look at the pictures and read the captions. Then write two questions in the left-hand side of the chart below. After you read the section, fill in the right-hand side of the chart.

Questions	What I Learned

Reading Support Resources   Reading Strategy • Chapter 15, Lesson 3

CHAPTER 15
Lesson 4 Summary
Destination: America

(*A More Perfect Union* pp. 462–467)

Thinking Focus: How did the influx of immigrants during the late 1800s affect American society?

Promise of America

More than 22 million immigrants came to the United States between 1860 and 1910. The first groups were mostly from Britain, Ireland, Germany, and Scandinavia. Later, people came from southern and eastern Europe. Many came to escape poverty. Others wanted to get away from being punished because of their religion or politics. Some wanted just to make money and go back home. But most came to stay. Immigration was encouraged by many states and companies.

Thousands of immigrants came to the West Coast from Japan, China, and the Philippines. Some of the Chinese came for the gold rush in California in 1849. Others followed to work on the railroads. People from southern China and Japan were getting away from the overpopulation and economic problems in their countries.

? What groups immigrated to America during the mid- to late 1800s?

Immigrants Become Americans

Many Americans did not want immigrants to come to this country to work. They did not like the immigrants' different customs, ways of dressing, and language. Immigrants had trouble with English. They often had to take the most difficult, dirty, underpaid jobs. It was also hard for immigrants to change their way of life. For example, many Jewish immigrants felt that they had to give up their traditions and identity to fit into American culture.

Summary continues on next page

Destination: America *(Lesson 4 Summary continued)*

For most immigrants, though, life in the United States was better than the life they had left behind. Many have made great contributions to the United States. Their work has helped this country to grow and be strong. Many immigrants such as Andrew Carnegie, Samuel Gompers, and Alexander Graham Bell changed industry forever. The food, culture, music, and art of immigrants have become a part of life in the United States.

? What problems did immigrants face in becoming Americans?

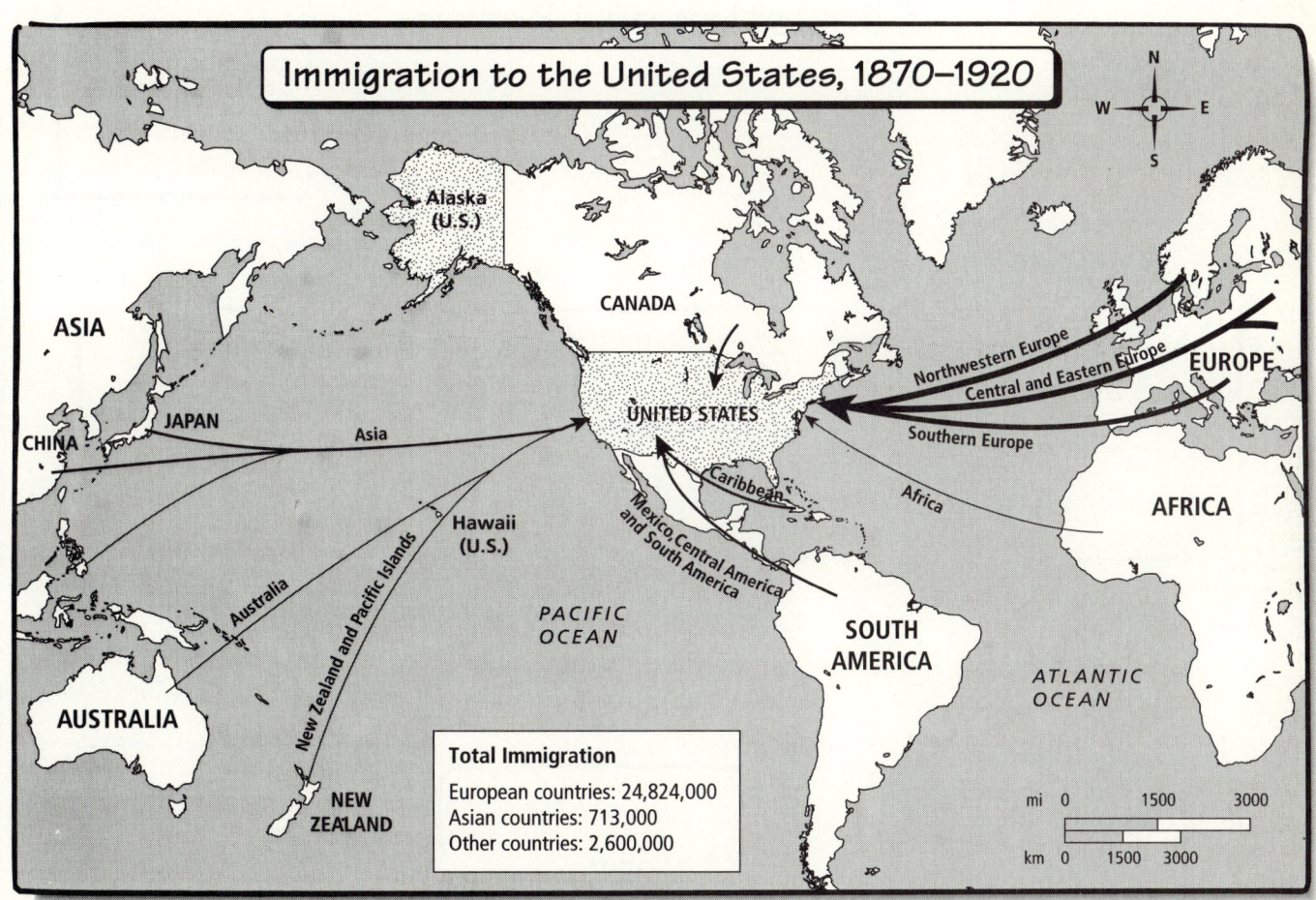

Use with *A More Perfect Union* Pages 470–495

Chapter Overview
The Gilded Age

Fill in the blank spaces below with information from the chapter.

When: 1868–1898

Who: robber barons, government officials, Mugwumps, Populists

Corruption and Reform

- [ ]
- Corruption in Business and Government
- [ ]

↓

Reform

- civil services replaces _____
- _____
- trusts and monopolies controlled
- Populist party

Name: _____ Date: _____

CHAPTER 16
Lesson 1 Preview
The Politics of Corruption

(*A More Perfect Union* pp. 472–476)

Dishonesty in Business and Government

- Robber Barons: offered bribes, bought votes
- Government Fraud: Union Pacific Credit Mobilier, cheated Indians
- Big City Politics: patronage, graft

1. Look at the graphic organizer above. Then read and answer the following questions:

   a. People who gained fortunes by illegal means were called "robber barons." What two corrupt, or dishonest, things did robber barons do?
   _____
   _____

   b. Name one group of Americans who were affected by government fraud.
   _____

   c. What two corrupt things did big city officials do?
   _____
   _____

2. Look at the photograph at the bottom of page 473 in your text. Compare it to the photograph at the bottom of page 475. How does the lifestyle of the people on page 473 compare with the lifestyle of the people on page 475? Write your answer below.
   _____
   _____
   _____
   _____

Reading Support Resources   Lesson Preview • Chapter 16, Lesson 1   **229**

CHAPTER 16

Lesson 1 Reading Strategy
The Politics of Corruption

(*A More Perfect Union* pp. 472–476)

Finding the Main Idea This reading strategy helps you organize and remember what you read. When you finish a selection, jot down the main idea and its supporting details.

1. Read the section "Big Business Attempts to Influence Politics." Which sentence below best expresses the main idea of the section? Circle the letter next to the best answer.

   a. During and after the Civil War, rich and powerful men made fortunes and tried to influence politics.

   b. After the Civil War, wealthy people built mansions and had expensive parties.

   c. People who gained fortunes illegally were called "robber barons."

2. Read the section "Scandals Plague Grant's Presidency." Which sentence below best expresses the main idea of the section? Circle the letter next to the best answer.

   a. During Grant's presidency, government officials were involved in fraud with railroad companies and scandals involving kickbacks.

   b. President Grant was honest, but people around him were not.

   c. A New York newspaper reported the Union Pacific Railroad fraud.

3. Write a detail about the scandals during Grant's presidency.

   _____

4. Read the section "Machine Politics Develop" on pages 475–476. Then fill in the chart below.

Main Idea	Supporting Details

CHAPTER 16

Lesson 1 Summary
The Politics of Corruption

(*A More Perfect Union* pp. 472–476)

Thinking Focus: What were some of the characteristics of American politics in the decades following the Civil War?

Big Business Attempts to Influence Politics

During the Civil War, many business leaders charged the government very high prices for war materials. They were able to do this because the government badly needed those materials. They kept overcharging, even after the war. Those who made a lot of money by being dishonest were called "robber barons." Men such as James Fisk, Jay Gould, and John D. Rockefeller bribed or threatened judges and members of Congress to write and explain laws that would support their business's needs. The robber barons were so rich that they showed off their wealth in extreme ways. For example, the average worker at that time earned about $10 a week. But a party thrown by a robber baron could cost as much as $200,000! Many Americans were upset by this situation and began to speak out against it. This period from about 1870 to 1900 was called the "Gilded Age."

How did business influence politics during the Gilded Age?

Scandals Plague Grant's Presidency

Ulysses S. Grant was elected President in 1868. He was an honest man, but he did not know much about politics. He was surrounded by dishonest and corrupt people who took advantage of their positions to cheat and steal. During the 1872 Credit Mobilier scandal, a group of railroad managers invented a company that didn't exist. They bribed Congressmen to put money aside for it. Then the managers took the all the money. There were other scandals, too. In 1873, the Secretary of War received **kickbacks** for helping to cheat some American

kickback
(kĭk′ băk′)
a payment made to a person in return for political or business favors

Summary continues on next page

Indians. President Grant's personal secretary blackmailed some whiskey makers who had not paid taxes. In another scandal, Congress voted itself a huge pay raise. People were so upset by this that Congress had to give up the raise.

? In what ways did members of Grant's administration use their positions for their personal gain?

Machine Politics Develop

While Grant was president, cities were growing very quickly. Many immigrants were moving to cities. They soon became crowded, dirty and dangerous to live in. City governments did not have money for water, fire, and police services. They also did not have leaders or organizations to take care of these things. Some people took advantage of this situation to gain political power for themselves. Men who had grown up in city neighborhoods offered food, jobs, and loans to people to get their votes. They also gave political favors, such as work contracts, in exchange for money or votes. This system is called **patronage**. This system grew into large **political machines**. Many corrupt leaders became very powerful. They rewarded themselves with **graft**. Perhaps the most famous political boss was William Marcy Tweed of New York City. He controlled the city's entire Democratic political machine. The headquarters of his operation was Tammany Hall. He and his friends stole about $200 million from the city between 1868 and 1871. He was arrested. But the machine continued to operate.

? In what sense were machine politics a direct response to conditions in American cities during the Gilded Age?

patronage
(pā′ trə-nĭj)
the practice of giving out government jobs in return for political support

political machine
(pə-lĭt′ ĭ-kəl mə-shēn′)
a powerful, tightly run political organization that controlled many American cities in the late 1800s and early 1900s

graft
(grăft)
money gained by elected or appointed officials through dishonest or illegal means

Growth of Political Bosses

Name: _____ Date: _____

CHAPTER 16
Lesson 2 Preview
The Reforming Impulse

(*A More Perfect Union* pp. 477–485)

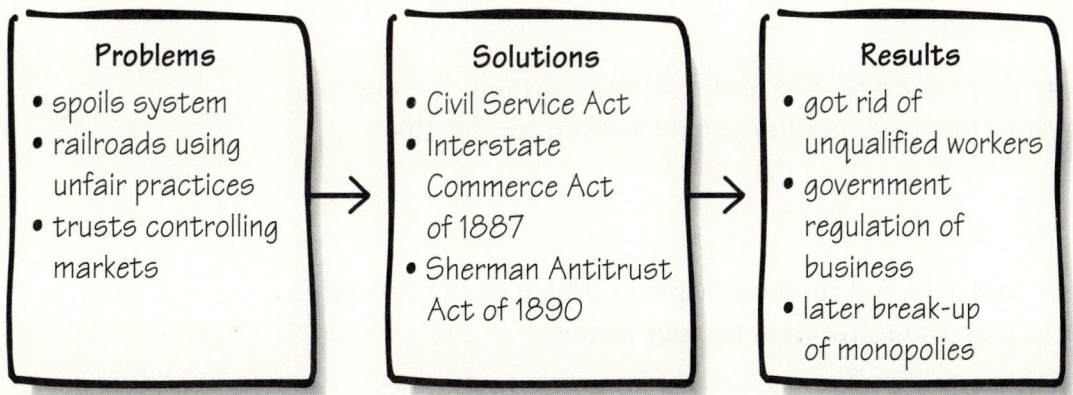

Laws that Solved Problems

Problems
- spoils system
- railroads using unfair practices
- trusts controlling markets

Solutions
- Civil Service Act
- Interstate Commerce Act of 1887
- Sherman Antitrust Act of 1890

Results
- got rid of unqualified workers
- government regulation of business
- later break-up of monopolies

1. **Look at the graphic organizer above to fill in the blanks below.**

    a. Two problems in society in the late 1800s were _____ and _____.

    b. As a result of laws passed, the government got rid of _____, began regulating _____, and later broke up _____.

2. **Look through lesson 2 on pages 477–485. Read the main section titles. Fill in the blanks below to list the main section titles.**

    The _____ Seek Reform

    Attacking the _____ System

    Regulating the _____

    _____ the Trusts

Name: _____   Date: _____

CHAPTER 16
Lesson 2 Reading Strategy
The Reforming Impulse

(*A More Perfect Union* pp. 477–485)

Using the Visuals This reading strategy helps you use photographs, maps, charts, and illustrations to help you understand what you read. As you read, be sure to study the visuals and carefully read the captions.

1. Look at the pictures on pages 478–479 and read the captions. In what two years did both Grover Cleveland and Benjamin Harrison run for the presidency?

   _____

2. Study the graph on page 481 and read the caption. Which of the following statements is true? Circle the letter next to your answer.

   a. Most of the nation's railroads were owned by small companies.
   b. The Pennsylvania Group owned 27,000 miles of railroad.
   c. Six companies owned more than half of the nation's railroads.

3. Study the graph on page 485 and read the caption. Which of the following statements is true? Circle the letter next to the best answer.

   a. American Hide and Leather owned 70 percent of the leather products industry.
   b. Western Union controlled 100 percent of the telegraph industry.
   c. American Sugar Refining Company and American Hide and Leather were both owned by the same person.

4. Using only the pictures and captions in the lesson, find answers to the questions listed in the chart below.

Question	Answer
Before the 1890s, why did drawings and engravings appear in newspapers?	
Who wrote a book exposing the unfair practices of the Standard Oil Company?	
What two animals became popular symbols for the Democratic and Republican parties?	

CHAPTER 16

Lesson 2 Summary
The Reforming Impulse

(*A More Perfect Union* pp. 477–485)

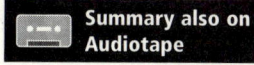

Thinking Focus: What political and business practices did reformers in the 1870s and 1880s want to change? Why?

The Mugwumps Seek Reform

In the late 1800s, there was little conflict or activity in politics. The government was filled with unqualified people who had gotten their jobs in return for political support. People began to demand reform of this spoils system. Among them was a group of powerful and well-educated Republicans who called themselves **Mugwumps**. They also wanted to reduce the protective tariff, which was a tax on imported items.

[?] Who were the Mugwumps and what features of the American political system did they seek to reform?

Attacking the Spoils System

Mugwumps and other reformers wanted to set up a **civil service** system. In this system, people who wanted to work for the government would have to take a test to prove they were qualified. Jobs would no longer be given in return for political favors or votes. The reformers also wanted to try to keep jobs away from immigrants and political party workers. One of the worst examples of the spoils system was the New York Customs House. Senator Roscoe Conkling ran it to finance his own political machine. President Rutherford B. Hayes found out that 200 people who were on the Customs House payroll did no work for it. In 1883, Congress passed the Civil Service Act. Now, only those who passed the civil service test could be hired. It also became illegal to fire civil service workers because of their political views.

[?] Why did reformers want to replace the spoils system with a civil service?

Mugwumps
(mŭg´ wŭmps´)
reformers in the Republican Party who wanted to get rid of government corruption during the Gilded Age

civil service
(sĭv´əl sûr´ vĭs)
jobs in government that are awarded on the basis of merit

Summary continues on next page

Regulating the Railroads

After the Civil War, the government gave land and money to railroad companies to help them connect the different regions of the country. The railroads took advantage of this special treatment. They bribed and threatened politicians to let them do what they wanted. Large railroads got rid of competitors, overcharged farmers, and gave large shippers secret discounts. Although state laws were passed against these unfair practices, many people did not want government to **regulate** the railroads. They believed such regulations went against the Fifth Amendment protection of private property. Even so, in 1887, Congress passed the Interstate Commerce Act. Although the Supreme Court made the law weaker, the Interstate Commerce Act was important. It gave the federal government the right to regulate business.

[?] For what reasons did the big railroad companies become targets of reform?

Restraining the Trusts

Reformers also wanted to control the power of the industrial **monopolies** and **trusts**. Monopolies and trusts controlled the whole market for their products or services. They could set the price and quality of the products. As a result, people paid higher prices for poor quality goods and service.

John D. Rockefeller directed an oil monopoly. He then formed the Standard Oil Trust. This allowed him to control the whole oil industry. It was hard for the reformers to fight the trusts. Finally, Congress passed the Sherman Antitrust Act of 1890. Its purpose was to limit the power of trusts. But lawyers for the trusts were often able to get around the law. Like the Interstate Commerce Act, this law would be used later to limit the power of big companies.

[?] In what way did monopolies and trusts act against the best interests of the people?

---

regulate
(rĕg´ yə-lāt´)
to control or manage based on established rules

monopoly
(mē-nŏp´ ə-lē)
a company that completely controls the market for a particular product or service

trust
(trŭst)
a combination of companies formed by legal agreement to reduce competition

CHAPTER 16

Lesson 3 Preview
The Populist Revolt

(*A More Perfect Union* pp. 486–491)

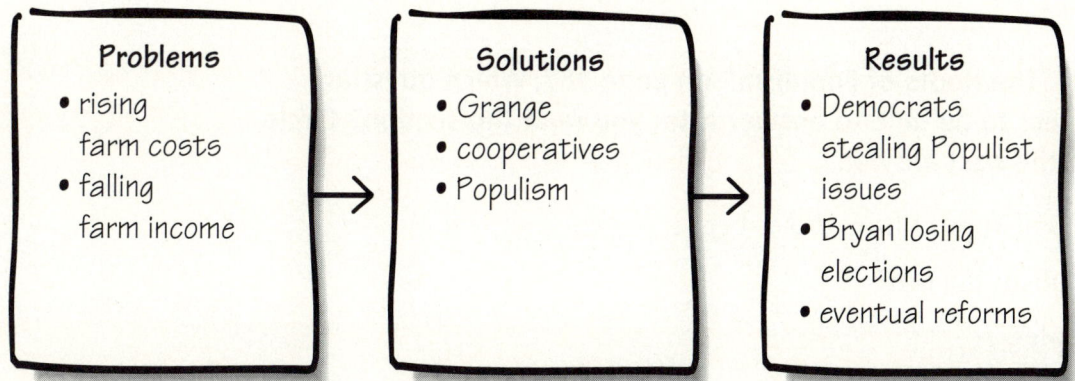

1. Look at the graphic organizer above. Then read the following sentences and fill in the blanks.

   Rising _____ and falling _____ were problems farmers faced in the 1890s. To solve these problems, farmers got together and organized the Grange movement. They also formed _____ to share farm machinery and shipping costs. In addition, a political movement called Populism represented farmers' interests. These solutions led to eventual _____.

2. Look at the map on page 491. What does the map show about the presidential election of 1896?

   _____
   _____
   _____

Reading Support Resources

Lesson Preview • **Chapter 16, Lesson 3** **237**

CHAPTER 16
Lesson 3 Reading Strategy
The Populist Revolt

(*A More Perfect Union* pp. 486–491)

Self-Question This reading strategy helps you stay focused on what you read. Ask yourself questions before you read a section. Then read to see if you can find the answer to your questions.

1. Read the heading "The Roots of Populism" on page 487. Which question below do you expect to be able to answer after you read the section? Circle the letter next to the best answer.

    a. What was Populism and how did it begin?

    b. Why did Populism die out?

    c. What is a revolt?

2. Read the red heading on page 489 and the blue headings that follow on pages 489 and 490. Write a question that you expect to be able to answer after you read the section.

    _____

3. Look at the map on page 491. Which question below can you answer by looking at the map? Circle the letter next to the best answer.

    a. Which candidate carried the South?

    b. Which candidate carried the New Mexico territory?

    c. Why did McKinley carry Kentucky?

4. Before you read the lesson, write two questions on the left-hand side of the chart. After you read the lesson, fill in the right-hand column of the chart.

Questions	What I Learned

CHAPTER 16
Lesson 3 Summary
The Populist Revolt
(*A More Perfect Union* pp. 486–491)

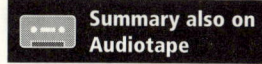

Thinking Focus: Why did American farmers decide to form their own political party in the 1890s?

The Roots of Populism

In the 1870s and 1880s, American farmers were in trouble. Their cost of doing business was going up and their profits were dropping. They had to pay property taxes. Railroads charged high prices to take farm products to markets. New, more efficient, and expensive farm machinery was developed. Most farmers had to borrow money, at high interest rates, to buy them. Although the machines helped farmers produce more food, prices fell because there was more food in the market than they could sell. Farmers slowly began to work together for change in a movement called **Populism**.

Farmers also believed that the goverment should circulate more paper money. The value of paper money depended on the amount of gold the government had. Bankers, however, believed in "hard money" that was backed by gold. The "hard money" policy became law in 1875. In 1878, farmers, laborers, and a few businessmen formed the Greenback-Labor Party to fight this policy. Farmers elected 14 members to Congress in 1878. Then they could change laws and policies that would help farmers.

❓ What economic and political factors led to the rise of the Populist movement?

Farmers Establish the Populist Party

Farmers set up **cooperatives** to save money on shipping and machinery. Many farmers also joined more radical groups called alliances to fight for higher prices and lower costs. In 1889, the two biggest alliances joined. They wanted to help farmers with such things as low-cost

Populism
(pŏp´ yə-lĭz´ əm)
a political movement that represented the interests of farmers in the 1890s

cooperative
(kō-ŏp´ ər-ə-tĭv)
an organization or association that is owned by those who use its facilities or services

Summary continues on next page

loans, regulation of the railroads, and an increase in the money supply. The new National Farmers' Alliance supported candidates who promised to help farmers. Once elected, however, many broke their promises. In 1892, the farmers set up the Populist Party. Their candidate for President lost, but others won—2 governors and 14 representatives in Congress.

? What measures did farmers take to lessen some of their economic hardships?

Populism Peaks and Fades

The failure of the economy gave the Populists a big boost. People began to think that Populism might work. The Democrats nominated William Jennings Bryan for President in 1896. He supported the Populist idea of issuing more silver coins to increase the money supply. Although the Populists supported Bryan, he kept away from them. He did not want other voters to think he was too radical. Bryan lost the election. The economy improved after the election, and in 1898, gold was discovered in Alaska. As a result, there was enough gold to back more paper money. Few people besides farmers had supported the Populists. All of these things led to the fall of the Populist Party.

? What factors contributed to the decline of the Populist Party?

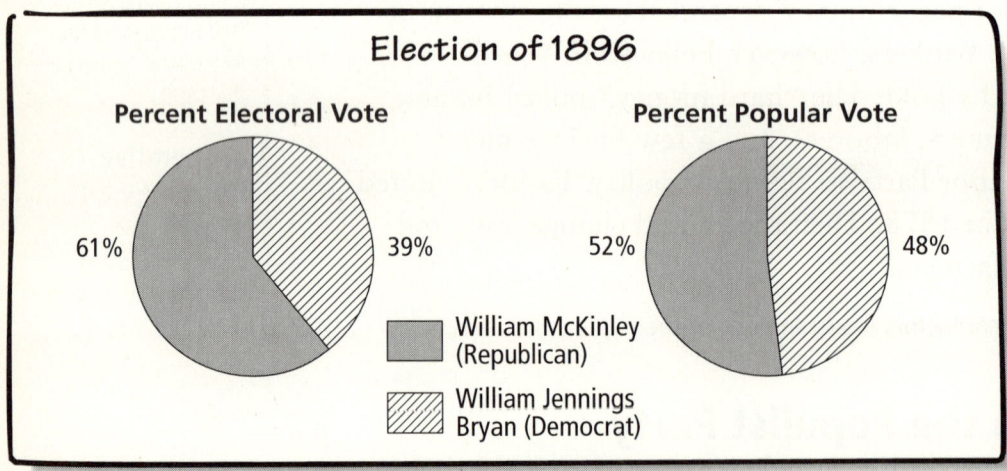

Use with *A More Perfect Union* Pages 496–525

Chapter Overview
The Reform Era

Fill in the blank spaces below with information from the chapter.

When: 1890–1920

Who: Progressives, muckrakers, reformers

Where: United States

An Era of Reform

Reform in Cities
- Progressives → settlement houses
- education
- city planning
- _____ → politics

Progressive Reform
- the "square deal"
- trust busting
- _____
- tariff and banking reform

_____
- Prohibition
- _____
- radicalism
- _____

Reading Support Resources

CHAPTER 17
Lesson 1 Preview
The Shame of the Cities

(*A More Perfect Union* pp. 498–506)

1. Look at the graphic organizer above. Muckrakers were journalists who wrote articles about social problems and government corruption. Progressivism was a nationwide reform movement. Which of the following effects was not a result of the work of muckrakers and Progressives? Circle the letter next to your answer.

   a. There was reform of city politics.

   b. There was reform in education.

   c. Settlement houses were built.

   d. Social problems increased.

2. Look at the pictures on pages 498 to 505 in your text and read the captions. Based on these pictures, write two or three sentences that describe some of the social problems that needed reform.

Name: _____   Date: _____

CHAPTER 17
Lesson 1 Reading Strategy
The Shame of the Cities

(*A More Perfect Union* pp. 498–506)

Sequence This reading strategy helps you follow what is happening in your reading. As you read, pay attention to dates and times, as well as to words such as before, finally, after, and then.

1. Read the section "A Time for Change." Put the events listed below in order by writing *1, 2,* and *3* in the blanks.

    ___ Jane Addams introduced the settlement house to the United States.

    ___ America had a laissez-faire policy toward government interference in business.

    ___ The Progressive movement got its name.

2. Read the section "Educational Reform." Which of the following conditions took place first? Circle the letter next to your choice.

    a. Schools emphasized learning by rote.

    b. Educational reforms took place.

    c. Businesses sent their employees to learn English.

3. Read the last two sections of the lesson, "City Planning" and "Reforming City Politics." Then fill out the chart to show the sequence of the main events.

Cause	Effect
First,	
Then,	
After that,	
Next,	
Finally,	

Reading Support Resources   Reading Strategy • **Chapter 17, Lesson 1**   **243**

CHAPTER 17

Lesson 1 Summary
The Shame of the Cities

(*A More Perfect Union* pp. 498–506)

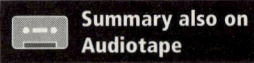

Thinking Focus: What caused the social problems and political corruption that were common features of American cities between 1890 and 1920?

A Time for Change

America always had a **laissez-faire** policy toward business. Businesses could make decisions and products without anyone checking on them. During a bad economic time in 1893, many companies raised prices and cut workers' pay, or wages. Working and living conditions were poor. The greed of businesses made people angry. They wanted society to change. Reformers joined a movement called **Progressivism**. Jane Addams, a reformer, began a settlement house in a poor Chicago neighborhood. She provided child care, education, and other services. Some journalists, called **muckrakers**, wrote about the unfair actions of businesses and monopolies, and the terrible conditions in the cities.

> What were the main social and economic conditions during the period 1890 to 1920 that inspired reformers?

Educational Reform

Schools in the 1800s required students to memorize their lessons. Students were not allowed to move around the classroom or talk to each other. Desks were bolted to the floor. Progressive reformers wanted schools to change. They wanted more people to get an education, including many of the immigrants who could not speak or write English. Progressives thought an education would "Americanize" them and help the immigrants to learn middle-class values. They also believed that businesses would benefit from having workers who could read and write English. Progressive educators were led by John Dewey. His ideas are still followed today. For example, he encouraged the idea of children learning by taking part in their lessons and through play.

> What features of 19th century American education did the Progressive movement reform?

laissez faire
(lĕs′ā fâr′)
a policy that opposes governmental regulation of industry or the economy

Progressivism
(prə-grĕs′ĭ-vĭz′əm)
a broad social, economic, and political reform movement that took place from about 1890 to 1920

muckraker
(mŭk′rāk′ər)
a journalist who tells others about political corruption and social problems

Summary continues on next page

The Shame of the Cities (Lesson 1 Summary continued)

City Planning

Most cities in the United States had not been planned. As a result, city life was horrible for many people. They lived in crowded **tenements** where poor conditions made life dangerous and unhealthy. Politicians either did not care about the conditions in the tenements, or could do little to change them. Progressives believed that cities could be pleasant and livable. They wanted **zoning laws** to make sure people didn't have to live near dirty factories. They wanted apartment buildings that were safe and had windows for air and light. In 1906, the Progressives formed an association to encourage cities to build public parks and playgrounds. They even wanted buildings in cities to be beautiful. This "city beautiful" movement inspired people such as Andrew Carnegie to help build large and beautiful buildings.

tenement
(tĕn′ə-mənt)
an apartment building that does not meet minimum standards of cleanliness, safety, and comfort

zoning law
(zōn′ĭng lô)
a law restricting areas of a city to a certain use, such as residential, commercial, or industrial

[?] In what ways did the Progressives believe that urban planning and zoning laws would help solve the "shame of the cities"?

Reforming City Politics

Poor city government often led to poor living conditions in most neighborhoods. Many cities were run by dishonest political bosses. These bosses were often not qualified to run the services that cities needed, such as fire and police protection. They were willing to trade favors for votes. Most of the immigrants living in cities did not speak English. They were willing to trade their votes for things such as food, jobs, or housing.

Progressive reformers changed the way cities were run. They got rid of the political bosses who ran small parts of the city and gave out favors. The reformers started city-wide elections. They elected small groups of people, called commissions, who had the right skills to run cities. Each commissioner was in charge of one department, such as the police department. Some commissions hired managers to run the city. These managers were professionals who had no political connections. Many American cities are run this way today.

[?] How did corrupt politicians increase the social and economic problems of the cities?

Name: _____ Date: _____

CHAPTER 17
Lesson 2 Preview
Progressive Reform

(*A More Perfect Union* pp. 507–512)

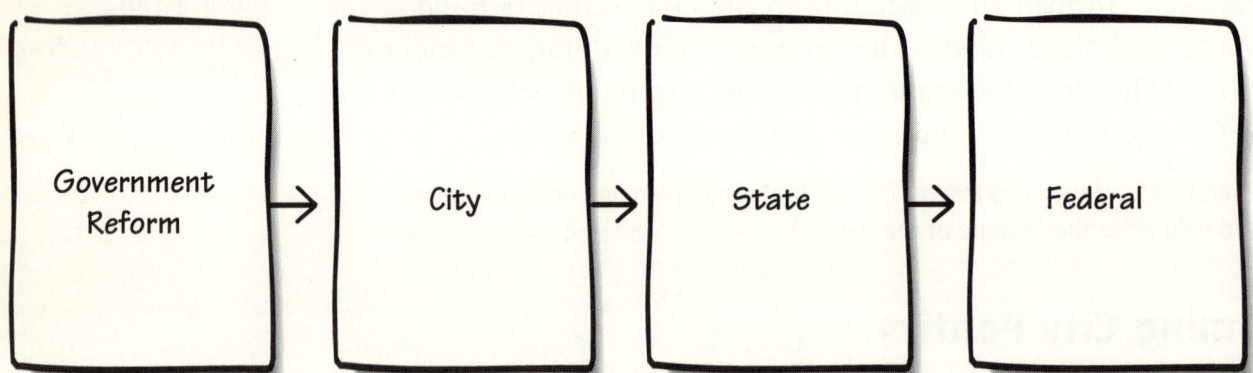

1. Look at the graphic organizer above. What three levels of government were reformed?
   _____
   _____
   _____

2. Look at the map on page 511. Read the caption and be sure you understand the key. Then answer the following questions.

   a. What two states voted for William Howard Taft?
      _____
      _____

   b. How many states voted Progressive?
      _____

246 Chapter 17, Lesson 2 • Lesson Preview

Name: _____   Date: _____

CHAPTER 17
Lesson 2 Reading Strategy
Progressive Reform

(*A More Perfect Union* pp. 507–512)

Evaluate This reading strategy helps you recognize the difference between facts and opinions. A fact is something that can be proven to be true. An opinion is a belief based on what a person thinks or feels.

1. Read the section "State Government Reform." Which statement below is an opinion? Circle the letter next to the best answer.

   a. The most important reforms took place in Wisconsin.
   b. Robert M. LaFollette of Wisconsin was a lawyer and former congressman.
   c. The initiative gave voters the power to start a bill with a petition.

2. Read pages 508–509. List three facts from your reading.

   _____
   _____
   _____

3. Read the section "Giving the Senate to the People." Is the following statement a fact or an opinion? Explain your answer.

   "Senators were more loyal to those who put them in power than they were to the voters."

   _____

4. Read the sections "The Bull Moose Party" and "Wilson Continues Reform Efforts." Fill out the following chart with facts about Theodore Roosevelt and Woodrow Wilson.

Facts About Theodore Roosevelt	Facts About Woodrow Wilson

Reading Support Resources

CHAPTER 17
Lesson 2 Summary
Progressive Reform

(*A More Perfect Union* pp. 507–512)

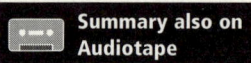

Thinking Focus: What kinds of changes in state and federal government resulted from Progressive reform?

State Government Reform

Progressives wanted state governments to pay more attention to the needs of the people. One reformer, Robert M. La Follette, was elected governor of Wisconsin in 1900. He held primary elections, which gave voters the chance to pick candidates. He changed the state job system so that people got jobs because they had the right skills. He made sure laws were passed that stopped businesses from giving money to political parties. He set up special groups to watch over the utilities and the railroads. La Follette's program became known as the "Wisconsin Idea." Other states later followed it. Many began using the secret ballot, the **initiative**, the **referendum**, and the **recall**. These three reforms allowed voters to take part in state government more directly.

❓ How did Robert La Follette's "Wisconsin Idea" spur reform of state governments?

The Federal Government Responds

Theodore Roosevelt, a Republican, began many reforms when he became President in 1901. He wanted laws to protect people by making meat, food, drugs, and medicines safe. Roosevelt sued monopolies that cheated people. He also began a program of **conservation** to save the wilderness.

Progressive reform was helped by two new amendments. The Sixteenth Amendment set up the federal income tax. This was a new way to get money to pay for government services. The Seventeenth Amendment called for the direct election of senators.

❓ What government reforms did Theodore Roosevelt institute at the federal level?

initiative
(ĭ-nĭsh´ ə-tĭv)
a way that lets citizens suggest a bill by signatures from registered voters on a petition

referendum
(rĕf´ə-rĕn´ dəm)
the way people can vote directly for or against a bill

recall
(rĭ-kôl´)
a special election that allows voters to remove an elected official from office before his or her term is finished

conservation
(kŏn´ sûr-vā´ shən)
the act or process of protecting and preserving natural resources and wilderness areas

Summary continues on next page

Progressive Reform *(Lesson 2 Summary continued)*

The Bull Moose Party

In 1908, Roosevelt decided not to run for President. William Howard Taft ran as the Republican nominee, and won. Taft carried out some reforms, but later became less willing to make changes. Roosevelt decided to run again in 1912. The Republican Party was split. Conservatives supported Taft, and Progressives supported Roosevelt. When Taft was nominated, Roosevelt and his supporters started a third party, the Bull Moose Party. In the election, the Republican vote was split between Republicans and the Bull Moose Party. As a result, the Democratic candidate, Woodrow Wilson, became president. The election was still a victory for the Progressives because both Wilson and Roosevelt had supported Progressive ideas.

[?] How did Roosevelt's "Bull Moose Party" contribute to a Progressive victory in the 1912 election?

Wilson Continues Reform Efforts

President Woodrow Wilson supported many Progressive reforms. He started a program called the "New Freedom." He wanted to protect people from big businesses. He lowered tariffs to make goods from other countries more affordable. He set up a national banking system with The Federal Reserve Act. Wilson also pushed Congress to accept the Clayton Antitrust Act, which made monopolies less powerful. He created the Federal Trade Commission, which worked to stop unfair practices in business. Wilson's reforms were important. But he still allowed racial segregation. He also did not support women's right to vote.

[?] What were President Woodrow Wilson's successes and failures in advancing Progressive causes?

CHAPTER 17
Lesson 3 Preview
Competing Crusades

(*A More Perfect Union* pp. 513–519)

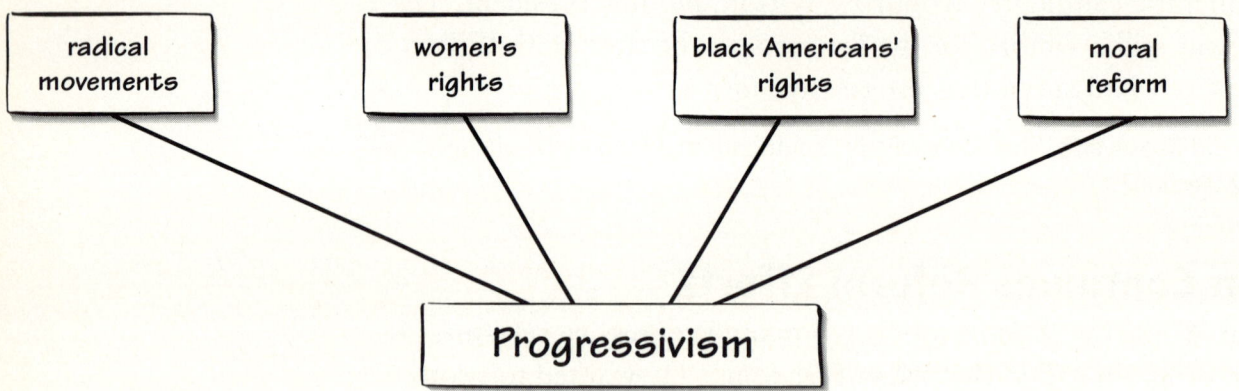

1. Look at the graphic organizer above. What four types of reforms were part of Progressivism?

   _____
   _____
   _____
   _____

2. Look at the pictures of women reformers on pages 513 and 517, and read the captions that go along with them. What two different approaches to reform do these pictures show?

   _____
   _____
   _____
   _____

CHAPTER 17
Lesson 3 Reading Strategy
Competing Crusades

(*A More Perfect Union* pp. 513–519)

Compare and Contrast This reading strategy helps you understand how events are similar and different. As you read about historical events, think about how they compare and contrast with events you already know.

1. Read the section "Moral Reform." How were the temperance movement and the fight against child labor similar? Circle the letter next to the best answer.

    a. Both began in the 1830s.

    b. Both led to Constitutional Amendments.

    c. Both were led by women.

2. Read the section "Radical Political Movements." How did radical political movements like Socialism differ from the reforms of the Progressives?

   _____

3. Read the sections "Women's Rights" and "Progressivism for Whites Only." Then fill in the chart below to help you compare the struggle of women and African Americans for civil rights.

	Women	African Americans
what they wanted		
what they achieved		
important leaders		

4. Use the information from your chart to write down one way the movements of women and African Americans were alike and one way they were different.

   Alike: _____

   Different: _____

Reading Support Resources Reading Strategy • Chapter 17, Lesson 3 **251**

CHAPTER 17
Lesson 3 Summary
Competing Crusades

(*A More Perfect Union* pp. 513–519)

Thinking Focus: What other social movements attempted to change American society during the Progressive Era, and what were their goals?

Moral Reform

Many women worked for change in American life. They led the movement to support **prohibition**. In 1917, the Eighteenth Amendment was passed, making it illegal to make and sell alcohol.

Women also worked to stop child labor. In the 1800s, people thought hard work was good for children. Poor families needed the money that their children could earn. Progressives believed that children should not work. The Child Labor Act of 1916 stopped some people from selling goods made with child labor. The Supreme Court, however, said the Child Labor Act took away children's right to sell their work. The Supreme Court did not support child labor laws until 1938.

? Why didn't the Child Labor Act work?

Radical Political Movements

Progressives wanted to change the political and economic system. Some groups thought the Progressives did not go far enough. Radical groups such as the **Socialists** gained support in the early 1900s. They wanted to replace capitalism and have the workers or the government control factories and businesses. **Anarchists** were more radical and used violence to force change. Some people in the labor movement had extreme views, too. The Industrial Workers of the World did not want workers to be paid wages. Unlike other unions, it included women, blacks, and immigrants.

? How did the goals of radical political movements differ from those of the Progressives?

prohibition
(prō´ə-bĭsh´ən)
the forbidding by law of the manufacture, transportation, sale, and possession of alcoholic beverages

socialist
(sō´shə-lĭst)
a person who supports an economic system in which the workers possess both political power and the means of producing and distributing goods

anarchist
(ăn´ər-kĭst)
a person who opposes all organized forms of government

Summary continues on next page

Competing Crusades *(Lesson 3 Summary continued)*

Women's Rights

Back in 1848, women tried to become **enfranchised**. But even by the 1890s, women still could not vote. Many people felt that women should stay home and not be involved in politics.

The National Women's Suffrage Association worked hard to get the right to vote. In 1917, members of the National Women's Party surrounded the White House. President Wilson had them arrested. When the women began a hunger strike, officials had them force-fed. People were angry. Wilson then changed his mind, and supported the women. But Congress would not support them, even though some states gave women the right to vote.

During World War I, women held many important jobs while men were at war. This helped to finally get the Nineteenth Amendment passed. It gave all women the right to vote.

> **enfranchise**
> (ĕn-frăn′ chīz′)
> to give the rights of citizenship, especially the right to vote

[?] How did the women's rights movement go about winning the right to vote for women?

Progressivism for Whites Only

Progressives did not think about black Americans. Violence against blacks was common in the South. Most Southern states did not allow blacks to vote, or said that blacks had to know how to read and write in order to vote. Sometimes people had to pay to vote. Southern laws also set up "separate but equal" systems that were not really equal. In *Plessy* v. *Ferguson*, the Supreme Court ruled that "separate but equal" public places, like schools, were legal.

Finally, however, white Progressives helped black leaders start the National Association for the Advancement of Colored People (NAACP). This organization still helps black Americans demand their civil rights.

[?] What impact did the Progressive movement have on the lives of black Americans?

Child Labor Reform

- **1912** — The Children's Bureau of the Department of Labor is formed.
- **1905–1907** — Most states pass child labor reform laws.
- **1916** — The Child Labor Act is passed.
- **1920** — The Nineteenth Amendment is accepted.
- **1938** — The Supreme Court upholds child labor laws.

Timeline: 1900 — 1910 — 1920 — 1930 — 1940

Use with *A More Perfect Union* Pages 526–559

Chapter Overview
America Emerges as a World Power

Fill in the blanks with information from the chapter.

When: 1850–1921

Where: The U.S. and abroad

Expansion and Conflict

Asia and the Pacific
- Alaska
- _____
- the "New Navy"
- trade with _____

Latin America
- _____
- Roosevelt Corollary
- Panama Canal
- tension with Mexico

World War I
- end of neutrality
- _____
- a new kind of warfare
- League of Nations

After the War
- labor unrest, race riots, violence
- "Red Scare"
- _____
- return to "normalcy"

Name: _____ Date: _____

CHAPTER 18
Lesson 1 Preview
International Expansion

(*A More Perfect Union* pp. 528–532)

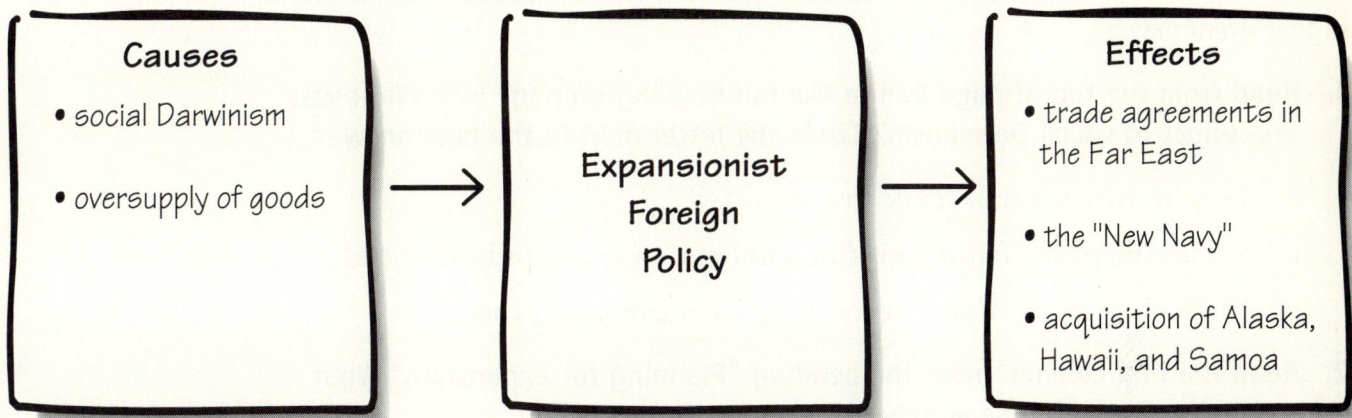

1. Look at the graphic organizer above. Then answer the following questions:

   a. What two things caused the United States to adopt a foreign policy based on international expansion?

   _____
   _____

   b. What three new territories did the United States acquire?

   _____
   _____
   _____

2. Look at the graph on page 529 of your text. Was trade becoming more important or less important from the years 1876 to 1914? Explain your answer.

   _____
   _____
   _____
   _____
   _____

Reading Support Resources   Lesson Preview • Chapter 18, Lesson 1   **255**

Name: Date:

CHAPTER 18
Lesson 1 Reading Strategy
International Expansion

(*A More Perfect Union* pp. 528–532)

Cause and Effect This reading strategy helps you understand events and why they occur. As you read, think about factors that caused an event. Then think about what the effects of that event may be.

1. Read from the top of page 528 to the red heading on page 529. What was one effect of social Darwinism? Circle the letter next to the best answer.

   a. Less healthy animals tended to die off.

   b. Some Americans felt justified in gaining power around the world.

   c. In 1899, Senator Albert Beveridge gave a campaign speech.

2. Read the first column under the heading "Planning for Expansion." What caused businesses to seek new markets for their goods?

   _____

3. Finish reading the section "Planning for Expansion." Which of the following was not an effect of American expansion? Circle the letter next to the best answer.

   a. The United States acquired Alaska.

   b. The "New Navy." was developed.

   c. Secretary Seward succeeded in developing a vast American empire.

4. Read the sections "Expanding Trade with Asia" and "Moving into the Pacific." Then fill in the chart below.

Cause	Effect
	Trade with China grows.
Europeans divide China into "spheres of influence".	
	Japanese ports are opened for trade with the West.
The U. S. wants "stepping stones" to China and Japan.	

CHAPTER 18

Lesson 1 Summary
International Expansion

(*A More Perfect Union* pp. 528–532)

Thinking Focus: What social and economic factors led the United States to pursue a policy of international expansion after the Civil War?

Justifying Expansion

In 1858, biologist Charles Darwin published a new theory. He said that some plants and animals develop to become more fit and more likely to survive. As a result, the plants and animals that are less fit die off. This theory was called "survival of the fittest."

Some people thought that Darwin's theory could be applied to nations. This idea was called "Social Darwinism." Social Darwinists claimed that some nations, such as the United States, were naturally stronger than others. Some Americans believed the United States had the right to control North America and other places around the world.

? How did social Darwinism influence America's outlook on the world in the last half of the 19th century?

Planning for Expansion

After the Civil War, American farms, mines, and factories produced more goods than Americans could buy. Businesses wanted to sell their extra goods to foreign countries. They were also interested in making money from the natural resources in Latin America and Asia. By the late 1800s, U.S. leaders started to expand U.S. trade and power. The U.S. Navy also began to rebuild its ships.

In 1867, Secretary of State William H. Seward helped the United States buy Alaska from Russia. Many members of Congress thought it was just an icy wasteland. But Alaska had copper, gold, and other valuable resources.

? What impact did economic conditions at home have on America's foreign trade in the late 1800s?

Summary continues on next page

International Expansion (Lesson 1 Summary continued)

Expanding Trade with Asia

By the mid-1800s, American merchants had made a lot of money trading with China. Now they wanted to trade with more Asian nations. After China lost a war with Japan in 1895, European nations planned to divide China into trading areas called "spheres of influence." This would not have let the United States trade with China. But in 1898, the Europeans accepted a U.S. plan called the Open Door Policy. Now China could remain independent and could trade with all nations, including the United States.

The United States also tried to set up trade with Japan. For nearly 200 years, Japan had refused to trade with any nation. In 1853, Commodore Matthew Perry went there with four warships. By showing Japan the power of the U.S. Navy, Perry was able to get a trade agreement for the United States. In 1882, an agreement was also signed with Korea.

? Why did the United States seek to establish trade relations with Asian countries?

Moving into the Pacific

The United States wanted to control some areas in the Pacific as steppingstones to China and Japan. In 1867, the United States claimed the Midway Islands. In 1878, it set up a naval station in the Samoan Islands. But the country it most wanted to control was Hawaii. Congress had placed a tax on Hawaiian sugar. This tax made sugar expensive and hurt business. American planters knew that if Hawaii became a part of the United States, sugar would not be taxed. They planned to overthrow the Hawaiian queen and then declare Hawaii an American **protectorate**. In 1893, with the support of U.S. Marines, the queen was forced to **abdicate**. Hawaii became a U.S. territory in 1898.

? In what way were smaller nations in the Pacific important to American expansionist plans?

---

protectorate
(prə-tĕk'tər-ĭt)
a country that is protected and partly controlled by a more powerful country

abdicate
(ăb'dĭ-kāt')
to officially give up the power to rule

Name: _____ Date: _____

CHAPTER 18
Lesson 2 Preview
Conflict and Conquest

(*A More Perfect Union* pp. 533–540)

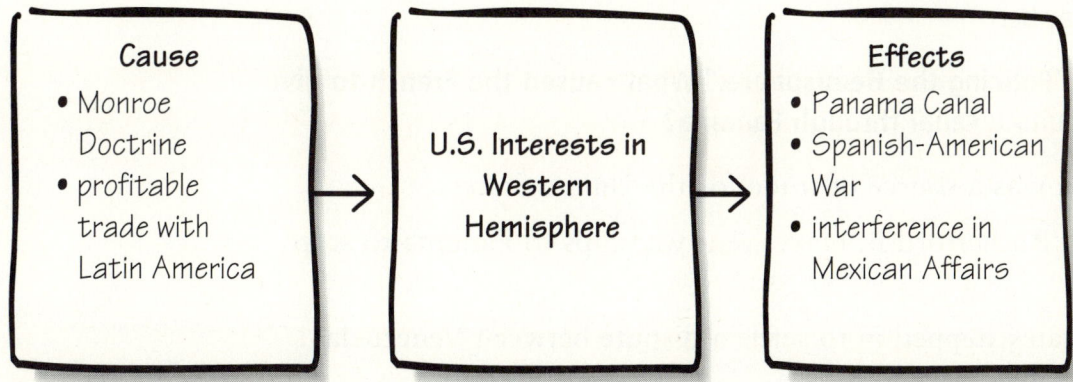

The United States in the Western Hemisphere

Cause
- Monroe Doctrine
- profitable trade with Latin America

→ U.S. Interests in Western Hemisphere →

Effects
- Panama Canal
- Spanish-American War
- interference in Mexican Affairs

1. **Study the graphic organizer above. Then read the following sentences and fill in the blanks.**

   a. The _____ Doctrine was one of the reasons that the United States had interests in the Western Hemisphere.

   b. The Spanish-American War was one of the _____ of U.S. interests in the Western Hemisphere.

2. **Read the lesson title and the red and blue headings in your text on pages 533 to 540. Use words from those headings to fill in the lesson outline below.**

   Conflict and Conquest

   I. Policing the _____

   II. _____ with Spain

       A. The Pressure for _____ Builds

       B. The Spanish-American War

       C. _____ Fight for _____

   III. Building the _____ Canal

   IV. Tension with _____

Reading Support Resources

Lesson Preview • Chapter 18, Lesson 2   **259**

Name: _____ Date: _____

CHAPTER 18

Lesson 2 Reading Strategy
Conflict and Conquest

(*A More Perfect Union* pp. 533–540)

Cause and Effect This reading strategy helps you understand events and why they occur. As you read, think about the factors that caused an event. Then think about what the effects of that event may be.

1. Read the section "Policing the Hemisphere." What caused the French to give up their plan to build a canal through Panama?

    a. Latin America was a source of trade for the United States.

    b. U.S. President Rutherford B. Hayes sent warships to Panama to stop the French.

    c. The United States stepped in to settle a dispute between Venezuela and Great Britain.

2. Read the section "Conflict With Spain." List two causes of the Spanish-American War.

   _____

   _____

3. List two effects of the Spanish-American War.

   _____

   _____

4. Read the section "Tension With Mexico." Then fill in the chart below.

Cause	Effect
	President Wilson orders U.S. Navy to take the port of Veracruz.
126 Mexicans die in battle with the U.S. and the Huerta government falls.	
	President Wilson sends troops into Mexico.

260 Chapter 18, Lesson 2 • Reading Strategy

CHAPTER 18

Lesson 2 Summary
Conflict and Conquest

(*A More Perfect Union* pp. 533–540)

Thinking Focus: What steps did U.S. Presidents take in the late 19th and early 20th centuries to keep European nations away from Latin America and to extend U.S. control over the region?

Policing the Hemisphere

In the late 1800s, Latin America was important to the United States as a trade partner and as protection from other countries. The United States used the Monroe Doctrine to keep foreign countries away from the area. For example, in 1878, the United States would not let France build a canal through Panama. In 1895, the United States helped Venezuela settle a dispute with Great Britain.

[?] Under what circumstances did the United States invoke the Monroe Doctrine in the late 1800s?

Conflict with Spain

In 1895, Cuba tried to free itself from Spain, but failed. To punish the Cubans, hundreds of thousands of people were imprisoned. Many died of starvation. When news of this got to the United States, some newspapers used **yellow journalism** to make Americans angry with Cuba.

In February 1898, an American warship named the *Maine* blew up in a Cuban harbor, killing more than 200 sailors. Some newspapers blamed the explosion on Spain.

On April 19, 1898, Congress declared Cuba free. It sent American soldiers to get Spain out of Cuba. This started the Spanish-American War. Spain lost the war and had to give up Puerto Rico, Guam, and the Philippines to the United States. The Filipinos fought the United States for independence, but lost. Some Americans were against this kind of **imperialism**.

[?] What events led the United States to declare war on Spain?

yellow journalism
(yĕl´ ō jûr´ nə-lĭz´ əm)
a style of newspaper of reporting stories using strong words and changing the truth.

imperialism
(ĭm-pîr´ ē-ə-lĭz´əm)
trying to set up to an empire by having power over other countries

Summary continues on next page

Conflict and Conquest *(Lesson 2 Summary continued)*

Building the Panama Canal

American businesses planned to build a canal through Panama. A canal would give the United States an easier route to Asia and Latin America as well as more power in Central America. The Panamanians wanted the canal built because it would bring them trade and money. But in 1903, Panama was a part of Colombia, and Colombia wouldn't sell the land for the canal. With the help of the United States, Panama revolted against Colombia and won. The United States could then build the canal.

In 1904, President Roosevelt added the "Roosevelt Corollary" to the Monroe Doctrine. It said that the United States had the right to get involved in events within Latin American nations.

[?] What was the importance of the Panama Canal to the United States?

Tension with Mexico

In 1913, General Victoriano Huerta murdered Mexico's democratic president and took over the country. President Woodrow Wilson was against Huerta's ideas. In 1914, members of the USS *Dolphin* were arrested for docking their ship in Mexico without asking permission. Wilson now had an excuse to try to get rid of Huerta. The U.S. Navy took over the port of Veracruz. A battle followed, and soon afterwards, Huerta's government fell.

The Mexican people were angry at what the United States did. A rebel named Francisco "Pancho" Villa held up a train in Chihuahua and killed 16 Americans who were on it. He also killed 19 Americans in New Mexico. In 1916, President Wilson sent troops to Mexico to catch Villa. They did not, and tensions remained between Mexico and the United States.

[?] Why did the United States intervene in Mexican affairs on several occasions between 1914 and 1917?

Name: _____ Date: _____

CHAPTER 18
Lesson 3 Preview
America at War

(*A More Perfect Union* pp. 541–546)

The United States Joins the War

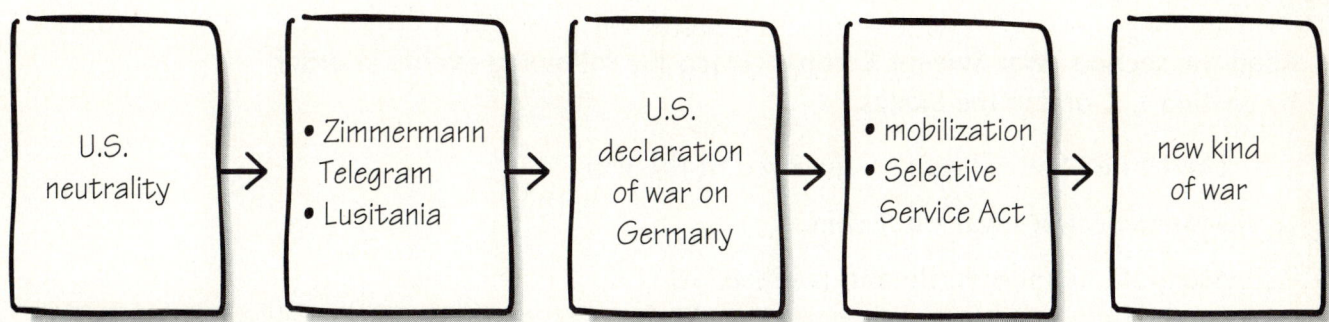

1. Look at the graphic organizer above. Then read the following list of events. Number the events in order according to which happened first, second, and so on.

   ___ mobilization

   ___ U.S. neutrality

   ___ Zimmermann Telegram

   ___ U.S. declaration of war on Germany

2. Look at the poster shown on page 543 in your text. Find one additional image in the lesson that shows how people were encouraged to take part in the war effort. Write the page number and explain your choice.

   _____

   _____

   _____

Name: _____ Date: _____

CHAPTER 18
Lesson 3 Reading Strategy
America at War

(*A More Perfect Union* pp. 541–546)

Sequence   This reading strategy helps you follow what is happening in your reading. As you read, pay attention to dates and times, as well as to words such as *before*, *finally*, *after*, and *then*.

1. Read the section "War Sweeps Europe." Place the following events in order by writing *1*, *2*, or *3* in the blanks.

   ___ The United States becomes involved in the war.

   ___ Austria declares war on Serbia.

   ___ Archduke Francis Ferdinand is killed.

2. Read the section "Entering the War." Place the following events in order by writing *1*, *2*, or *3* in the blanks.

   ___ the interception of the "Zimmermann Telegram"

   ___ the sinking of the *Lusitania*

   ___ the United States official declaration of war

3. Read the section "Fighting the War." Then complete the timeline below.

   April 6, 1917 _____ _____ Nov. 11, 1918

   Nearly 10 million men have registered for the draft.

   _____   _____

CHAPTER 18
Lesson 3 Summary
America at War

(*A More Perfect Union* pp. 541–546)

Thinking Focus: What kept the United States out of World War I initially, and what prompted it to enter the war in 1917 on the side of the Allies?

War Sweeps Europe

During the late 1800s and early 1900s, Europeans were nervous about any single country having too much power. To protect themselves, they formed alliances. Members agreed to help each other fight other countries if necessary. There were two European alliances:

- The Triple Alliance members were Germany, Austria-Hungary, and Italy.
- The Triple Entente members were Britain, France, and Russia.

In 1908, Austria took over Bosnia from Serbia. This made many Bosnians very angry. On June 28, 1914, a Serbian student shot and killed the Archduke Francis Ferdinand of Austria and his wife in Sarajevo, Bosnia. Austria declared war on Serbia. Within weeks, all the major powers of Europe were at war.

? What factors and events led to the outbreak of World War I?

Events Leading up to World War I

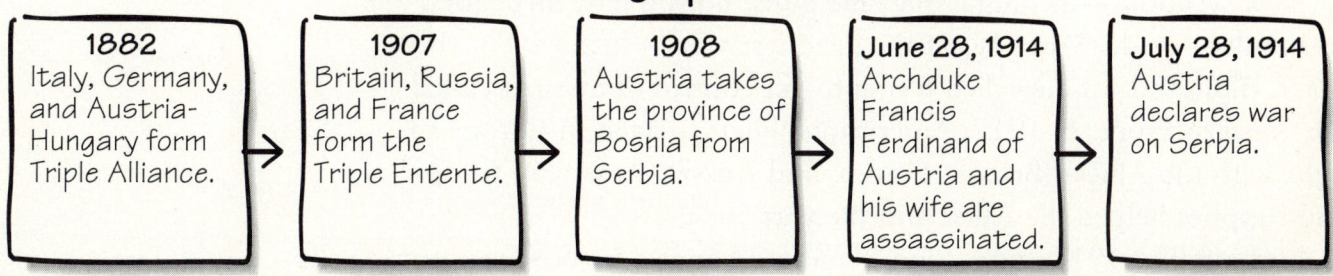

Summary continues on next page

America at War (Lesson 3 Summary continued)

Entering the War

President Woodrow Wilson did not want to take sides in the war in Europe. Most Americans wanted to stay out of it. Some Americans were divided about who they should support.

On May 7, 1915, a British passenger ship, *Lusitania*, was sunk by a German submarine. More than 1,200 people died, including 128 Americans. Germany had attacked the ship because they thought it was carrying American-made weapons to the British. Soon after, Americans began to push President Wilson to enter the war.

In February 1917, Britain discovered a secret message, the "Zimmermann Telegram." It asked Mexico to fight with Germany against the United States if the Americans entered the war. This was proof that Germany was plotting against the United States. President Wilson was forced to give up neutrality. On April 6, 1917, the U.S. Congress declared war on Germany.

[?] What caused President Wilson to turn his back on neutrality and declare war on Germany?

Fighting the War

When the United States entered the war, it had to **mobilize** an army. The army would have to be trained quickly, and U.S. factories would have to start making war materials. Congress passed the Selective Service Act, which made all men between the ages of 21 and 30 register for military service. By June 1917, nearly 10 million men had registered. Hundreds of thousands of these men were African Americans.

New weapons—including machine guns, poison gas, torpedoes, and tanks—made World War I the deadliest war in history. For three years, thousands of men died trying to get control of an area called the Western Front. In 1917, American soldiers arrived in Europe to fight with the Allies—Britain, France, and Russia. American troops and supplies helped the Allies win the war.

In the fall of 1918, more than a million Americans took part in a final push that stopped the German army. On November 11th, both sides signed an **armistice** ending the war.

[?] What impact did the United States' entry into the war have on the fighting in Europe?

mobilize
(mō´ bə-līz´)
to prepare troops and supplies for war

armistice
(är´ mĭ-stĭs)
a temporary peace agreement

Name: _____   Date: _____

CHAPTER 18
Lesson 4 Preview
Impact of the War

(*A More Perfect Union* pp. 547–553)

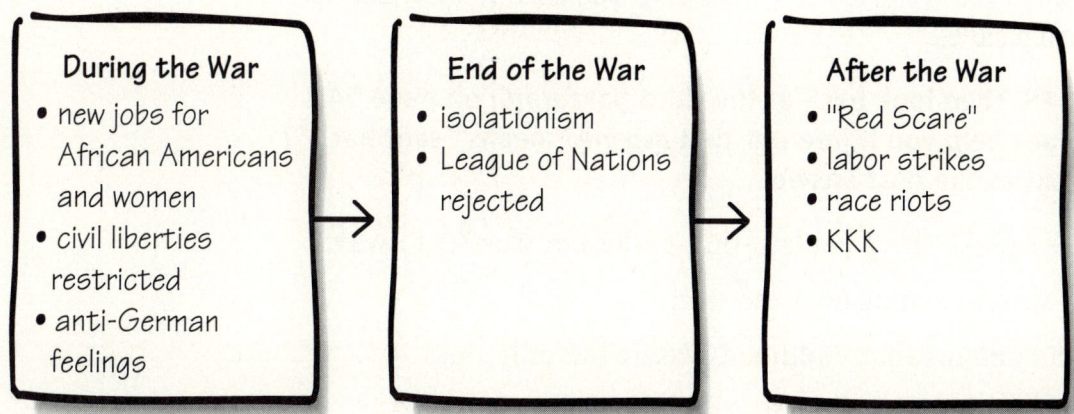

1. **Study the graphic organizer above. Then read the following sentences and fill in the blanks.**

   a. African Americans and women gained new jobs _____ the war.

   b. The United States rejected the League of _____ at the end of the war.

   c. _____ the war, there were _____ strikes.

2. **Look at the map on page 550 in your text and read the caption. Write the names of the two countries that lost the most territory as a result of the war.**

   _____

   _____

Name: _____ Date: _____

CHAPTER 18
Lesson 4 Reading Strategy
Impact of the War

(*A More Perfect Union* pp. 547–553)

Think About Words This reading strategy helps you figure out the meaning of new words. When you come to an unfamiliar word, look for word parts you already know and use clues such as context and pictures.

1. Read pages 547–549. Then look back at the third paragraph on page 547. How do context clues help you figure out that *deported* means "sent back"? Circle the letter next to the best answer.

   a. The words "to Russia" help explain that Goldman was sent away.

   b. Goldman had spoken out against the war.

   c. The paragraph explains that Goldman wasn't the only one who was deported.

2. Read the section "Retreating from World Affairs" on pages 551–552. What part of the word *isolationism* is a word that you already know?

   _____

   How does knowing a part of this word help you figure out what *isolationism* means?

   _____

3. Read the section "Aftermath of the War." Choose a word from the section that is new to you. Then fill in as much of the chart below as you can to help you figure out what the word means.

   WORD: _____

   clues from the reading: _____

   clues from the pictures: _____

   similar words I already know: _____

   parts of words I already know: _____

   the word means _____

268 Chapter 18, Lesson 4 • Reading Strategy   Reading Support Resources

CHAPTER 18
Lesson 4 Summary
Impact of the War

(*A More Perfect Union* pp. 547–553)

Thinking Focus: What impact did World War I have on American society during and after the war?

War at Home

Most Americans supported the war, but some spoke out against it. In 1918, Congress passed the Sedition Act to stop **dissent**. This made it a crime to speak against the government or its symbols, such as the flag. Those who spoke against the war were punished.

Because of the war, Americans who were born in other countries were distrusted, or treated badly without any reason. The war did, however, offer new opportunities for women and blacks. Workers were needed because so many men had left to fight in the war. For the first time, women got the chance to prove they could do any type of job. Black Americans, too, were offered good factory jobs that had not been open to them before.

? What was life like for different groups of Americans who stayed at home during the war?

dissent
(dĭ-sĕnt´)
disagreement of opinion with an authority, such as a government

reparations
(rĕp´ə-rā´shənz)
payments made by defeated nations as repayment for the damages they caused in war

The Treaty of Versailles

After the war ended, President Woodrow Wilson developed a peace plan known as the Fourteen Points. It called for problems between nations to be settled without going to war. Wilson also wanted to set up a League of Nations to make sure that members would respect each others' national limits.

France and England didn't agree with Wilson's plan. They wanted to punish Germany for all that they had suffered. The Treaty of Versailles made Germany take full blame for the war, give up land, and pay $15 billion in **reparations** to the Allies. Most Germans thought the treaty was harsh and unfair.

? In what way did President Wilson attempt to shape peace terms after the war?

Summary continues on next page

Impact of the War *(Lesson 4 Summary continued)*

Retreating from World Affairs

The Treaty of Versailles called for the League of Nations to be set up. Wilson hoped the League would help nations stay at peace. Republican Senators did not like the idea that a threat to any one member of the League would be seen as a threat to all. They thought that as a member of the League, the United States would be forced to fight in foreign wars. The Republicans wanted a policy of **isolationism**. Without their votes, the Treaty and the League of Nations could not be approved by the U.S. government. The public supported the idea, but the Senators held out. In March 1920, the Senate rejected the League of Nations. Although the League was created, the United States was not a member.

> **isolationism**
> (ī´sə-lā´ shə-nĭz´əm)
> the idea that a nation should avoid alliances with other nations and not get involved in the affairs of other nations

[?] Why did the United States adopt a policy of isolationism after the war?

The Aftermath of War

In 1919, factory workers went on strike because of low wages and long hours. More than 25 race riots broke out. Most of them were caused by whites demanding that black Americans give up the good jobs they had gotten during the war.

After the war some Americans also feared that the Russian Communists might try to take over the United States. Americans worried that immigrants from Russia or Eastern Europe were spies. During the "Red Scare" of 1919, over 6,000 Americans were arrested. Many of them were immigrants. They were charged with plotting against the government. Almost all were found not guilty.

Many Americans had been upset by the war and the strikes, riots, and arrests that followed. A Republican senator from Ohio, Warren G. Harding entered the 1920 presidential race asking for a return to "normalcy." The people liked this idea, and Harding easily won the presidency.

[?] What internal problems disrupted American society in the postwar period?

Use with *A More Perfect Union* Pages 562–589

Chapter Overview
Pluralism

Fill in the blank spaces below with information from the chapter.

A Land of Immigrants

Immigration Laws
- Chinese Exclusion Act, 1882
- _____, 1921
- _____, 1924
- Immigration Act of 1965

Main Groups Immigrating
- before 1900 _____
- early 1900s _____
- 1960s to today _____

Immigration Issues Today
- assimilation
- _____
- bilingual education
- continuing enrichment of American culture

Reading Support Resources   Chapter Overview • Chapter 19 **271**

Name: _____ Date: _____

CHAPTER 19

Lesson 1 Preview
A Land of Immigrants

(*A More Perfect Union* pp. 564–570)

U.S. Immigration Policy, 1882-1924

Chinese Exclusion Act, 1882 → Immigration Act, 1891 → Literacy Act, 1917 → Emergency Quota Act, 1921 → National Origins Act, 1924

1. Look at the graphic organizer above. Then answer the following questions:

   a. How many years passed between the Chinese Exclusion Act and the Immigration Act?
   _____

   b. In what year was the Literacy Act passed?
   _____

   c. What acts were passed in 1921 and 1924?
   _____
   _____

2. Read the red and blue headings on pages 564 to 570 of your text. What do these headings suggest about Americans' changing views toward immigration?
   _____
   _____
   _____
   _____

Name: Date:

CHAPTER 19

Lesson 1 Reading Strategy
A Land of Immigrants

(*A More Perfect Union* pp. 564–570)

Self-Question This reading strategy helps you stay focused on what you read. Ask yourself questions before you read a section. Then read to see if you can find the answer to your questions.

1. The chart below shows what kinds of questions you might ask as you prepare to read the section "Coming to America." As you read that section, look for the answers to these questions and fill in the chart.

Coming to America	
Who came to America?	
Why did they come to America?	
What happened after they got to America?	

2. Read the red heading on page 566. Which question below do you expect will be answered by reading the section? Circle the letter next to the best answer.

   a. What kinds of festivals were celebrated by immigrants?

   b. How have immigrants enriched American culture?

   c. Why did the U.S. government pass laws to limit immigration?

3. Read the red and blue headings on pages 569–570. Write a question that you expect to be able to answer after you read the section.

   _____

   _____

4. Read the section and look for the answer to your question. Write your answer, or something else that you learned, in the space below.

   _____

   _____

   _____

Reading Support Resources

CHAPTER 19

Lesson 1 Summary
A Land of Immigrants

(*A More Perfect Union* pp. 564–570)

Thinking Focus: How did U.S. immigration policy change between colonial days and 1960?

Coming to America

Scientists believe that the first group of people to come to America were from Asia. Their descendants became known as American Indians. The next group of immigrants came from Mexico to the Southwest in the late 1500s. Thousands more immigrants arrived, mostly from Europe, from the 1600s to the 1900s. Immigrants came to get away from bad economic or political situations in their homelands. They hoped to build a better life in the United States. Members of the same ethnic groups tended to settle in the same cities or neighborhoods. As a result, ethnic communities grew throughout the United States. Prejudice sometimes played a part in determining where ethnic groups lived and worked. But immigrants were needed to help settle the land, build cities, and work in factories, mines, and on the railroads.

? Explain why the United States is called a land of immigrants.

Resistance to Immigration

Until 1880, most immigrants came from northern and western Europe. They were Protestant and spoke English or a similar language. They quickly blended into American society. Conflicts with immigrants first became a problem when many Chinese came to the west to work on the railroads and in the mines. Many people did not like that the Chinese language, customs and beliefs were different from their own. This led to the Chinese Exclusion Act of 1882, which allowed only a few Chinese into the United States. Later, limits were put on immigrants from other Asian countries.

Anti-immigration feelings continued to grow. Some Americans

Summary continues on next page

A Land of Immigrants (Lesson 1 Summary continued)

feared that immigrants would change American culture and traditions. People were also afraid that immigrants would work for lower pay and take jobs away from Americans. New laws were passed to make it more difficult for people to move to this country.

? Why did people in the United States tend to fear immigrants in the early 1900s?

The Closing Door

After World War I ended, Americans feared that European immigrants would pour into the United States. Congress passed the Emergency Quota Act of 1921. This law set up a **quota** for the number of people allowed to immigrate from each country. The quota was set at 3 percent of the group's foreign-born population living in the United States in 1910.

In 1924, Congress replaced the 1921 Act with the National Origins Act. This reduced the quota to 2 percent of those present in 1890. The law greatly cut immigration by eastern and southern Europeans. It favored immigrants from northern and western Europe. But it did not affect those coming from countries in the Western Hemisphere. In the late 1930s, quota rules were loosened a little, and political **asylum** was offered to some highly educated Europeans.

After the end of World War II in 1945, the United States once again relaxed its quotas. It took in thousands of **refugees**. Many refugees came from eastern Europe, which was now governed by communists.

quota
(kwō´ tə)
the number of people of a certain nationality allowed to enter the United States in one year

asylum
(ə-sī´ ləm)
political protection

refugee
(rĕf´yōō-jē´)
a person who has left his or her country after facing oppression or great hardship

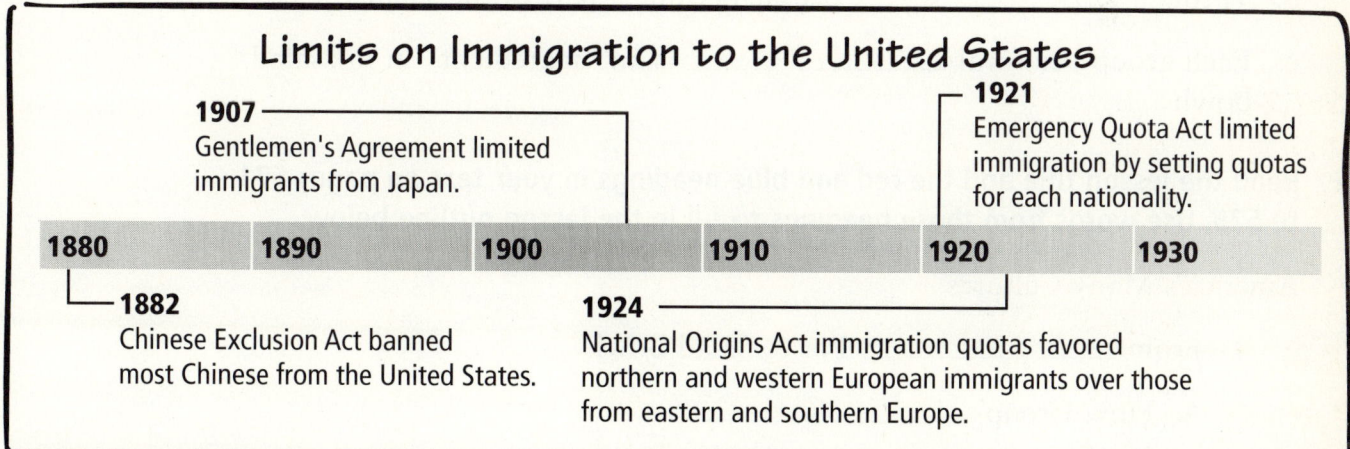

Limits on Immigration to the United States

- **1882** Chinese Exclusion Act banned most Chinese from the United States.
- **1907** Gentlemen's Agreement limited immigrants from Japan.
- **1921** Emergency Quota Act limited immigration by setting quotas for each nationality.
- **1924** National Origins Act immigration quotas favored northern and western European immigrants over those from eastern and southern Europe.

? What effect did the quota system have on immigration?

CHAPTER 19
Lesson 2 Preview
America's Many Cultures

(*A More Perfect Union* pp. 571–576)

How the U.S. Is Like a Salad Bowl

1. Look at the graphic organizer above. Use the following words to fill in the blanks below.

   | assimilation   heritage   salad |

   a. America's many groups of people mix like ingredients in a _____ bowl.

   b. Through _____, people become a part of the salad.

   c. Each group's cultural _____ is an "ingredient" in the salad bowl.

2. Read the lesson title and the red and blue headings in your text on pages 571 to 576. Use words from those headings to fill in the lesson outline below.

   America's Many Cultures

   I. From _____ Pot to Salad Bowl

      A. How Groups _____

      B. For Many, Hard Work Brings _____

   II. _____ to America

      A. Coping in a _____ Country

      B. The United States _____

Name: _____ Date: _____

CHAPTER 19
Lesson 2 Reading Strategy
America's Many Cultures

(*A More Perfect Union* pp. 571–576)

Finding the Main Idea This reading strategy helps you organize and remember what you read. When you finish a selection, jot down the main idea and its supporting details.

1. Read the section "From Melting Pot to Salad Bowl." Which sentence below best expresses the main idea of the section? Circle the letter next to the best answer.

    a. The culture of the United States is made up of many interconnected cultures.

    b. The Hmong were mainly farmers from the country of Laos.

    c. Mexican Americans have been in the United States for many years.

2. Read the first paragraph under the heading "Adjusting to America." Then write the main idea of the paragraph.

    _____

3. Finish reading the section "Adjusting to America." Write two details that support the following main idea: "New immigrants benefit from help in adjusting to their new lives."

    _____
    _____

4. Fill in the chart below with the main idea and at least two supporting ideas from the section "The United States Enriched."

Main Idea	Supporting Details

Reading Support Resources   Reading Strategy • Chapter 19, Lesson 2   **277**

CHAPTER 19

Lesson 2 Summary
America's Many Cultures

(*A More Perfect Union* pp. 571–576)

Thinking Focus: What are some of the benefits and challenges of being an immigrant in the United States?

From Melting Pot to Salad Bowl

For many years, America was called the "melting pot." This was because of the idea that the customs of new immigrants "melted" down and blended into a single American culture. Today many people compare the United States to a salad bowl. Like a salad, the United States is made of many different "ingredients," or cultures. America's different cultures mix together, but they also remain separate.

When an immigrant culture and a local culture meet, each adapts to the customs of the other. Most immigrants choose to assimilate, or blend into, American culture. But many also hold onto parts of their own culture and identity.

Work and education helped many immigrants blend into American society. Older immigrants often accepted the fact that they would not be able to get the most from America for themselves. Instead, they hoped that by working hard, their children would become successful. Immigrants often worked long hours at low-paying jobs and spent little money on themselves. They saved as much money as they could for their children's education. They believed that education was the key to success in the United States.

[?] What attitudes did many immigrants have toward education?

Adjusting to America

Adjusting to life in the United States is usually easier for the children than for parents or grandparents. Older people often find it hard to give up their culture and language. Children often help their older relatives by translating English for them. Churches and community groups can help immigrants hold onto their ethnic identity.

Summary continues on next page

Some groups find it difficult to assimilate because they have left their families behind. One person may come to the United States to earn enough money to bring the rest of the family a few years later. Once families are together, assimilation can be easier. Immigrants, such as Mexican Americans, who are close to family members in their home country, often do not assimilate as much. Other groups have had trouble because of racial prejudice.

Immigrants have added to the variety and diversity of American life. They have helped shape the meaning of the word *American*. They have contributed to all aspects of American life.

[?] Why did some immigrants find it difficult to become assimilated?

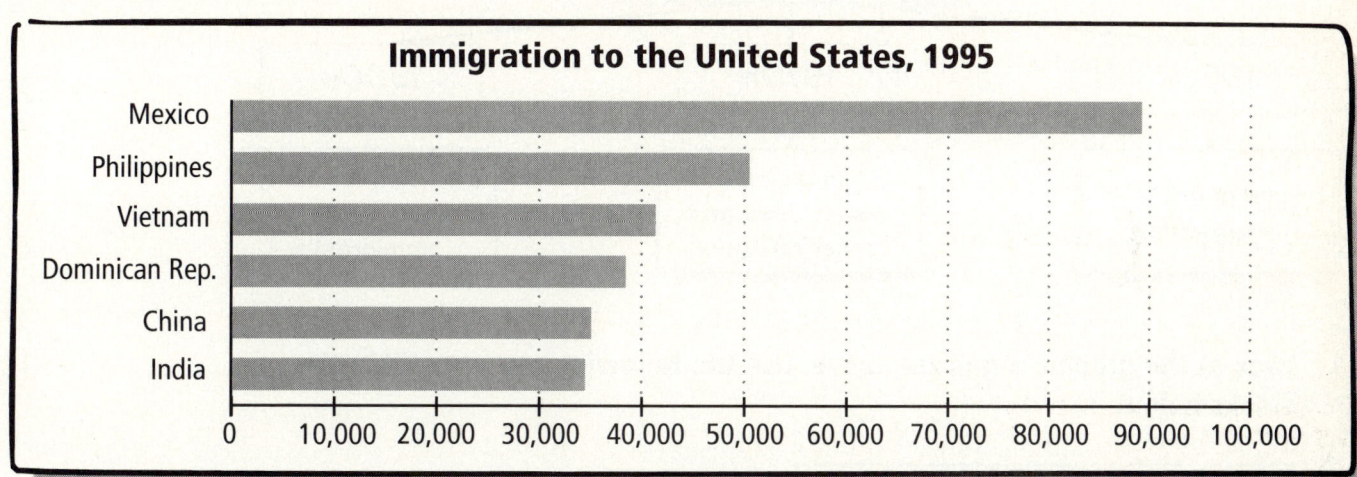

Name: _____ Date: _____

CHAPTER 19

Lesson 3 Preview
The Gates Reopened

(*A More Perfect Union* pp. 578–583)

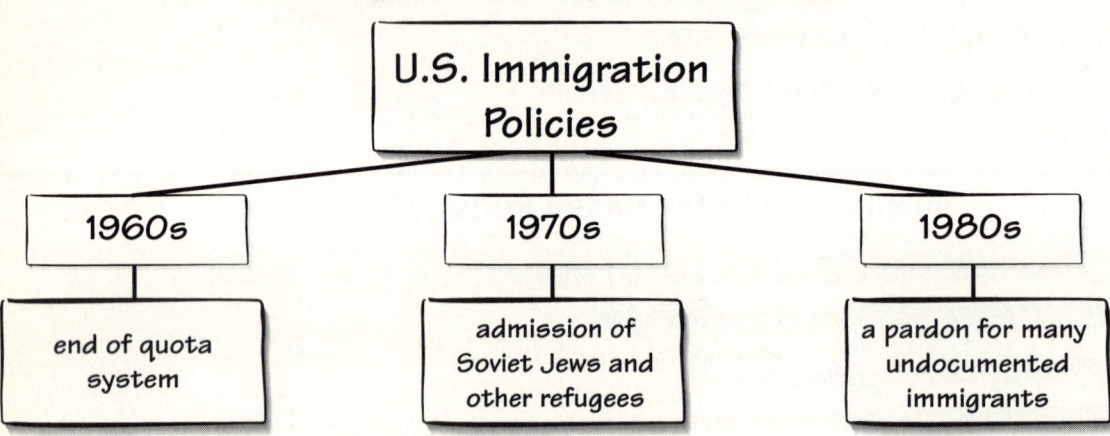

1. Look at the graphic organizer above. Use the following terms to fill in the blanks below.

   | refugees   pardon   quota |

   a. In the 1960s, a new law was passed that ended the _____ system.

   b. In the 1970s, the United States began admitting growing numbers of _____.

   c. In the 1980s, a law was passed that gave a _____ to many undocumented workers.

2. Look at the photograph on page 579 and read the caption. Find another photo in the lesson that shows more "boat people." Write down the page number of the photo. Then write the name of the city and country the people have just arrived in.

   _____

   _____

   _____

Name: _____ Date: _____

CHAPTER 19
Lesson 3 Reading Strategy
The Gates Reopened

(*A More Perfect Union* pp. 578–583)

Sequence This reading strategy helps you follow what is happening in your reading. As you read, pay attention to dates and times, as well as to words such as *before*, *finally*, *after*, and *then*.

1. Read the section "Expanding Opportunities for Immigrants." Place the following events in order by writing *1*, *2*, and *3* in the blanks.

   ___ Many Vietnamese, Cambodians, and Laotians flee their countries.

   ___ President Lyndon B. Johnson signs a new immigration law.

   ___ President John F. Kennedy is assassinated.

2. Read the section "Undocumented Immigration." Then place the following items in order by writing *1*, *2*, and *3* in the blanks.

   ___ *Braceros* get temporary permits to work in the United States.

   ___ Thousands of migrant workers apply for legal immigration.

   ___ The Immigration Reform and Control Act is passed.

3. Study the circle graphs on pages 580 and 581. Write a sentence describing the changes in immigration to the United States.

   _____

4. Read the section "Other Challenges of Immigration." Then complete the timeline below.

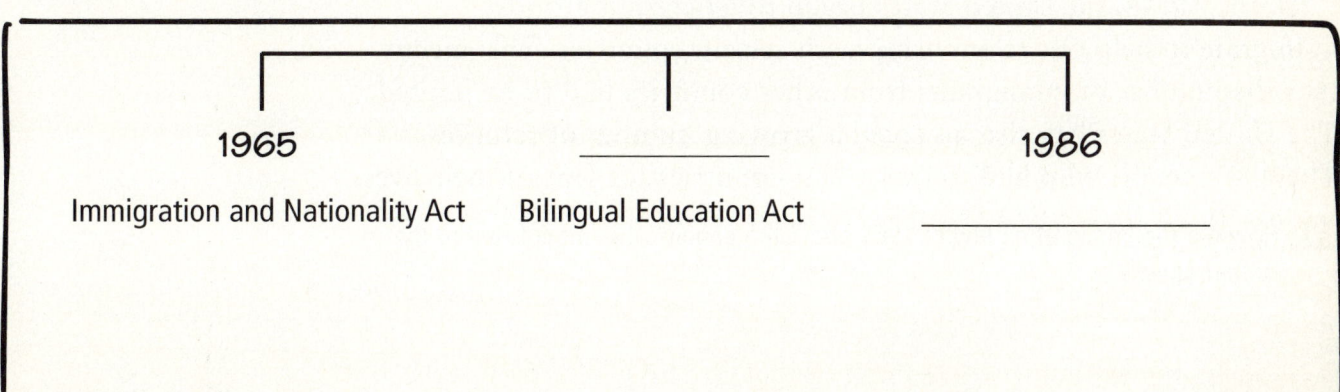

1965 — Immigration and Nationality Act
____ — Bilingual Education Act
1986 — ____

CHAPTER 19

Lesson 3 Summary
The Gates Reopened

(*A More Perfect Union* pp. 578–583)

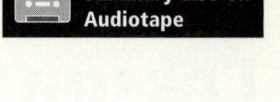
Summary also on Audiotape

Thinking Focus: How did the pattern of immigration to the United States change after the 1960s?

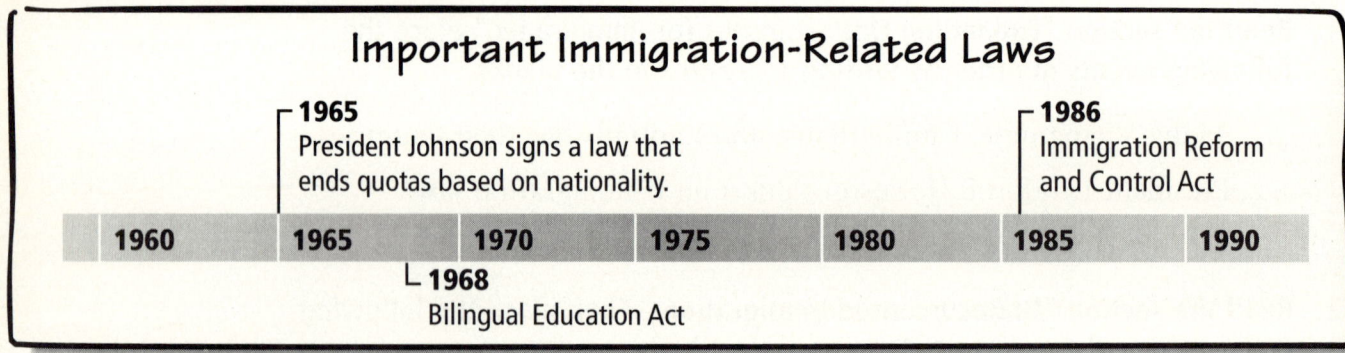

Important Immigration-Related Laws

- 1965: President Johnson signs a law that ends quotas based on nationality.
- 1968: Bilingual Education Act
- 1986: Immigration Reform and Control Act

Expanding Opportunities for Immigrants

In 1965, President Lyndon B. Johnson signed a new immigration law. This law ended the quota system. It admitted immigrants on the basis of their skills and their family ties to people already living in the United States. This law was more fair than the old quota system. It was not fair, however, to people from Asia, Africa, and Latin America. Immigration from those regions had not been allowed earlier, or was very limited. As a result, there were very few people from those areas already living in the United States.

In the 1970s, the United States began to let certain groups immigrate to help our relationship with certain countries. This meant that the number of immigrants from other countries had to be limited. The United States has also accepted a growing number of refugees. These are people who had to leave their countries for fear of their lives.

? How did the immigration law of 1965 affect the people who immigrated to the United States?

Summary continues on next page

The Gates Reopened (Lesson 3 Summary continued)

Undocumented Immigration

During World War II, the United States needed workers because many men were away fighting. Mexicans were hired to work on farms with temporary work permits. They were supposed to go back to Mexico, but many stayed in the United States as **undocumented immigrants.**

Undocumented workers enter the United States from Mexico and other countries. If they are caught they can be sent back to their own country. Most workers are willing to take the chance. Their U.S. jobs pay little, but the wages are better than those they could earn in their own countries.

In 1986, Congress passed the Immigration Reform and Control Act. This law said that all undocumented immigrants who could prove they'd been living and working in the United States since 1982 could become legal immigrants. Special rules were also made for **migrant workers.** Migrant workers who had spent at least 90 days in the Unites States between May 1, 1985, and May 1, 1986, could become legal immigrants.

[?] How did some undocumented workers gain the right to stay in the United States?

Other Challenges of Immigration

Today, most immigrants come from Asia and Latin America. Many do not speak English. In 1968, Congress passed the Bilingual Education Act. It says that subjects should be taught in English and in the students' native language. People who support **bilingual education** believe it helps immigrant children to learn English more easily. It also lets immigrants keep their culture. But some people feel that using two languages does not help students learn English and keeps them separate from society. They would like new laws that require classes to be taught in English only. They would like English declared the official language of the United States.

[?] What different views do people have on bilingual education?

---

undocumented immigrant
(ŭn-dŏk´ yə-mənt´əd ĭm´ ĭ-grənt)
an immigrant who enters the United States without permission and does not have a passport or visa

migrant worker
(mī´ grənt wûr´ kər)
a person who travels across the United States planting and harvesting crops as jobs are available

bilingual education
(bī-lĭng´ gwəl ĕj´ ə-kā´ shən)
teaching in two languages

Use with *A More Perfect Union* Pages 590–620

Chapter Overview
Modern American Democracy

Fill in the blank spaces below with information from the chapter.

Toward Liberty and Justice for All

Citizenship and Voting Rights

- 1790 ▷ Citizenship granted to any "free white person of good character."
- 1868 ▷ _____
- 1920 ▷ Women win voting rights
- _____ ▷ Indian citizenship
- 1970 ▷ _____

Civil Rights

- 1964 ▷ Civil Rights Act
- 1965 ▷ _____
- 1971 ▷ _____
- _____ ▷ Equal Opportunity Act
- 1975 ▷ _____

284 Chapter 20 • Chapter Overview

CHAPTER 20
Lesson 1 Preview
A Government of Citizens

(*A More Perfect Union* pp. 592–597)

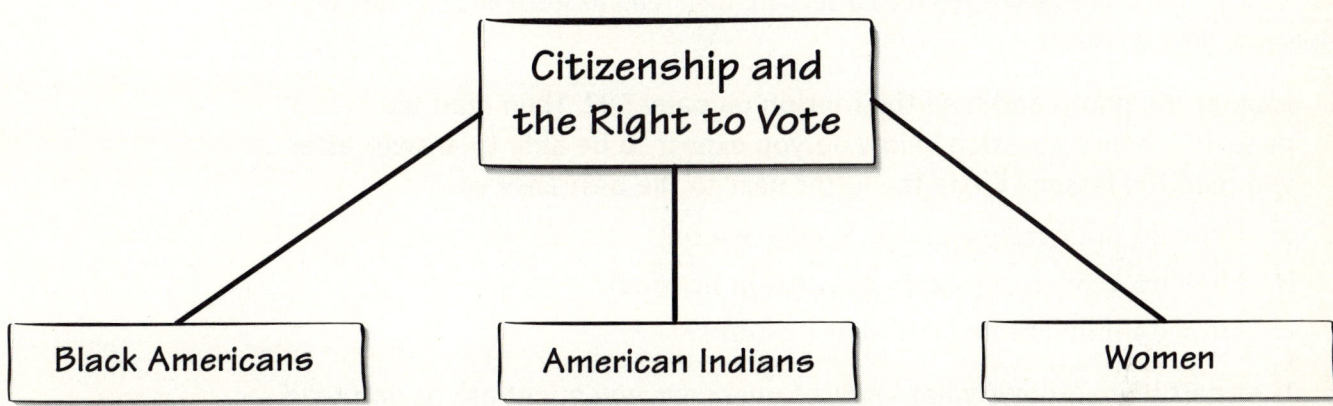

1. Look at the graphic organizer above. What three groups of people already living in the United States were the last to gain U.S. citizenship and the right to vote?

   _____

   _____

2. Look at the timeline on page 595 in your text. Then read the following sentences and fill in the blanks.

   The Civil Rights Act that led to black Americans gaining cititzenship was passed in _____.

   In _____, black men were granted the right to vote. The _____ gave both black and white women the right to vote in _____. American Indians were given the right to vote in _____. The _____ eliminated literacy tests and poll taxes, which were used to keep minorities from voting.

Name: _____ Date: _____

CHAPTER 20
Lesson 1 Reading Strategy
A Government of Citizens

(*A More Perfect Union* pp. 592–597)

Self-Question This reading strategy helps you stay focused on what you read. Ask yourself questions before you read a section. Then read to see if you can find the answer to your questions.

1. Look at the photo and read the caption on page 592. Then read the rest of page 592. Which question below do you expect to be able to answer after you read the lesson? Circle the letter next to the best answer.

   a. How do immigrants gain U.S. citizenship?
   b. How do U.S. citizens gain citizenship in Israel?
   c. How do immigrants learn new customs?

2. The chart below shows what kinds of questions you might ask as you read the section "Citizenship Defined." As you read, look for the answers to these questions and fill in the chart.

Citizenship	
What is a citizen?	
What rights and responsibilities come with being a citizen?	
How can a person become a citizen of the United States?	

3. Read the red and blue headings and look at the pictures on pages 595–596. Which question below do you expect to be able to answer after you read the lesson? Circle the letter next to the best answer.

   a. What was the civil rights movement?
   b. Which groups of Americans have gained the right to vote since the late 1800s?
   c. What is a democracy?

4. Read the first paragraph under the heading "Ideal Versus Reality." Write a question in the space below that you expect might be answered as you read the section.

_____

286 Chapter 20, Lesson 1 • Reading Strategy   Reading Support Resources

CHAPTER 20
Lesson 1 Summary
A Government of Citizens

(*A More Perfect Union* pp. 592–597)

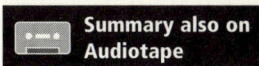

Thinking Focus: In what ways has the definition of citizenship and the rights associated with it expanded in the United States since 1787?

Citizenship Defined

A **citizen** is a person who owes loyalty to and receives protection from a country's government. In the United States, citizens are responsible for choosing their leaders. One can become a citizen of the United States by one of three ways:

- being born in this country
- having at least one parent who is an American citizen
- **naturalization**

To become naturalized you must do the following:

- live in the United States for at least five years
- prove you can read and write
- prove you are of good character
- understand the U.S. political system
- have never belonged to a group that wanted to overthrow the U.S. government.

? What does it mean to be a citizen of the United States?

citizen
(sĭt´ ĭ-zən)
a person who, by birth or naturalization, owes loyalty to and receives protection from a nation's government

naturalization
(năch´ ə-rəl-ĭ-zā´ shən)
the process by which a citizen of one country becomes a citizen of another country

Citizenship Expanded

The Constitution does not define citizenship. In 1790, Congress passed a law that gave citizenship to any "free white person" of "good character" who had lived for over a year in a state and who promised to support the U.S. Constitution. This definition kept African Americans and American Indians from citizenship. It was later used to deny citizenship to Asians.

It was not until 1868, three years after slavery ended, that the Fourteenth Amendment gave citizenship to black Americans. A few American Indians gained citizenship rights in 1887. The Indian

Summary continues on next page

A Government of Citizens *(Lesson 1 Summary continued)*

Citizenship, or Snyder, Act of 1924 gave American Indians born in the United States citizenship.

[?] What groups of Americans have won their citizenship since 1787?

Voting Rights Expanded

For many years, states decided who could vote. Most states made owning property a requirement for voting. People thought that this was unfair. By the late 1820s, most states no longer had this requirement. Voting rights were given to all white men.

Many western states let women vote in state and local elections. In the early 1900s, these same rights were won in many other states. In 1920, the Nineteenth Amendment gave the right to vote to all women.

In 1870, the Fifteenth Amendment gave black Americans the right to vote. But many states did not let blacks vote until the 1960s. In 1924, American Indians were given the right to vote. But it was not until the late 1950s that all states allowed American Indians to vote. In 1971, the Twenty-Sixth Amendment gave all citizens aged 18 and older the right to vote.

[?] What groups of Americans have won the right to vote since 1787?

Ideal Versus Reality

Many Americans were denied their rights as citizens because of prejudice and discrimination even though there were laws against this. In the South, whites set up ways to keep blacks from voting. They set up a poll tax that most black citizens could not afford to pay. In some states, black Americans had to take reading and writing tests that were almost impossible to pass. Laws also kept blacks and whites separate. Other laws denied blacks equal opportunities to good schools and jobs.

Voting was made very hard for American Indians too. Most lived far away from where they had to vote, and they did not have a way to get there. And although no one prevented women from voting, women also faced discrimination.

[?] How have Americans sometimes been denied the rights legally guaranteed to them by the Constitution?

CHAPTER 20
Lesson 2 Preview
Putting the Constitution to Work

(*A More Perfect Union* pp. 600–608)

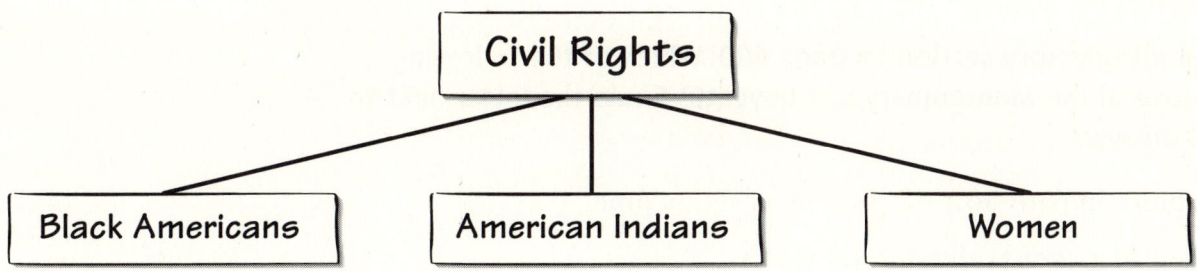

Americans Who Have Gained Rights

1. **Study the graphic organizer above. Use the following words to fill in the blanks below.**

   | rights   Americans   Indians   civil |

   a. During the civil _____ movement, black _____ began to challenge segregation laws.

   b. Black Americans made gains during the _____ rights movement.

   c. These gains encouraged American _____ and women to also demand their civil rights.

2. **Look at the photographs on page 606 in your text. Describe the difference between the women shown in the top photo and those shown in the bottom photo.**

   _____
   _____
   _____
   _____
   _____
   _____

Name: _____   Date: _____

CHAPTER 20
Lesson 2 Reading Strategy
Putting the Constitution to Work

(*A More Perfect Union* pp. 600–608)

Cause and Effect This reading strategy helps you understand events and why they occur. As you read, think about the factors that caused an event. Then think about what the effects of that event may be.

1. Read the introductory section on page 600. Which of the following was a cause of the Montgomery bus boycott? Circle the letter next to the best answer.

    a. The bus company lost 65 percent of its income.

    b. Black Americans walked to their jobs.

    c. Rosa Parks was arrested for refusing to give up her seat on a bus.

2. Read the sections "The Rights of Citizens" and "The Civil Rights Movement." What was one effect of the case *Brown v. Board of Education*?

    a. People watched the events of the civil rights movement on television.

    b. Schools could no longer be segregated.

    c. People swam in segregated swimming pools.

3. Read the section "American Indians Make Gains." What caused American Indian leaders to push for new laws to help their people?

    _____

4. Read the sections "The Fight for Women's Rights" and "The Ongoing Struggle for Justice." Then fill in the chart below.

Cause	Effect
Betty Friedan publishes *The Feminine Mystique*.	
	Equal Rights Amendment is defeated.
Japanese Americans are unfairly placed in detention camps during World War II.	

CHAPTER 20
Lesson 2 Summary
Putting the Constitution to Work

(*A More Perfect Union* pp. 600–608)

Thinking Focus: How have some groups of Americans used the Constitution to obtain the rights and freedoms previously denied them?

The Rights of Citizens

The Bill of Rights guaranteed basic freedoms to every American citizen, but said nothing about the states having to obey these amendments. The Fourteenth Amendment changed this. It said that states could not "deprive any person of life, liberty, or property, without due process of law; nor deny to any person . . . the equal protection of the law." This means that no government can take away the freedoms guaranteed by the Bill of Rights. It also lets citizens challenge unfair laws.

> In what ways does the Constitution guarantee American citizens certain basic rights?

The Civil Rights Movement

A system called segregation separated blacks from whites. During the 1960s, many blacks and whites began to break segregation laws in order to change them. For example, they had **sit-ins** at lunch counters, refusing to leave until they were served. Based on the Fourteenth Amendment, the Supreme Court ruled that segregation laws were illegal.

In 1963, Martin Luther King, Jr., gave an important speech. He spoke of a dream in which all American citizens had the same freedoms. In 1964, the Civil Rights Act was passed. Soon after, state laws that stopped black Americans from voting were made illegal.

> What strategies did black Americans use to win their civil rights?

sit-in
(sĭt=ĭn)
a nonviolent form of protest in which people occupy a room, building, or a place outdoors in order to pressure others to meet their demands

Summary continues on next page

Putting the Constitution to Work *(Lesson 2 Summary continued)*

American Indians Make Gains

American Indians faced prejudice and discrimination. The civil rights movement encouraged them to form political groups and fight for change. They held protests and marches. They went to court to claim the land that they had lost to the government. They succeeded in winning back some lands, or in being paid for them.

[?] How did American Indians win greater control over their lives and regain territory lost in the 18th and 19th centuries?

The Fight for Women's Rights

Getting the right to vote did not do away with discrimination toward women. In the 1960s, women began to demand equal rights. In 1971, the Supreme Court ruled that unequal treatment based only on a person's sex was illegal. In 1972, The Equal Employment Opportunity Act called for equal pay for equal work. The Educational Amendment of 1972 said that women's college athletics had to receive the same financial support as men's programs. Women now work in many jobs that were once only open to men. Women also take an active role in politics and government.

[?] What gains did women make as a result of the revival of the women's movement?

The Ongoing Struggle for Justice

Sometimes there is a gap between a nation's ideals and real events. For example, during World War II, thousands of Japanese Americans were relocated to prison-like camps. The government was afraid that they would not be loyal to the United States during the war. In 1988, Congress apologized for what it had done. When people understand the Constitution, they can challenge unfairness and use the political process for change.

[?] In what sense is the effort to guarantee all Americans their constitutional rights a never-ending process?

Name: _____ Date: _____

CHAPTER 20
Lesson 3 Preview
Making a Difference

(*A More Perfect Union* pp. 609–613)

A Citizen's Responsibilities

1. **Look at the graphic organizer above. Then read the following sentences and fill in the blanks.**

    a. One of a citizen's _____ is to be informed.

    b. Another one of a citizen's responsibilities is to be _____.

2. **Read the lesson title and the red and blue headings in your text on pages 609 to 613. Use words from those headings to fill in the lesson outline below.**

    Making a Difference

    I. _____ Who Made a Difference

        A. A Sense of _____

        B. _____ Getting Involved

    II. Rights Involve _____

        A. Getting Involved

        B. _____ to Keep

Name: _____ Date: _____

CHAPTER 20
Lesson 3 Reading Strategy
Making a Difference

(*A More Perfect Union* pp. 609–613)

Finding the Main Idea This reading strategy helps you organize and remember what you read. When you finish a selection, jot down the main idea and its supporting details.

1. Look at the picture and read the text on page 609. Which sentence below best expresses the main idea of the selection? Circle the letter next to the best answer.

    a. Food From the 'Hood donates twenty-five percent of their produce to the needy.

    b. The best way to expand a business is by offering new products.

    c. Food From the 'Hood is a student-run business that gives food to the needy and earns money for college scholarships.

2. Read the section "Citizens Who Made a Difference." Which sentence below best expresses the main idea of the section? Circle the letter next to the best answer.

    a. Jane Addams became one of the most important reformers of her time.

    b. Ordinary people can have a huge impact on society when they become active in public affairs.

    c. Thousands of middle school students participate in a special program called CityYouth: Education and Community in Action.

3. Read section "Rights Involve Responsibilities." Then fill in the chart below.

Main Idea	Supporting Details

CHAPTER 20
Lesson 3 Summary
Making a Difference

(*A More Perfect Union* pp. 609–613)

Thinking Focus: Why is it important to be a responsible, active citizen?

Citizens Who Made a Difference

In 1961, President John F. Kennedy urged Americans to "ask not what your country can do for you; ask what you can do for your country." He was asking ordinary Americans to get involved in public affairs. Throughout American history, citizens have helped society in many ways. Some, like Frederick Douglass and Elizabeth Cady Stanton, have fought for civil rights and women's rights. Others, like Jane Addams, have worked to improve life for poor people living in the cities.

Students can also make a difference. Thousands of middle school students are part of a program called CityYouth: Education and Community in Action. Through this program, students in communities across the country work together for positive change and to develop a sense of **civic responsibility**. Their projects include community safety, cleaning parks and rivers, adopting senior centers, and collecting clothing for those in need.

[?] How have ordinary American citizens made the nation a better place in which to live?

civic responsibility
(sĭv´ĭk rĭ-spŏn´sə-bĭl´ĭ-tē)
a sense of duty to work for the good of one's community

Rights Involve Responsibilities

A government whose power comes from the people is only as good as its citizens. As citizens, Americans have certain responsibilities. Citizens must understand their government and know their rights. They must also vote, take part in the political process, and know about the issues.

Summary continues on next page

Even though you aren't old enough to vote, you can still be active in politics and public affairs. Taking a role in student government is one good way of learning how the political process works. You can also join organizations like Teen Age Republicans or the Young Democrats of America. As a member, you might pass out campaign flyers or make phone calls to voters.

Young people can also have a say in international, national, and local issues by joining an organization. For example, Amnesty International works for human rights throughout the world. Students Against Drunk Driving (SADD) helps students teach other teenagers about the dangers of drinking and driving. To become involved in local issues, you might join an organization that works for better public transportation or that raises money for the homeless. You could also tutor people who cannot read.

During the 20th century, Americans have worked hard to make the United States a nation of "liberty and justice for all." But to give liberty and justice to all, the United States will always need informed and responsible citizens.

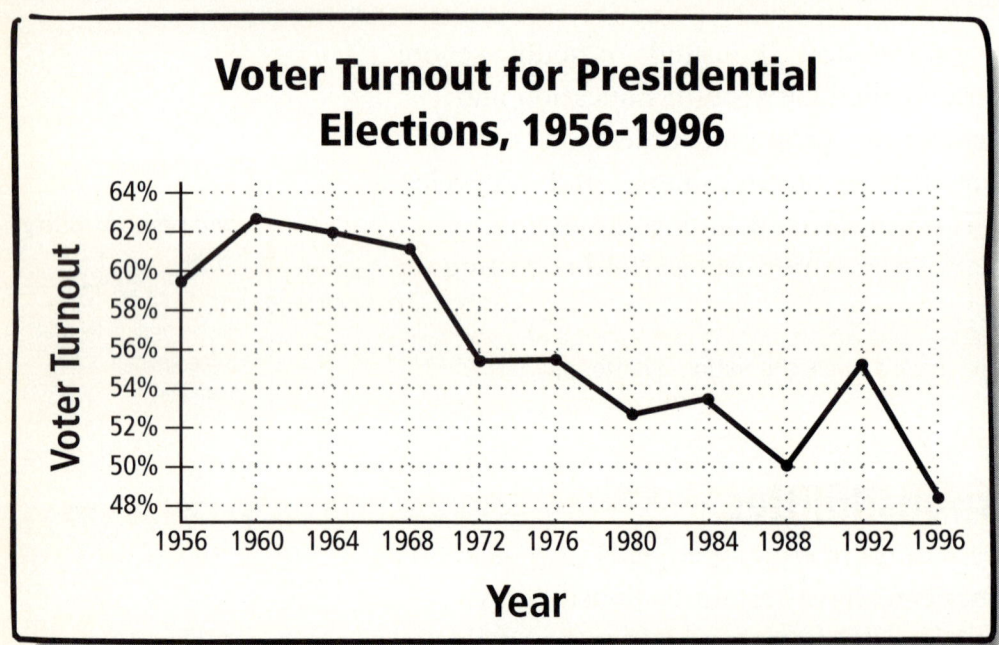

? What responsibilities does being a good American citizen include?